Feminizing Political Institutions

Feminizing Political Institutions

How Women Change Perceptions of Politics and Improve Democracy

Nichole M. Bauer

OXFORD
UNIVERSITY PRESS

Oxford University Press is a department of the University of Oxford.
It furthers the University's objective of excellence in research, scholarship,
and education by publishing worldwide. Oxford is a registered trade mark of
Oxford University Press in the UK and in certain other countries.

Published in the United States of America by Oxford University Press
198 Madison Avenue, New York, NY 10016, United States of America.

CIP data is on file at the Library of Congress.

ISBN 9780197841525

DOI: 10.1093/9780197841556.001.0001

Printed by Marquis Book Printing, Canada

The manufacturer's authorized representative in the EU for product safety is
Oxford University Press España S.A. of Parque Empresarial San Fernando de Henares,
Avenida de Castilla, 2 – 28830 Madrid (www.oup.es/en or product.safety@oup.com).
OUP España S.A. also acts as importer into Spain of products made by the manufacturer.

To Henry, a constant source of joy.

Contents

List of Figures

List of Tables

Acknowledgments

An underlying assumption behind my scholarship on gender and voter decision-making is that having more women in masculine institutions will have a transformative effect on those institutions. This assumption may stem, in part, from very wishful thinking about the effects of women's representation in political institutions but other institutions outside of politics. For example, academia and most political science departments, including my own, are majority-men institution with few to no women in senior positions. My own political science department has only had one woman serve at the rank of full professor, as of the fall of 2025, since the department was founded some 120 years ago. Having been in academia for over a decade, I can appreciate how difficult it is for women to change political science departments and to make them places that are more inclusive for women, people of color, and other under-represented groups. I want to take a moment to acknowledge all the women who have tried to "femininize" masculine institutions from political science departments to political bodies. But also, men can choose to create more inclusive institutions, and I hope more will make this choice. Instigating institutional change is hard, and women cannot and should not have to carry this burden alone.

I started working on this project six years ago when I was finishing my last book. I was incredibly fortunate to receive a Louisiana Board of Regents Support Fund, Research Competitiveness Subprogram Grant that supported the data collections for this book. I am certainly indebted to this funding program. There would be no book without this grant support. I'd also like to thank Ann Whitmer, a grants guru of sorts at LSU. In the fall of 2019, I met with Ann and asked about any grants I could apply for even if getting funding was a long-shot. Ann encouraged me to apply for the Research Competitiveness Subprogram Grant, and devoted a lot of time to helping me put together a budget and refine my proposal. Ann is, literally, the most helpful person I have ever encountered in academia. I am not being hyperbolic in this declaration. I also used support from the Remal Das and Lachmi Devi Bhatia Memorial Professorship and the D. Jensen Holliday Professorship.

Part of my Board of Regents grant was used to support the creation of the Gender & Politics Research Lab at LSU. A team of undergraduate and graduate students who worked with me on completing various parts of the data collections for this book include Katelyn Davis and Daniela Sestich who did a lot of the early heavy lifting on collecting data about women in local political office that I used in Chapter 2. There are a lot of other students who have worked with me in the lab and if I try to list them all, I will surely forget someone. Nevertheless, I appreciate the energy, enthusiasm, and comradery from everyone who comes through GPRL! I am so excited to keep working with you all in the years ahead. The lab is decidedly a feminized institution persisting in a very masculinized department.

While I was working on this book project, my then LSU colleague Jeong Kim proposed a women's writing group. This led to the WIPS Wednesday Writing Group. I spent a lot of time at French Truck in Baton Rouge writing and complaining about this project with many women including Jeong Kim, the writing group founder, Anna Gunderson, my trusty and reliable writing partner for so long, along with Emily Rains, Lindsey Pruett, and other women at LSU who dropped in to write together over the years. I miss writing with you all so very much every Wednesday from 9 am until about noon.

I wrote the last chapter of this book while at a writing retreat with Jennie Sweet-Cushman and Erin Cassese. Writing at the beach proved to be more productive than one might think. But also, Jennie and Erin provided, and still provide, me with endless personal and professional support. They listen to my petty complaints, and that is truly an invaluable service. I have many petty complaints.

Belinda Davis certainly deserves more than a short paragraph in my book acknowledgements. She is a loyal friend, a constant voice of reason, mentor, reliable ride home when it rains, and all-around inspiring human being. I appreciate Belinda's persistence in creating positive change in Baton Rouge, Louisiana, and at LSU. Your efforts deserve much more recognition.

I was also fortunate enough to present my research for this book through several invited talks and conferences where discussants and audience members provided helpful insights along with excellent questions about my theory. Jenn Merolla was a discussant for this project when I wrote the very first iteration of what would become Chapter 3. Jenn always has the most thoughtful and helpful guidance. I also presented this work as part of the Experimental Study of Politics and Psychology speaker series at Rutgers University, through the research symposium at Stony Brook University, and a small gender workshop at the University of Houston. The opportunity to present this research when it was still in an early stage helped me refine my ideas and sharpen my arguments.

I am so very fortunate to have such a strong personal and professional support system, and there are many others deserving of recognition including

Jazzmyn Moultrie who provided care for my child when he was just a little, bitty guy. Angela Chnapko at Oxford who was excited and intrigued by the idea for this book. Fanny Ramirez and Ruth Moon through our grievance hotline group chat. Martina Santia who I describe to people as a former student, current friend. I also want to recognize all my co-authors over the last five years who listened to me talk about this project at some point. I am so lucky that I have too many excellent co-authors to list here.

Finishing this book was a race. In the fall of 2023, I was lucky to be on sabbatical which afforded me ample time to sit down and write this thing. I also had a very firm end of the fall semester deadline not because my sabbatical would end, but because I was set to give birth. The very real deadline of bringing a new human into the world certainly provided me the motivation needed to just get this thing done. I finished the first draft of this book and sent it off to Angela for review just two weeks before Henry made it into the world. Anna Gunderson deserves a second mention here, along with Drew Berens, for packing my hospital bag when the timeline for Henry's birth was unexpectedly moved up. It is my understanding that Emily Rains provided support via text in this endeavour.

Henry, you are an endless source of joy and love. You charm everyone you encounter. I hope your friendliness, enthusiasm, and constant joy never end.

1

Gender Stereotypes and Women's Representation

A remarkable event occurred in January 1912 in the town of Kanab, Utah, a small agricultural hamlet of just 911 people at the time, located in southern Utah just north of the Arizona border. The town's newly elected council began a new term. All five elected members of the council were women: Mary Woolley Chamberlain held the position of chairwoman, Luella McAllister served as Treasurer, Tamar Hamblin was the clerk, with Blanche Hamblin[1] and Ada Seegmiller serving as councilors. The election of the all-women council, one of the first all-women bodies of government in the United States, is striking as it occurred a full six years before ratification of the 19th Amendment giving women the right to vote—though women had the right to vote when Utah achieved statehood in 1896 (Teele 2019). These five women did not put themselves forward to run for the city council, but rather a group of men put the women on the ticket as a joke. Apparently, putting women in charge was just that laughable. The candidacies of these women were never meant to be taken seriously. Politics, after all, was an endeavor for men.

Reflecting later in her life on the election of the all-women council, the council chairwoman Mary Woolley Chamberlain explained the dynamics that led to the five women winning election:

In these little towns there is not salary enough in any of the offices to justify men to devote their time to them, and as their other work calls them away from home most of the time, the affairs of the town were often sadly neglected, so on the morning of Election Day 1911 the first three men at the polls suggested that they make up a ticket of women, which they did, more as a burlesque than anything else, but we were every one elected by a large majority.[2]

[1] The historical record is not entirely clear on whether Tamar Hamblin and Blanche Hamblin were related or just coincidentally shared the same surname.

[2] https://www.deseret.com/2018/3/23/20642137/how-kanab-s-1911-all-women-town-council-went-from-disgusted-to-making-history#the-kanab-all-woman-town-council-served-from-1911-to-1913-left-to-right-luella-mcallister-treasurer-blanche-hamblin-councilor-mary-w-chamberlain-mayor-tamar-hamblin-clerk-ada-seegmiller-councilor

Feminizing Political Institutions. Nichole M. Bauer, Oxford University Press. © Nichole M. Bauer (2026).
DOI: 10.1093/9780197841556.003.0001

Upon hearing of her victory, Chamberlain reported that she felt "disgusted" and "unqualified" for the job. Chamberlain's sentiments are still common among women over a century later. Women are far more likely to doubt their qualifications for political office compared to similarly situated men (Crowder-Meyer 2020) and the masculinity of politics deters women from running for elected office (Kanthak and Woon 2015; Stoddard and Preece 2015). Chamberlain and the four other winning women only decided to accept the job on the city council after positive encouragement from their fathers and other prominent men in the town.

During the two-year period the town council governed Kanab, the all-women council was incredibly productive. The women passed ordinances governing who could do business in the town as well as rules to govern these businesses. The women also set about "cleaning up" the town through laws designed to restrict vices such as gambling and drinking. Indeed, the women were active in the temperance movement—not uncommon for women at the time (Fletcher 2008). The high level of productivity of the all-women council mirrors findings from research today that women in political office are, in fact, highly productive lawmakers (Lazarus and Steigerwalt 2018; Holman, Mahoney, and Hurler 2022). The focus of the women on social and morality issues also fits with research showing that women have distinct issue agendas that differ from the issue agendas of men in office (Swers 1998; Atkinson and Windett 2019). As the council's two-year term came to an end, many in the town reflected on the women's legacy noting that they had "done more for the town than all the male Boards they have ever had."[3] Only one of the five women ran for re-election, Ada Seegmiller, and she won,[4] but the other women on the council hoped their successful time in political power would encourage more women to pursue positions on the council. As far as I can tell, Kanab, Utah, has yet to elect another all-women town council,[5] and as of 2025, the Kanab City Council had no woman serving. The Kanab City Council of 1912 marked a unique moment in history when women held onto political power. This all-women government was neither the first nor the last.[6]

---

[3] Quotation comes from https://www.deseret.com/2018/3/23/20642137/how-kanab-s-1911-all-women-town-council-went-from-disgusted-to-making-history/.

[4] While Seegmiller ran for and won re-election, she resigned from her position in the second-term, though the historical record is not clear as to what prompted her resignation.

[5] https://kanab.utah.gov/2169/City-Council

[6] There are several cities that beat out Kanab, Utah. Syracuse, Kansas, elected an all-women city government in 1887, the same year that women gained the right to vote in city and school elections in the state. A few years later, Edgerton, Kansas, also elected an all-women town council. The local newspaper declared the city to have a "petticoat government."

In the modern era, other towns and cities voted in slates of all-women. In 2018, heralded as a "Year of the Woman," Los Altos, California, elected an all-women town council making Los Altos the third Californian town in the state's history to have an all-women council.[7] California previously elected all-women councils in 1992, the first "Year of the Woman" nationwide (Cook and Wilcox 1994), in Pacifica, and in 2017, in Blue Lake. Carmel, Indiana, a suburb north of Indianapolis, also elected an all-women town council in 2018. In 2020, Las Cruces, New Mexico, elected an all-women city council. The latest all-women city council came in 2023 in St. Paul, Minnesota, where not only are all the council members women, but six of the eight council members are women of color. This list is not, by any means, a complete list of all the all-women town or city councils, but it is still considered newsworthy to find instances of all-women legislative bodies more than 100 years after some of the first all-women local governments held power.

Women's descriptive representation is at a relatively high level in the US compared to past years. Kamala Harris in 2020 became the first woman to win and serve as the vice president, and in 2024, Harris became the first Black woman and first South Asian woman to receive the nomination of a major political party in the United States for the presidency. Of course, Harris did not win the presidency, but her candidacy was still an important moment for women's descriptive and symbolic representation. The presence of women is especially felt in legislative political institutions where women steadily increased their ranks over the last three decades. At the start of the 2025 legislative term, women in Congress held 28 percent of seats, an increase from 23.6 percent of seats in 2020, and a number that holds steady from the last legislative term.[8] Women also made major gains in state legislatures holding an average of 33 percent of seats across all fifty states[9]—though there is considerable variable across the fifty states. Nevada has had a majority-women upper and lower house for several years, and women currently hold majorities, or just to majorities, in the state legislatures of Arizona, New Mexico, and Colorado.

In the last decade, women continued to successfully run for and win office, and many of these gains came from women of color. The 2018 midterm elected dubbed a "Pink Wave" election was led largely by the victories of women of color.[10] Just after the 2024 presidential elections, women of color

---

hold sixty-one seats across both the House and the Senate. These gains included the election of two Black women to the US Senate, Angela Alsobrooks of Maryland and Lisa Blunt Rochester of Delaware. This is the first time two Black women served in the Senate at the same time. Indeed, politics is slowly becoming far more diverse in the gender and ethnoracial diversity of those who hold political office.

The United States is, in many ways, catching up to other countries where women's rates of representation are somewhat better. Women's representation is at or near parity in several nations including Rwanda where women hold 63.8 percent of seats in the lower chamber and 53.9 percent of seats in the upper chamber, Mexico where women hold 50.2 percent of seats in the national legislature, Sweden where women's representation is at 45 percent, as well as Finland, Spain, Norway, and New Zealand where women hold more than 40 percent of seats in the national legislatures. Many of these gains globally are due, in part, to the establishment of quota systems. Women's rise to power is not just isolated to legislative offices. Women serve in executive-level offices at record rates as well. Mexico not only has a majority-women legislature, thanks to a gender quota law that went into effect in 2018, but Mexico currently has a woman, Claudia Sheinbaum, elected as president. As of January 2025, twenty-five countries had a woman serving as the head of state.[11]

Theories of representation offer a useful lens for understanding the broader effects of women in elected political office. The concept of descriptive representation argues that political institutions should mirror the demographic characteristics of those that they represent (Pitkin 1967; Mansbridge 2003, 1999; Dovi 2002; Schwindt-Bayer and Mishler 2005). The value of descriptive representation is that all citizens will see themselves physically represented, and these perceptions should increase political efficacy, trust in government, and democratic legitimacy (Clayton, O'Brien, and Piscopo 2023b, 2019; Montoya et al. 2022; Kao et al. 2024). With descriptive representation comes an expectation of substantive representation based on shared groups' interests (Mansbridge 1999; Dovi 2002). Research suggests that women make good on these expectations of representing their gender and/or ethnorace groups (Swers 1998; Bratton and Haynie 1999). Women's representation can also have a symbolic effect (Pitkin 1967) such as role-modeling effects on young women and girls (Schneider, Sweet-Cushman, and Gordon 2023; Wolbrecht and Campbell 2017).

Intersectional models of representation show the positive substantive and symbolic benefits that accrue from the presence of individuals who hold

---

[11] https://www.unwomen.org/en/what-we-do/leadership-and-political-participation/facts-and-figures

multiple minoritized identities (Bejarano et al. 2021; Brown 2014b; Brown and Gershon 2017; Cargile, Merolla, and Schroedel 2016; Gay and Tate 1998). These models of intersectional representation consider the presence of not only women of color in institutions but also other minoritized groups based on social class status, gender identity, and other identity markers (Bergersen, Klar, and Schmitt 2018; Moureau, Nuño-Pérez, and Sanchez 2019). When individuals are represented by people with whom they share a minoritized identity, people's willingness to participate in government, levels of trust, and efficacy increase among these individuals most likely to face historical marginalization (Brown 2014b; Montoya et al. 2022). These are unique benefits that come from intersectional representation, and do not come from women's increased presence alone. I argue that another benefit of women's overall increased representation, including women of color, is the ability of women in government to transform the stereotypic perceptions people hold of political institutions.

Politics, from campaign processes to institutions, is largely perceived through the lens of "white-masculinity" (Hawkesworth 2003; Brown 2014a; Dittmar 2015). Hawkesworth (2003) explains the process of "racing-gendering" political institutions arguing:

> The term, *racing-gendering,* attempts to foreground the intricate interactions of racialization and gendering in the political production of distinctive groups of men and women. Racing-gendering involves the production of differences, political asymmetries, and social hierarchies that simultaneously create the dominant and subordinate ... The processes that produce a white male, for example, will differ from, while being fully implicated in, the processes that produce a Black man, a Latino, a Native American man, a white woman, a Black woman, a Latina, an Asian American woman, or a Native American woman (p. 531, italics in original).

The dominance of white men in political office leads to the privileging of behaviors more likely to be attributed to and valued in white men. The processes that lead to the reproduction of raced-gendered processes in political institutions are not, as Dittmar (2015) argues and demonstrates in her analyses of the gendered processes embedded in political campaigns, "immune to change" (p. 11). As the demographic characteristics of political institutions become more diverse, it is possible that the raced-gendered perceptions people hold of political institutions will change. In other words, people see political institutions as dominated by "white-masculinity" because, in part, most politicians are white men. If fewer white men hold political office, it is possible that these notions of politics as white and masculine will change as well. In this book, I develop and test a theory of institutional stereotype change which connects women's descriptive representation to shifts in the white-masculine stereotypes that people associate with political institutions.

Rises in the descriptive representation of women of color will, I argue, not only shift the masculine perceptions of political institutions but will also shift the perception that political institutions are governed by norms of whiteness. Indeed, a white racial identity often serves as an implicit benchmark for how candidates and elected officials should behave (Bauer 2020a; Schneider and Bos 2011). I base my argument about women of color's descriptive representation on the ways that individuals apply and consider stereotypes in the context of women of color (Cargile 2023; Harris-Perry 2013) and based on the ways that women of color embody both feminine and masculine stereotypes in their representational styles (Brown 2014a). I argue that women of color are better positioned to breakdown the white-masculine perceptions of institutions compared to men of color because of their intersectional identities. Certainly, men of color's descriptive representation has the potential to alter the racialized perceptions of political institutions (see, e.g., Clark (2019)). However, the stereotypes and experiences associated with men of color often replicate norms and perceptions of masculinity (Schneider and Bos 2011). Of course, masculinity, when applied to Black men, is very different from the masculinity performed by and attributed to white men (Peffley, Jon, and Sniderman 1997; Berinsky et al. 2011).

People often apply a mix of feminine and masculine traits to Latinas, Black women, and Asian women in leadership roles (Gonzalez and Bauer 2022; Qi, Kim, and Bauer 2023; Lien and Filler 2022). Part of this mixed stereotype content comes from the dual roles that women of color fill as mothers, home-makers, and economic providers active in the workforce (Harris-Perry 2013), along with the displays of femininity and masculinity on the part of women of color in elected office. Visible displays of, for example, Representative Alexandria Ocasio-Cortez or Ayanna Pressley, advocating aggressively for healthcare reform or better social services for veterans, fit into both feminine and masculine stereotypes. This is a case of advocating on feminine issues for minoritized groups using a masculine style of representation. Indeed, the ability of women of color to blend stereotypes about race and gender lead to the creation of unique stereotypes about Latinas, Black women, or Asian women in leadership roles. This blend of femininity and masculinity is part of what I argue will give women of color the ability to breakdown both the gendered and the raced stereotypes applied to political institutions.

To develop my theory of institutional stereotype change, I address several research questions throughout this book: (1) *Do individuals stereotype political institutions that are more diverse along racial and gender lines as less masculine and less white compared to institutions that under-represent women and people of color? (2) Are the feminizing effects of more diverse institutions more likely to be felt at different types of political office? (3) How does changing the stereotypic perceptions the public holds of political institutions change the way women and men engage in political participation and evaluate political institutions? and (4) How do the news media communicate the feminizing effects of women's descriptive representation?*

To answer these questions, I develop and test a theory of institutional stereotype change. This theory, briefly, argues that when the visible demographic characteristics of a political institution change to include more women and people of color, the raced-gendered stereotypes associated with those institutions will also change. People will associate institutions with more women as having more feminine qualities relative to institutions dominated by men which people will associate with masculine stereotypes. Stereotypes of political institutions, based on my theory, will change from masculine to feminine when there are more women in these institutions. I argue that women's increased descriptive representation not only has the potential to erode the masculinity of politics, but that women of color can erode the *white-masculinity* that dominates political institutions.

There are two central puzzles in the literature that lead me to develop this theory of institutional stereotype change: First, past scholarship implicitly assumes that the white-masculine stereotypes associated with politics are not likely to change; second, research produces mixed findings on how and whether women's descriptive representation matters. These two puzzles, or gaps in the literature, can, in part, be resolved by considering how women's descriptive representation changes the masculine stereotypes people hold of political institutions.

I ground this concept of institutional stereotype change in theories adapted from social psychology and organizational behavior. I argue that *who* serves in an institution shapes the public impressions formed of that institution. The visible images of who is in political office signal the stereotypic traits, behaviors, and qualities embodied by that institution. In this first chapter, I start by explaining the complicated relationship between gender stereotypes, perceptions of women and men leaders, and how masculinity defines political leadership. Next, I outline what we know, and do not know, about the broad effects of women's descriptive representation. Women's descriptive representation is thought to improve how regular people think about and engage in politics (Hinojosa and Kittilson 2020), but research offers mixed findings about these effects (Atkeson 2003; Wolak 2020c). I argue that if women's descriptive representation is going to affect how people engage in politics, then women's descriptive representation must first change the stereotypes people associate with political institutions. A central premise of my theory of institutional stereotype change is that women's descriptive representation is increasing in ways that alter the gendered and racialized lens through which people view political institutions. Before delving into the literature on women's descriptive representation, I provide a brief note on some of the key terms I use in this book.

Some Brief Notes on Terminology

There are several terms I use in this book that require some explanation to help guide readers: woman over female, ethnorace, and woman/people of color. First, I use the term woman as both a noun and an adjective. Scholars on politics and gender often use woman as a noun, i.e., a woman running for office, and use female as an adjective, i.e., a female candidate (see, e.g., my past scholarship Bauer (2015a)). These linguistic conventions are shifting as many scholars opt to use woman as both a noun and an adjective (Dolan 2010). I opt for the use of woman because female is a term that refers to the biological sex of a person as being female (Bittner and Goodyear-Grant 2017). Being a woman does not necessarily mean that a person has the biological markers that would lead them to be assigned the sex female at birth. I use woman/women to acknowledge that when I talk about women in representation, I only know their presented gender. Most women who identify as a woman in politics have a cis-gender identity where their gender identity matches their biological sex. The one exception to this linguistic choice is in the text of the experimental treatment where I refer to majority-female institutions because this is how the news media frequently refer to women's descriptive representation. Of course, not all women have this match between biological sex and gender identity; the representation of trans women and trans men is increasing in recent years. In short, I use women to acknowledge that I am only relying on the outward presentation of an elected representative's gender identity with no knowledge of their biological sex, but much of this book considers women's representation for cis-gendered women.

Second, I use the term ethnorace where many scholars often use the term "racial/ethnic" as in racial/ethnic diversity. I use the term ethnorace to refer to non-white people, whether regular people or people in elected political office. I use this term following research on race and ethnicity in political science and sociology (Bejarano et al. 2021; Bobo and Mickey-Pabello 2020; Grumbach,

Sahn, and Staszak 2022; Omi and Winant 2014; Bauer and Cargile 2023). The term ethnorace offers a way to refer to people belonging to either a racial or ethnic minority group, which can be but are not always overlapping categories.

Third, I use the term women of color to refer to women belonging to a minoritized ethnorace group such as a Black woman or a Latina (Gonzalez and Bauer 2022). I do not mean to imply that all women of color have the same experiences or the same effect on people through their descriptive representation. I use the term to differentiate how Black women, Latinas, Asian-American & Pacific Islander, and other women from a minoritized background might have different effects on institutions relative to white women (for an insightful discussion on the utility of this term, see Greene, Matos, and Sanbonmatsu (2021)). When it is theoretically and empirically important to distinguish between Black women, Latinas, and other women from minoritized ethnorace backgrounds, I use more specific ethnorace identifiers over the term women of color. When I aim to differentiate between white women and non-white women, I use the term women of color.

Fourth, the central focus of this book identifies the effects of women's descriptive representation, a term that I use considerably. Women's descriptive representation refers to the numeric presence of women in a legislative or executive office. Descriptive representation of women would occur if, for example, the US House was 51.8 percent women, as the American population is 51.8 percent women. Because I use this term a lot in this book, and it is a somewhat clunky term, I use the abbreviation, WDR, to refer to women's descriptive representation.

Can Stereotypes about Political Institutions Change?

Gender stereotypes, broadly, represent the way individuals classify people into feminine and masculine categories (Deaux and Lewis 1984). Feminine stereotypes characterize women as caring and empathetic (Prentice and Carranza 2002); in politics, voters stereotype women candidates as having a high level of expertise on issues that reinforce these traits such as education or healthcare policy (Schneider 2014). People think women candidates will prioritize healthcare issues because healthcare is an issue associated with compassion, and women are thought to be more compassionate than men (Huddy and Terkildsen 1993b). Masculine stereotypes characterize men as assertive and dominant (Vinkenburg et al. 2011); as such, voters attribute men with masculine issues such as defense and the military

(Holman, Merolla, and Zechmeister 2016). The link between masculine traits and issues comes from the perception that masculine traits are needed to be good at masculine issues (Holman, Merolla, and Zechmeister 2021). The traits associated with masculinity and men are also traits associated with political leadership and the traits associated with femininity and women are incongruent with political leadership (Bos, Schneider, and Utz 2017; Sweet-Cushman 2022). These stereotypes are deeply embedded and intertwined in how we think about women's and men's public and private roles, and how we conceptualize leadership inside and outside of politics.

Political leadership is commonly thought of through the lens of masculinity, more specifically through the lens of white-masculinity. Individuals think about white men when they think about identifying political leaders (Bauer 2020a; Bos et al. 2022), associate masculine traits as the most desired traits in a leader (Conroy 2015; Funk 1999; Aaldering and van der Pas 2020), and rate masculine issues as the most important political issues during an election cycle (Holman et al. 2019). The positive qualities associated most strongly with masculinity, such as toughness, are ascribed most frequently to and valued in white men (Schneider and Bos 2011). Toughness in men of color, in particular Black men, is considered to be a much more negative quality (Terkildsen 1993; Peffley, Jon, and Sniderman 1997). Much of the past scholarship on the role of gender and politics focuses on how political institutions limit the ability of women to enter into the political system as candidates (Crowder-Meyer and Lauderdale 2014; Crowder-Meyer 2013; Sanbonmatsu 2006; Lawless 2012; Bonneau and Kanthak 2020), perceptual challenges from the electorate (Bankert 2020; Bracic, Israel-Trummel, and Shortle 2019; Cassese and Holman 2019), and the success of women as elected officeholders (Anzia and Berry 2011; Volden, Wiseman, and Wittmer 2018; Mahoney 2018).

The masculine process of campaigning, such as engaging in negative attacks or self-promotion, deters women from pursuing political careers (Fox and Lawless 2011; Dittmar 2015; Kanthak and Woon 2014; Schneider et al. 2016). The white-masculinity of politics attracts individuals, including women, who identify as having more masculine rather than feminine traits as political candidates (Oliver and Conroy 2017) and this leads to higher rates of participation among individuals with those same masculine qualities, this means participation from more masculine women and more masculine men, at the individual level (McDermott 2016; Dynes et al. 2021). A central thread in this scholarship is that gender stereotypes frequently play a prominent role in women's ability to enter the masculine political system.

While masculinity appears to dominate perceptions of political leadership, it is thought that some types of institutions may be more feminine relative to other types of institutions. Some research argues that voters will value feminine traits more in lower levels of office, such as city councils (Huddy and Terkildsen 1993a), and that voters value feminine issues in gubernatorial offices (Fox and Oxley 2003). Other research argues that voters will see legislative institutions as more feminine because these offices are fundamentally group-based decision-making bodies compared to executive offices (Dolan and Lynch 2016). And still yet another body of scholarship argues that all political offices seen as more masculine (Sweet-Cushman 2022) and voters prefer candidates who emphasize masculine traits (Bauer 2020b). The extent to which masculine and feminine perceptions of institutions may shift based on levels of WDR at different levels of office is another point of conflict and ambiguity in the extant scholarship.

Current scholarship has not yet considered how people attribute white-masculine stereotypes to political institutions and how these white-masculine perceptions can change. To be sure, scholars have documented how white-masculinity guides the experiences of women and women of color in political institutions (Hawkesworth 2003; Brown 2014a; Dittmar 2015), but this scholarship is largely constrained to the gender and politics subfield. I consider how stereotypes of white-masculinity can be undone to create more feminine and more inclusive perceptions of institutions. Social psychology research shows that gender stereotypes are not static but subject to shift along with social and cultural changes (Diekman and Eagly 2000). Stereotypes about women of color also evolve over time. Harris-Perry (2013) charts how three stereotypic tropes about Black women, the mammie, Jezebel, and Sapphire stereotypes, developed with the shifting roles of Black women first as enslaved people and then as members of the workforce and as heads of households. As women of color move into different institutions, the stereotypes associated with those institutions will also change in tandem. The dual social roles held by women of color uniquely position this group to alter raced-gendered perceptions of institutions, especially when compared to men of color who have not always documented these dual feminine and masculine roles. Women of color are better positioned than men of color to change raced-gendered stereotypes because men of color are not similarly situated in both feminine and masculine social roles. Stereotypes about men of color often reinforce masculine stereotypes (Schneider and Bos 2011) though masculine stereotypes applied to men of color do not convey the same meaning as they do in the context of white men (Dawson 2001).

The association between leadership and white-masculinity is one that predates American democracy, and it is an entrenched association that evolved from the way that communities divided labor between women and men many millennia ago (Eagly 1987). Essentially, leadership became masculine because leadership required physical strength and the ability to leave communities for long periods of time and men were best suited to fill these roles compared to women because they did not have to worry about pregnancy and childbirth. These separate roles for women and men where women were relegated to fulfilling communal, or caregiving, tasks and men engaged in power-seeking, or agentic tasks, became more ingrained over time. In practice, many women engaged in agentic tasks and many men engaged in communal tasks; but the idea of leadership as masculine persisted over millennia.

Physical strength, as in the ability to fight physical battles with an enemy, is not necessary for political leadership in the modern era. Yet, the image of leadership as white and masculine persists. This association between leadership and white-masculinity comes, in part, from the dominance of white men in political leadership roles. White men hold most elected offices in the US, indeed nearly three-quarters of all officeholders are men, and the US has yet to elect a woman to the presidency. White men not only dominate political leadership roles but also set up institutions that exclude women from leadership roles (Hawkesworth 2003). Campaign processes condition voters to give men, and masculinity, an advantage in decision-making (Bauer 2020a; Dittmar 2015). Over the last century, many of the formal barriers that once limited women's access to political participation and political office have fallen away. As women, especially women of color, make gains in representation, it is important to determine if the strongly masculine associations voters hold of political leadership and political institutions can be changed. Few scholars consider how these stereotypic perceptions might change with changes in the demographic characteristics of political institutions.

The white-masculinity of politics has negative consequences for women's inclusion in politics. One of the most frequently cited barriers to women's political participation, especially women's participation as candidates, is the belief that they must conform to masculine behavioral norms, such as being argumentative and aggressive, to run for political office or even volunteer for a campaign (Crowder-Meyer 2020; Kanthak and Woon 2015; Stoddard and Preece 2015). The people most likely to participate in politics are often those who see themselves through the lens of masculinity (McDermott 2016) and political rhetoric often implicitly centers "whiteness" as a central identity (Jardina 2019).

The incongruence between the feminine stereotypes associated with women and the masculine stereotypes of leadership has a conditional but negative effect on the success of women political candidates depending on the types of strategies candidates deploy during their political campaigns (Bauer 2015a; Krupnikov and Bauer 2014; Bauer 2019; Cassese and Holman 2018; Ditonto 2019; Ditonto 2017; Ditonto, Hamilton, and Redlawsk 2014) and characteristics of individual voters (Bauer 2015b; Cassese and Barnes 2019; Cassese and Holman 2019; Valentino, Wayne, and Oceno 2018; Bracic, Israel-Trummel, and Shortle 2019; Bankert 2020). The strategic messages that work best for women and men on the campaign trail are those that highlight positive masculine traits, such as strength and experience, which also align with the normative expectations of good political leadership (Bauer 2019)[12] and these findings are consistent regardless of the level of office at stake (Bauer 2020b) or the partisanship of the woman (Bauer 2018).

The behavioral norms expected of politicians and candidates are not just masculine norms, they are norms that also fit into standards of *white-masculinity*. There is a very big perceptual difference between a white man who is aggressive and a Black man who is aggressive. There is also a difference in the ascription of these traits to women and women of color (Gonzalez and Bauer 2022). An aggressive white woman conjures up different images relative to an aggressive Black woman. Likewise, masculine attributes applied to men of color differ from those applied to white men. Aggression in Black men can trigger threatening associations with violence and criminality while aggression in white men is less likely to have this same type of connotation (Peffley, Jon, and Sniderman 1997). These raced-gendered standards for leadership affect perceptions of our political institutions such that institutions meant to be representative of the American population are institutions associated with white-masculinity both in the traits ascribed to the body and in the demographic composition. These perceptions are limiting for the representation of women and people of color.

The unique intersection of gender and race can create opportunities for women of color to capitalize on conventionally masculine qualities, such as strength, and stereotypically feminine qualities at the same time (Cargile, Merolla, and Schroedel 2016; Gershon and Monforti 2021). How women of color talk about the qualities they bring to political office and how women of color engage in representation can, potentially, overturn the white-masculine stereotypes that voters hold for political leadership. Take for example the

---

[12] For an exception, see Anzia and Bernhard (2022) who find that feminine traits benefit women in local races though my past research suggests that masculine traits are more valuable for women in local races (Bauer 2020b).

women of color elected to the US Congress in the 2018 midterm elections. These women, collectively called "the squad," embrace a somewhat masculine style of leadership through their unapologetic and assertive advocacy for their districts, their states, and people belonging to minoritized groups more broadly. These women, such as Rashida Tlaib or Ilhan Omar, are not just parroting the behaviors of white men in political office but they are doing something with the potential to be much more transformative. Women of color in Congress use a masculine style of leadership to advocate for policies and groups that align with the feminine stereotypic expectations held for women more generally. It is the attribution of both feminine and masculine traits to women of color along with the unique leadership styles of these women that can best position them to undo the white-masculine stereotypes associated with political leadership and lead individuals to form a more gender and racially inclusive perception of political institutions. The dual attribution of feminine and masculine stereotypes uniquely positions women of color to break down the white-masculinity of institutions, especially compared to men of color. Stereotypes about men of color include masculine qualities (Schneider and Bos 2011).

A constant thread throughout current scholarship is that individuals do not value femininity in women candidates and feminine qualities are not exactly a boon to men either (Bauer 2017). This scholarship assumes that the raced-gendered stereotypes held about politics, and political leadership, more broadly do not change. Social psychology research, however, argues that stereotypes can change, and the stereotypes of organizations change when the people in those organizations change (Glick, Wilk, and Perreault 1995; Kanter 1977b). The idea of applying gender stereotypes to political institutions and considering how perceptions of institutions change over time is relatively untested in the political science scholarship. I fill this intellectual gap in this book.

Past scholarship assumes that the stereotypes associated with political institutions are unlikely to change. However, stereotypes constantly evolve. The stereotypes associated with women changed over time to include not just feminine traits but both feminine and masculine traits to reflect the dual roles women fill as homemakers and economic providers (Diekman and Eagly 2000). The stereotypes of corporations and businesses change to include and value more feminine qualities when more women enter these organizations (Kanter 1977b; Acker 1992). Young people are more likely to see women political leaders as having the masculine traits voters value in political leaders (Taylor-Robinson and Geva 2023), though there are still many who see women as lacking masculine traits (Bauer 2020a). Having more women in small decision-making bodies changes who speaks in small group settings and how these groups make decisions (Mendelberg, Karpowitz, and Goedert 2014; Karpowitz and Mendelberg 2014; Arnesen and Peters 2018). Research on Nevada's majority-women state legislature finds evidence of institutional behaviors shifting to be more inclusive and to fit more strongly into feminine stereotypes (Sweet-Cushman, Gill, and Zorn 2025). Chapter 2 goes into more detail on when, why, and how stereotypes of organizations shift. However, the key point for this book is that few scholars consider how and when stereotypes in politics change. The theory of institutional stereotype change I develop presents a novel framework for understanding the forces that lead to shifts in stereotypes about political institutions.

In this book, I focus on how increasing the gender and ethnoracial diversity of holding political office can break down the raced-gendered stereotypes people hold of political institutions. I center my theory and analyses around women and women of color's descriptive representation because increasing the representation of these groups has the greatest potential to undo the negative masculine stereotypes voters hold of political institutions. This is not to say that men of color are also not under-represented. They are. Nor it is to say that men of color cannot undo the negative masculine stereotypes voters hold about political bodies. They certainly can. But the stereotypes voters hold of, for example, Black men politicians still have considerable overlap with the stereotypes held of politicians more generally (Schneider and Bos 2011). Thus, stereotypes about men of color may, unintentionally, reinforce the existing masculine stereotypes. I argue that women are best positioned to break down the gendered perceptions of political institutions because their very presence in elected office presents a direct contrast and challenge to the norm of men as leaders. Women of color are best positioned to break down the interlocking raced-gendered stereotypes of political institutions. Women of color, to gain a voice in men-dominated institutions guided by norms of racial exclusion, must disrupt politics as usual (Ford Dowe 2020), and their disruption to these raced-gendered norms can reshape how individuals think about political institutions.

Women's Descriptive Representation: Does It Matter?

Increasing women's presence in political institutions is thought to produce benefits for descriptive, symbolic, and substantive representation. Descriptive representation occurs when the members serving in elected bodies mirror the composition of those they represent (Pitkin 1967). Voters often prefer candidates and leaders who look like them. Women voters, in general, prefer women represent them in political office (Plutzer and Zipp 1996; Zipp and Plutzer 1985; Sanbonmatsu 2002a); voters of color prefer representatives and leaders who share their ethnoracial identity (White, Laird, and Allen 2014; Tate 2018); and women voters of color are supportive of representatives who are also women of color (Philpot and Walton 2007; Bejarano 2013; Lemi 2020). Improving descriptive representation matters because members from traditionally minoritized groups, including women, minorities, and the working class (Mansbridge 1999; Gay and Tate 1998; Tate 2018; Barnes and Saxton 2019), should be more likely to see legislative institutions that descriptively represent them as more legitimate institutions (Clayton, O'Brien, and Piscopo 2019; Wolak 2020c; Arnesen and Peters 2018). Citizens who see democratic institutions as more legitimate institutions will be more likely to participate in democracy through voting, activism, and running for political office (West 2017; Wolak 2017).

Women in political leadership roles also provide the benefits of symbolic representation. Evidence suggests that having women on the ballot can lead to a role-modeling effect where women see women run for office and then increase their own interest in running for office (Ladam, Harden, and Windett 2018; Bonneau and Kanthak 2020; Sweet-Cushman 2019; Schneider, Sweet-Cushman, and Gordon 2023). These role-modeling effects can be especially powerful among young girls (Campbell and Wolbrecht 2006; Wolbrecht and Campbell 2017; Campbell and Wolbrecht 2020; Ladam, Harden, and Windett 2018). Hillary Clinton's 2016 presidential campaign engaged many young girls excited about the prospect of having a woman president, and the role-modeling effect of having Clinton run, even though she did not win, can affect the political ambition of these young girls two and three decades down the road (Wolbrecht and Campbell 2017). Just having more women on the ballot, even if those women do not win political office, is thought to improve women's political interest, political knowledge, and likelihood of participating in the campaign process (Fridkin and Kenney 2014; Atkeson 2003)—though other research demonstrates a null effect (Wolak 2020c; Dolan 2006). More recent scholarship shows that WDR can be especially important and powerful at local levels of office (Clayton, O'Brien, and Piscopo 2023b). The benefits from having more women on the ballot as candidates occur even when women still hold a minority of spots on the ballot and a minority of seats in elected legislatures.

The entrance of women into political institutions can dramatically alter how those institutions operate. Women in legislatures provide substantive representation by advocating for other women, girls, and minoritized communities through the policies they prioritize and by giving voice to the stories of these under-represented groups (Swers 1998; Pearson and Dancey 2011; Dietrich, Hayes, and O'Brien 2019; Weeks 2022). Women are also particularly adept at constituency service. Women are more likely to respond to constituent service requests, but the lawmaker most likely to respond to constituent service requests is a woman of color (Lowande, Ritchie, and Lauterbach 2019; Bauer and Cargile 2023). Women lawmakers are highly effective at bringing women's issues to the forefront of the policy agenda (Osborn 2012; Dittmar, Sanbonmatsu, and Carroll 2018; Bryant and Hellwege 2018). This is especially true of women of color who represent the interests of women and minoritized ethnorace groups (Brown 2014a; Bratton 2006; Bratton and Haynie 1999; Bratton, Haynie, and Reingold 2007; Scott et al. 2021). Institutional barriers, such as seniority norms, often affect the ability of women to ensure that women's issues, such as equal pay legislation, become law. Women work to ensure that bills on women's issues are passed into law by forming alliances with men lawmakers who navigate women's issue bills through the legislative process (Volden, Wiseman, and Wittmer 2013; Atkinson and Windett 2019; Holman, Mahoney, and Hurler 2022; Holman and Mahoney 2019). Women's ability to change the behavior of men colleagues through informal pressures such as speeches (Nugent 2019; Dietrich, Hayes, and O'Brien 2019) is important because it suggests that institutional norms are not as "sticky" as past research suggests.

The literature on bureaucratic representation finds that women's representation in street-level institutions can powerfully affect those who engage with these institutions (Keiser et al. 2002; Keiser and Wilkins 2004; Keiser 2010). Some of this literature argues that these gains happen when bureaucracies work on women's issues or issues that disproportionately affect women such as social welfare policies or sexual assault (Keiser and Wilkins 2004; Davis, Livermore, and Lim 2011). The scope of women's presence includes the positive influence of women math teachers at the high school level on the performance of adolescent girls' math scores. Keiser et al. (2002) show an empirical relationship here between having a woman math teacher and improved scores for girls on exams. But it is not clear *how* this process happens. In other words, are the women teachers teaching math differently than men who teach math? I would argue that the key to this effect is not necessarily whether women teach math differently but whether women math teachers change the perception of whether math is a domain for girls and that girls are good at or whether math is a domain for boys. This change in the gendered perception of math is the possible mechanism by which positive outcomes occur.

Quota systems increase women's representation, but they also change the composition of legislative institutions and the way these institutions function. Legislatures with quota systems have higher levels of descriptive representation as these bodies are more diverse (Barnes and Holman 2020)—an important outcome for democratic legitimacy and accountability. Smith, Warming, and Hennings (2016) measured the stereotypic beliefs about women, men, and political leadership in Latin America based on where countries had greater representation of women often, though not always, using gender quotas. The authors found that having more women in office, even without gender quotas, reduced the extent to which people held onto stereotypic beliefs about women's and men's roles—though these effects varied based on individual- and country-level variation. Other work measures the impact of women's representation through gender quotas looking at whether having more women in office decreased bias toward women on the ballot among voters in subsequent elections with some authors finding a positive effect for reducing bias (Paola, Scoppa, and Lombardo 2010) and other authors finding a null effect (Clayton 2018). This scholarship suggests that having more women in political office has the potential to change the extent to which individuals endorse stereotypic beliefs about women and men broadly or are willing to support women running for political office. However, this work does not directly measure whether stereotypic beliefs about institutions also change in response to women's increased representation.

The effects of WDR on individual levels of political engagement are less clear. Past work offers inconsistent conclusions on whether WDR leads women, and men, to become more engaged in politics with some research arguing for a positive effect for the increased representation of women (Clayton, O'Brien, and Piscopo 2019; Fridkin and Kenney 2014; Hinojosa and Kittilson 2020; Schwindt-Bayer 2010; Barnes and Taylor-Robinson 2018; Karp and Banducci 2008; Verge, Wisehomeier, and Espirito-Santo 2020; Goyal and Sells 2024) and other work finding a null or conditional effect (Wolak 2020c; Atkeson 2003; Wolak 2015; Broockman 2014; Dolan 2006; Lawless 2004; Huber and Gunderson 2023). I argue that key to identifying whether women's representation enhances political engagement is whether the masculine stereotypes of politics shift to become more feminine. Current research has yet to consider these feminizing processes.

The most common empirical approach to measuring the effects of WDR pairs survey data with observational data on women's rates of representation (see, e.g., Wolak (2020c); Atkeson (2003); Dolan (2006); Gunderson and Huber (2024); Hinojosa and Kittilson (2020); Barnes and Taylor-Robinson (2018)). This approach, sometimes, show a statistical relationship between the number of women in office and women's increased participation. But the causal relationship is not always tested in this research. Atkeson (2003) argues that when women run for office in *visible* campaigns, they can affect political engagement, but visibility is the key causal factor. Atkeson's test of visibility is the competitiveness of the election. This is not an unreasonable way to gauge visibility, but there are no measures to precisely get at how much information people had about women candidates or the level of news coverage the women candidates received—all of which can affect who is aware of women's candidacies. I argue that the missing link in past research to explain when and to what extent WDR will lead to more engagement in politics is whether having more women in government changes the gendered perceptions people hold about political institutions. My research tests the causal mechanisms between WDR and increased political engagement.

Institutions seen as more feminine will, according to my theory, lead to higher levels of political engagement among both women and men in the electorate for two key reasons. First, more feminine institutions will be seen as more inclusive bodies. Past work finds that the masculinity of politics tends to attract people who have more masculine traits than feminine traits, and this masculinity effect occurs among average citizens engaged in regular political participation, such as voting (McDermott 2016), and among those who run for political office (Conroy and Oliver 2020; Oliver and Conroy 2017). The results are that people who embody more feminine traits in their daily lives feel that politics is not a place for them. More feminine institutions will not deter those with dominantly masculine traits but will lead individuals for whom feminine traits are dominant to participate more in political processes. Second, feminine institutions will embody traits and behavioral characteristics that will increase individual levels of external political efficacy, or the idea that government will listen to people like them. Stauffer (2021) finds that even when people think that there are a lot of women in government, even if that is not necessarily accurate, people have higher levels of political efficacy. I argue that this increased efficacy effect comes not just from the presence of women in institutions but from the shift in the stereotypes associated with those institutions.

I build my theory of institutional stereotype change on two sets of scholarship. First, I consider research in the business and organization literatures on the effects of women entering the labor force. The seminal scholarship in this area is the work of Kanter (1977b, 1977a) who argued that as women enter masculine business organizations, the masculine norms of that organization break down. This scholarship led to the conclusion that when women reach a *critical mass* of 15 percent, masculine norms will erode (Dahlerup 2006).

The origins of the very precise 15 percent metric are not entirely clear as Kanter never says *how many* women constituent enough women, but the benchmark offered a useful tool for early scholars of gender and politics to assess the effects of women. The notion of a 15 percent critical mass in political institutions has largely fallen by the wayside and given rise to the concept of women as critical actors (MacDonald and O'Brien 2011; Childs and Krook 2009, 2008; Grey 2006; Tremblay 2006; Dahlerup 2006; Childs and Krook 2006). Women can operate as critical actors even if their numeric presence is less than 15 percent.

Second, I build on recent scholarship tracking the effects of WDR—starting with Hinojosa and Kittilson (2020). Hinojosa and Kittilson (2020) argue that women's collective representation will increase the feelings of political connectedness among women in the electorate; I expand on this argument to test how women's collective representation shifts the impressions people form about political institutions directly. The connection between stereotypes and institutions is one that few studies directly test (for an exception see Hawkesworth (2003)). Hinojosa and Kittilson (2020) argue that the effect of women's collective representation should be the strongest among women, but in their empirical analyses of women's representation in Uruguay, they find that both women and men have greater political connectedness. I build on this finding to test how women's representation increases political engagement among people who see themselves as having more feminine than masculine qualities. I argue, based on the findings from Hinojosa and Kittilson, that the effect of increasing WDR should be felt among women, men, and people with feminine and masculine personality attributes. Documenting these more expansive effects is especially important as McDermott (2016) argues that the gaps in who participates in politics is not so much a gap between women and men but a gap between people with masculine and people with feminine qualities.

Third, the participatory effects will be the strongest when WDR is visible, building on an argument tested first by Atkeson (2003) but built on by others (Fridkin and Kenney 2014; Burden, Ono, and Yamada 2017). The *visibility* benchmark has some roots in the critical mass scholarship first advanced by Kanter (1977a, b). Rather than benchmarking women's descriptive representation to a precise proportion, the visibility concept argues that the public's increased awareness of women's descriptive representation can change the relationship the public has with political institutions. The visibility of high-profile women in politics is part of the argument developed by Burden, Ono, and Yamada (2017) to explain why people are less resistant to electing more women to political office. These authors argue that the high-profile role of Hillary Clinton in public life has helped to make women's representation more visible. Hinojosa and Kittilson offer a useful way for me to test assumptions about women's visibility in office.

I center my research on institutional stereotypes for several reasons. First, there is scant scholarship on whether institutional stereotypes *can* change. While there are excellent theories in political science showing how political institutions came to have their current raced-gendered associations as white-masculine institutions (Hawkesworth 2003; Brown 2014a; Dittmar 2015), this research has yet to examine how these associations shift when political institutions become more diverse. Weeks (2022) shows that the implementation of quotas for women in parliaments not only increases the number of women in office but also increases the set of policies passed that rectify gender inequities. Past scholarship shows that the presence of women in elected office changes the outputs of political institutions, but this work has not yet connected these shifts to the gendered lens people use to evaluate political institutions. Second, the stereotypes voters hold of political institutions and the raced-gendered nature of those stereotypes affect who participates in politics in terms of candidates and citizens. The white-masculinity of politics attracts individuals who share these qualities, and it is not just that politics attracts white men, though it does, but it is that politics attracts women and men and people of color who see themselves as having *more* masculine traits rather than feminine traits (McDermott 2016; Oliver and Conroy 2017). Thus, the masculine nature of our political institutions excludes not just women, but women, men, and women and men of color who see themselves as having qualities such as being warm, gentle, or caring rather than tough, aggressive, and assertive. In other words, our political institutions, in their current form, are excluding a lot more people than past scholarship previously thought.

Masculinity not only limits who participates in politics but negatively affects how people think about political institutions. It is no secret that public approval of political institutions plummeted to new lows in recent decades. People report disliking the gamesmanship, aggressiveness, and grandstanding involved in politics (Hibbing and Theiss-Morse 2002), and it is noteworthy that these are all stereotypically masculine behaviors and qualities. I argue that part of why people hate political institutions is that these institutions are heavily steeped in performing norms of white-masculinity that can be harmful to creating well-functioning democratic systems. The masculinity of politics undermines democratic goals and norms. It is not only important that people report hating the masculine qualities of political institutions, but also important that people report wanting to see more feminine behaviors out of political institutions, such as compromise (Wolak 2020a). More feminine political institutions have the potential to be more inclusive if individuals start to think about political institutions in different ways.

Overview of Chapters

Chapter 2 delves more deeply into the theory of institutional stereotype change. I draw on literature from social psychology, organizational behavior, and behavioral economics to identify how the numeric presence of women or men in an institution affects the stereotypic lens through which people see that institution. I outline the major tenets of my theory of institutional stereotype change and outline each of the major hypotheses tested through the remaining chapter. I delineate and elaborate on all the hypotheses the empirical chapters will test. Here, I not only explain how the public came to identify political institutions as masculine institutions, but I also make the argument that the white-masculinity of political institutions is a critical part of why many Americans opt out of political participation and why the public holds these institutions (i.e., Congress) in such low esteem.

Chapter 3 addresses the first major question guiding this book: *Do individuals stereotype political institutions that are more diverse along racial and gender lines as less masculine and less white compared to institutions that under-represent women and people of color?* I focus on testing how women's presence, alone, can change the gendered perceptions of political institutions from masculine to feminine. The experiments in Chapter 3 vary whether institutions are majority-women or majority-men and the level of office at stake, a legislative or an executive institution. This feature of the study design in Chapter 3 also lends insights into the book's third major question: *Are the feminizing effects of more diverse institutions more likely to be felt at different types of political office?* The experiments presented in this chapter show that people see majority-women legislative and executive institutions as more feminine than majority-men institutions.

Chapter 4 focuses on the distinct impact of women of color's descriptive representation in political institutions. Women's representation, more generally, has the power to undo the *masculine* stereotypes of political office, but it is women of color that are uniquely positioned, due to their intersectional identities, to undo both the raced and gendered perceptions of political institutions. I develop a theory for how women of color uniquely transform and undo the raced-gendered perceptions of political institutions, and I test this theory with a series of survey experiments. I conduct a series of experiments to track how the presence of women of color affects the gendered and racialized traits associated with political institutions. These experiments also show that the increased representation of women of color increases individual feelings of trust and confidence in political institutions. Moreover, people see institutions that represent women of color well as better able to work on a variety of political issues that affect the daily lives of individuals, especially individuals belonging to minoritized groups.

Chapter 5 tackles the third question grounding this manuscript: *How does changing the stereotypic perceptions the public holds of political institutions change the way women and men engage in political participation and evaluate political institutions?* I argue that more feminine political institutions will lead to higher perceptions of institutional trust and legitimacy. Past scholarship finds mixed effects for whether women's increased representation does, in fact, lead to positive effects among individual perceptions of political institutions (Clayton, O'Brien, and Piscopo 2019; Wolak 2020c; Atkeson 2003). A reason for these mixed findings is that past work fails to consider this process of stereotypic change. If women enter political institutions at increased rates but do not lead voters to see these institutions as less masculine, then it is unlikely that women's representation will have positive effects on voters. However, if women change stereotypic perceptions of institutions, then it is likely that people will view political institutions more positively, and can increase their own levels of political engagement. I test these outcomes drawing on the experimental tests presented in Chapters 3 and 4.

Chapter 6 addresses the final question of this book: *How do the news media communicate the feminizing effects of WDR?* I propose a framework of feminine and masculine political process in news coverage to explain when and how the news media will shift the frames used to talk about the process by which Congress, and other key political actors, considers, negotiates, and passes legislation. Past work shows quite clearly that the news media rely on frames of conflict and gridlock (Meeks 2013), all stereotypically masculine behaviors, to cover political processes—and these frames turn individuals off politics. Breaking down the white-masculine stereotypes of political institutions will shift how the news media talk about the political process to rely on feminine political process frames. Feminine political process frames, a new concept I introduce in this book, highlight compromise and consensus-building over fighting and obstructionism. I show how the use of feminine process frames emerges by tracking news coverage of Congress and its passage of key legislation such as budgets from 2007 through to the present. I match these time frames with data on women's representation in Congress which includes periods with Nancy Pelosi as Speaker of the House and the leader of the Democratic Party. With more women in political office, the news media will, I argue and show, be more likely to receive information about feminine stereotypic behaviors from Congress and will also get a more balanced picture of how legislative processes work.

The final chapter presents a summary of the key findings from this book about the effect of women's presence in political institutions on the way individuals see these political institutions through a racial and gendered lens. Perceptions of political institutions matter. If individuals see political institutions as exclusionary places primarily for white men, then individuals who are women and people of color may be less likely to participate in these institutions due to lower levels of trust, credibility, and political efficacy. Moreover, the white-masculine stereotypic perception of political institutions can depress political participation from those who do not share these qualities, namely non-white individuals, and those who do not see themselves as having masculine qualities. Changing these narrow perceptions of political institutions can occur through women's increased descriptive representation. Individuals see institutions that represent more women and more women of color as less masculine and more feminine, and this outcome increases political participation and engagement. Chapter 7 outlines the key implications of this research and identifies new lines of inquiries that can build on the theory of institutional stereotype change presented here. Indeed, the findings in this book about how to undo narrow and damaging perceptions of political institutions apply to other white-masculine institutions that under-represent women and people of color.

2

The Gendered (Political) Pictures in Our Minds

At the 2019 State of the Union address, the women of Congress attended the event donned in white suits and white dresses for the occasion. The choice to wear white was a strategic one meant to harken to the suffragists of the early twentieth century who protested, marched, and advocated for women's right to vote while wearing white. For the suffragists, wearing white was a symbolic choice meant to signify women's moral purity.[1] A key plank of the suffragist argument was that women were morally superior to men embodying traits like honesty and trust (McConnaughy 2013; Teele 2019). The suffragists argued that these positive qualities, which fit into conventional feminine stereotypes (Prentice and Carranza 2002), made them particularly well-suited to participate in political life through voting. In other words, allowing women to participate in democracy could, perhaps, give political institutions more feminine qualities. At this time, politics already had an association with negative masculine qualities with a reputation for corruption (Scott 1969)—and this perception has been slow to shift.

The women wearing white at the State of the Union in 2019 used their attire to draw attention to the marginalized status of women in social, political, and economic life rather than women's moral purity. More specifically, the women, mostly Democratic women, who wore white in 2019 did so in solidarity with the women leading the charge in the #MeToo movement. The #MeToo and Times Up movement gained traction in 2017 through 2018 and was a public reckoning holding powerful men who abused and harassed women accountable for their actions (Ghosh et al. 2022). The #MeToo movement occurred across many public institutions including the entertainment industry, the news media, state legislatures, and the US Congress. A *New York Times* investigation found that 201 men in powerful positions lost their jobs and some faced criminal charges for harassing and abusing women.[2] Congress was not immune as nearly a

[1] https://www.teenvogue.com/story/history-of-color-white-womens-suffrage-movement
[2] https://www.nytimes.com/interactive/2018/10/23/us/metoo-replacements.html

Feminizing Political Institutions. Nichole M. Bauer, Oxford University Press. © Nichole M. Bauer (2026).
DOI: 10.1093/9780197841556.003.0002

dozen men resigned or lost their re-election bids in 2018 because of sexual harassment allegations. The #MeToo scandal not only shed light on the bad behavior of men in power but on how institutions protect those men. State legislatures across the country re-vamped their policies around workplace sexual harassment to better protect survivors (Mahoney, Kearney, and Shaffer 2020). Congress faced scrutiny for a burdensome sexual harassment-reporting process that required survivors to undergo counseling before any official investigation or punishment for the perpetrator could begin. Instead of protecting the most vulnerable, over-worked, and often poorly paid staffers and unpaid interns, the institution protected those in power. The #MeToo movement forced Congress, and other institutions, to change their policies to better prevent abuse and to protest those who report abuse.

At the first State of the Union after the 2018-midterms, the record-setting numbers of women in Congress, and allied men, decided to make a bold statement through their white attire. News coverage the day after the State of the Union featured photos of the women wearing white. Headlines from major papers read: "State of the Union: Here's Why Women Are Wearing White" from *Time* magazine, "Democratic women send political message by wearing white to State of the Union," in *USA Today,* and "Why Democratic Women Wore White at State of the Union," in the *New York Times.* The white clothing stood out against the dark, black, gray, and navy suits worn by most members of Congress. The image of the women in white was certainly a striking one that led to public discussions about the broader status and role of women within politics. Indeed, the images people hold of political institutions are shaped by *who* serves in those institutions.

Individuals form opinions about issues, people, and political institutions based on what Walter Lippman referred to as the "pictures in our heads" (1922). These pictures are the mental representations people conjure up when thinking about a particular subject. For example, if you ask people to think about a nurse, chances are good that most people will think about a woman wearing white and caring for other people. When many people think about political leaders, they conjure images of men, mostly white men (Bauer 2020a), and the association between white men and leadership becomes ingrained in how people think early in childhood (Bos et al. 2022). The visible representations people see matters for the impressions they form (Paivio 1979). Visual representations of politics are rife with gendered images that often reinforce masculine stereotypes (Carpinella and Bauer 2021) and these images can affect evaluations of candidates and leaders (Bauer and Carpinella 2018; Boussalis et al. 2021).

Individuals receive information about political institutions through visual cues including the photos of members of Congress or the president as well as the types of news stories written about the actors in these key political institutions and through social media. Research by Bos, Doorn, and Nelson (2018) found that images of political leaders frequently include images of women—suggesting visibility and perhaps an over-representation of women. These visual cues and the information people get about politics through the news media affect the way people think about politics (Cappella and Jamieson 1996). My theory of institutional stereotype change argues that when people start to see visible representations, listen to, or read news stories about women in politics, the "pictures in their heads" will shift from masculinity to femininity. This chapter provides more detail on how and why political institutions are associated with characteristics defined by white-masculinity. I outline my central theory behind how women's descriptive representation can shift the white-masculine images people hold of institutions to include more feminine qualities, and I preview each of the hypotheses I test in the subsequent chapters. Before moving onto my tests of stereotype change in Chapter 3, I conclude this chapter with three short empirical analyses. First, I review descriptive data on women's rates of representation in the US. Second, I track news coverage of women's descriptive representation after the 2024 election. Third, I then offer a short empirical test to confirm that people do, in fact, think of most political institutions through the lens of masculinity.

How Political Institutions Became Raced-Gender Institutions

Gender and race underlie how people think about political leaders in both implicit and explicit ways. Implicitly, when individuals think about leaders, they tend to think about white men. Oxley et al. (2020) asked children throughout the US to draw images of the presidency, a visible leadership role that many children learn about in American politics from a young age. The authors aimed to see whether Obama's presidency as the first Black president coupled with Hillary Clinton's historic presidential run shifted the stereotypic images people hold of white-masculine leadership. The authors found that most school age children drew images of white men as leaders, even though many of these children had only lived under the Obama presidency. In research for my first book, *The Qualifications Gap*, I asked an adult sample to find images of political leaders on the internet, and individuals overwhelmingly found images of white men as indicative of typical leaders (Bauer 2020a). The image of white men as leaders are continually reinforced by their dominance in political leadership roles, but the origins of these raced-gendered associations extend much deeper.

Social role theory uses an evolutionary perspective to track how stereotypes about women and stereotypes about men developed (Eagly 1987). Gender stereotypes map onto the separate roles designated for women and for men (Eagly and Karau 2002), and these roles lead to broad stereotypes about institutions, organizations, and professions (Glick and Fiske 1996). Social role theory offers a useful lens for understanding how masculinity came to dominate political leadership roles (Schneider and Bos 2019). Leadership roles are associated with masculinity, and these roles developed from the division of labor between men and women in the formation of very early communities that existed several millennia ago (Eagly 1987). When people first formed communities, these communities needed to divide the tasks necessary for ensuring the community's survival. Such tasks include hunting, gathering food, and producing children. The biological abilities of women and men dictated divisions of labor. For women, their reproductive roles defined their social roles. Even after pregnancy and the act of childbirth ended, childcare placed inordinate demands on women's bodies through behaviors such as breast feeding required to nurture and care for children—and these extra caregiving roles performed by women persist today (Hochschild and Machung 1990).

Tasks performed by men included hunting and protecting communities. Because men did not become pregnant and did not shoulder childcare responsibilities, they performed tasks that allowed them to be away from their families and communities for long periods of time (Wood and Eagly 2012). Oftentimes, hunting for food required men to temporarily leave their communities, and taking a baby or a toddler hunting was not safe or practical. Of course, in these early communities, women still performed a lot of tasks that required physical strength, like farming, but they did so while staying closer to home. These hunting and protection tasks men performed evolved into broader leadership roles while women's roles evolved to relegate them to the home (Eagly and Karau 2002). These role divisions between women and men evolved over time into the familiar feminine and masculine stereotypes that persist today.

This evolutionary and historic account for the development of women's and men's roles explains the processes by which masculinity became aligned with political leadership, but it does not account for the association with leadership and whiteness. In the American context, whiteness, masculinity, and political leadership are bound together in unique ways through the nation's history with slavery, Jim Crowe laws, and other practices that stoked racial prejudice and segregation. Stereotypes about race, especially stereotypes about Black men as violent or lazy, developed in the American context to justify the chattel slave system that fueled the American economic system in the early years of the country's founding (Acharya, Blackwell, and Sen 2018; Valentino, Hutchings, and White 2002; Sears and Valentino 2005). The development and enforcement of these negative racial stereotypes led to the perception that only white men had the qualities necessary to fill pivotal leadership roles, and leadership became, in the American context, associated with white-masculinity.

While serving in leadership roles, the men in charge create rules, norms, and processes that serve to solidify their positions in these roles of power while excluding others (Fenno 1962; Cox and McCubbins 1993; Rohde 1991; Hawkesworth 2003; Karpowitz and Mendelberg 2014; Barnes 2016; Phillips 2023). Take, for instance, the norm of giving deference to seniority when assigning committee chair positions (Krehbiel 1990). This practice reflects a patriarchal rule structure that favors men. At face value, the norm does not appear all that raced or gendered but the norm has a gendered dimension. Men start their political careers earlier than women and have more time to build seniority while women start political careers later due to life-cycle demands, namely, the burdens of child-rearing and the second-shift (Burrell 1994; Lazarus, Steigerwalt, and Clark 2023). Women because they start their careers later take more time to reach the seniority level needed to be able to use that seniority to stake out a position as committee chair. Seniority norms reinforce hierarchical power relationships which is a central principle underlying the structure of gender relationships (Acker 1992). The seniority rule ensures that men in Congress get to chair powerful committees thereby locking more junior women out of key leadership roles (Senk 2023).

A recent example of the raced-gendered norms of Congress is the unlikely alliance of Democrat Brittany Petersen, of Colorado's 3rd district, and Republican Anna Paulina Luna, of Florida's 13th district, at the start of the 119th Congress. Representative Pettersen, at the start of 2025, was in the latter stages of pregnancy, and she was set to give birth in early February. Rules in the US House required that all members physically be present to vote on rules, legislation, and other House business. Because Representative Pettersen was so close to giving birth, she could not be physically present to vote. Representative Pettersen, working with Republican Anna Paulina Luna, petitioned House Speaker Mike Johnson to allow proxy voting when House members are absent for childbirth and childcare. The rule change would have applied to both women and men. Speaker Johnson's response was an emphatic no on the rule change arguing that the original Congress did not allow for proxy voting for people giving birth, so the current Congress could not allow it. Of course, the first US Congress included only white men.[3]

Congress also displays masculine behavior in more overt ways. The use of filibusters, either active filibusters with a legislator speaking on the floor or just obstructing legislation, reflects an agentic display of power where one person, often but not always a man brings legislative work to a halt, singlehandedly. Senator Tommy Tuberville, a Republican from Alabama, used the threat of a filibuster to block the nomination of some 400 military leaders to higher positions to try and force the Pentagon to change its policy on access to abortion for servicemembers. The blockade of these military appointments and Tuberville's refusal to relent even when facing pressure from co-partisans represent a very masculine way of exercising power. It is also worth noting that Tuberville is using a masculine practice, the filibuster, to protest a masculine institution, the military, over a policy that disproportionately affects women.

More overt displays of power and strength are not unusual in legislatures around the globe as evidenced through studies of legislative brawls (Batto and Beaulieu 2020). It has been some 170 years since one member of Congress beat another member with a cane. However, threats of violence, an extreme form of masculinity, are not a relic of the past.[4] In a single 24-hour period in November 2023, there were multiple incidents of members of Congress engaging in or threatening to engage in physical force against another person. Senator Markwayne Mullin of Oklahoma appeared to challenge the Teamsters President Sean O'Brien to a physical fight during a Senate hearing.[5] Senator Mullin even stood up and started to remove his wedding ring presumably so he could throw a bunch at the witness. A Republican representative from Tennessee accused then recently unseated House Speaker Kevin McCarthy of elbowing him in the back while passing one another in a crowded hallway.[6] Representative James Comer of Kentucky called Representative Jared Moskowitz of Florida a "smurf"[7] because Representative Moskowitz was

---

[3] As of June 2025, the new rule for proxy voting did not come to pass and a compromise arrangement was worked out between Representative Luna and Speaker Johnson to allow vote pairing when members are absent for childbirth and childcare reasons.

[4] This caning occurred on May 22, 1856, when South Carolina Representative Preston Brooks beat Senator Charles Sumner until he was unconscious. The caning occurred over a dispute about admitting Kansas as a free state or a slave state. See the US Senate website for more information: https://www.senate.gov/artandhistory/history/minute/The_Caning_of_Senator_Charles_Sumner.htm#:~:text=On%20May%2022%2C%201856%2C%20the,beat%20a%20senator%20into%20unconsciousness.

[5] https://www.usatoday.com/story/news/politics/2023/11/14/markwayne-mullin-teamsters-sean-obrian-fight-senate/71580882007/

[6] https://www.msnbc.com/morning-joe/watch/-he-was-shoved-reporter-details-mccarthy-allegedly-hitting-colleague-197908549680

[7] For those unfamiliar, the smurfs were a cartoon from the 1980s that featured very small and very blue beings, though they were smurfs not people. See https://en.wikipedia.org/wiki/The_Smurfs for more on smurfs.

wearing a blue suit.[8] These displays of aggression, both physical and verbal, reinforce white-masculine norms of behavior in Congress—though these examples do not exactly demonstrate behavior in line with norms of "good leadership."

The over-valuing of masculinity can lead to the under-valuing of femininity in the institution. Of course, it is not always the case that femininity is under-valued or on display in political institutions. Former Speaker of the House John Boehner was well-known, some might say infamous, for crying while in public office. A cursory search on YouTube for the phrase "John Boehner crying" produces 2350 videos of the former speaker shedding tears—and many of these videos are compilations. Insightful commentaries[9] of Boehner's tears point out that he usually cried about things that related to him, such as his meeting with the pope, and not shedding tears in a display of empathy for other people—which fits with masculine stereotypes given the inward focus of his emotions. The displays of tears by Boehner contrast with the almost display of tears by then presidential candidate Hillary Clinton in 2008. Clinton did not actually shed tears when she appeared in front of supporters in New Hampshire, but the appearance of emotion haunted her presidential campaign. Displays of feminine behavior in masculine institutions, when they happen, often occur from men, and are seen as aberrations from the norm. Displays of feminine behaviors by women are often seen as disqualifying.

Crying is a more irregular form of a feminine behavior that one would not necessarily expect to see often on display in political institutions. There are other more stereotypically feminine behaviors that fit with behaviors that are normatively desirable in politics (Guttmann and Thompson 2012), such as building compromise and consensus to pass legislation. Women's stereotypic behaviors promote compromise while men's stereotypic behaviors promote conflict when in leadership roles (Eagly and Carli 2003a; Vinkenburg et al. 2011). Compromise is a behavior that the public says they want to see more of from Congress (Wolak 2020a). When the news media cover congressional behavior, the narrative often is one about conflict and not one about compromise (Cappella and Jamieson 1996). A dominant media narrative about conflict incentivizes political leaders to instigate conflict as a means of gaining news coverage which can bolster a politician's reputation and name recognition.

The association between masculinity and political leadership is reinforced through multiple feedback channels in political life from the visible presence

---

[8] https://thehill.com/homenews/house/4309288-moskowitz-comer-tense-exchange/
[9] https://www.politico.com/magazine/story/2013/12/weeper-of-the-house-john-boehner-cries-100557

of men in media coverage (Baitinger 2015) to the conflict-driven tone of media discourse (Klar and Krupnikov 2016). These forces coalesce to shape the white-masculine image people hold of political institutions. The next section outlines how these entrenched stereotypes can be overturned.

The Logic of Dismantling Institutional Stereotypes

This book advances a theory of institutional stereotype change that delineates the conditions under which the raced-gendered perceptions individuals have about political institutions will change to become less entrenched with white-masculinity. A strong body of scholarship exists tracing how political institutions in the US are raced-gendered institutions (Hawkesworth 2003; Brown 2014a), and these racing and gendering processes are intertwined. Indeed, the raced-gendered dynamics of institutions lead some women legislators to subtly subvert these masculine norms to behave in ways that resemble feminine steroetypes but also are not as visible (Eatough and Preece 2025; Barnes 2016; Anzia and Berry 2011).

I argue that the primary catalyst for undoing the raced-gendered stereotyping of political institutions is through increasing the diversity of who serves in elected political office. When women's and women of color's descriptive representation increases, the raced-gendered perceptions of political institutions will break down. Evidence of these breakdowns will occur through the way individuals stereotype political institutions, increased political participation from those who are conventionally least likely to participate, and improved institutional trust and credibility.

Economics research finds that the gendered perceptions of occupations can change (Levanon, England, and Allison 2009). The dominance of one gender or racial group in a social role or occupation strongly predicts the gender stereotypes associated with that role or occupation (Glick, Wilk, and Perreault 1995). The military is associated with masculinity, in part, because most service members are men. Likewise, the field of nursing is classified as a feminine profession because, in part, most nurses are women. When the balance of men to women in a profession changes, the stereotypic impressions people have of that profession also changes. These shifts can occur from feminine to masculine and masculine to feminine. For example, up until the last 100 years, most babies were delivered by midwives, and these midwives were women (Varney and Thompson 2016). As the medical industry became more formalized requiring medical degrees and licenses, the field of obstetrics emerged and was initially dominated by men (Summey and

Hurst 1986).[10] The medical field, especially being a doctor, is perceived over-all as a masculine profession. The stereotypes of those groups will transfer from the individuals to the institution. Yoder and Schleicher (1996) explains: "What made medical school masculine in the 1970s was not the tasks physicians did (job content) and not the personal characteristics of doctors (personality), but simply the basic demographic fact that most medical practitioners were men" (p. 174). An example of a shift from masculine to feminine is the field of real estate. Just a half-century ago, most real estate agents were men. As women increasingly entered the workforce, real estate became an attractive option, in part, because it allowed for the kind of flexibility women need to balance their professional life with their family life, or to manage the proverbial second-shift. The field of real estate, especially when it comes to helping people purchase homes, is one where feminine qualities, like having strong interpersonal relationship-building skills, are seen as an advantage.

Social psychology research suggests broad over-time changes in the stereo-typic beliefs held about women are possible. In a half-decade, women went from being primarily homemakers and mothers to having careers while often still being homemakers and mothers (Eagly et al. 2020). Diekman and Eagly (2000) found that stereotypes about women in the present and future include a mix of feminine and masculine qualities, whereas stereotypes about women from the past more narrowly focused on traditional feminine qualities. These shifts occurred due to women's entrance into the labor force and women taking on more stereotypically masculine roles in stereotypically masculine institutions. Important to note is that Diekman and Eagly (2000) do not find a similar shift for men largely because men's social roles have not expanded. Even with changes in stereotypes about women, there are still marked differences in the stereotypes held of women and men (Haines, Deaux, and Lofaro 2016; Eagly et al. 2020). The key catalyst in this stereotype change is women's increased presence in conventionally masculine institutions.

The gendered lens through which people evaluate an institution or an organization is shaped by *who* serves in that institution (Glick, Wilk, and Perreault 1995; Glick 1991; Acker 1990; Kanter 1977b). For most of American history, it is white men who served in political office and in key leadership roles (Brown 2014a; Rosenthal 1995). White men, even with women's representation at a high level, still hold most elected offices in the US and are most political candidates in elections. My theory of dismantling masculine stereotypes centers on the descriptive representation of under-represented

---

[10] The obstetrics-gynecology specialization has, in the last decade, become more gender-balanced and appears to tilt toward more women. https://www.ama-assn.org/medical-students/specialty-profiles/how-medical-specialties-vary-gender

groups increasing in a noticeable and visible fashion. I test how WDR will change both the raced and gendered stereotypes of institutions. In this way, the stereotypes and perceptions of an institution are tied to the individuals who serve in that institution. However, my argument of stereotype change is not a case of people simply applying the stereotypes of those in an institution to the institution. The stereotypes people hold of men are not the exact same as the stereotypes people hold of political institutions—though there is considerable overlap. Men are stereotyped as being physically strong (Koenig et al. 2011) but I do not expect people will stereotype political institutions as physically strong. Physical strength is not an attribute that is relevant or applicable to a political institution. I expect some overlap in the stereotypes people apply to women and to majority-women institutions, but institutional stereotypes are separate constructs from the stereotypes about women more generally.

Preview of Key Predictions

In this section, I outline the basic logic behind my empirical predictions below and provide a fuller theoretic account for these predictions in the following empirical chapters. Table 2.1 previews each prediction, the empirical test used for the prediction, and the chapter in which the hypothesis test occurs.

The shift toward more feminine political institutions will start with changes in the gender balance of who serves in political institutions. These changes will then lead to a shift in the traits that individuals associate with an institution. I argue that a substantial increase in WDR can change the stereotypes associated with political institutions. The question of what constitutes a substantial increase is not a question of how many women are enough, but how visible women are in institutions (Hinojosa and Kittilson 2020; Atkeson 2003). I argue that visible gains in WDR will affect the stereotypic views that individuals hold of political institutions. The gendered shifts hypothesis delineate this effect below:

Gendered Shifts Prediction: Higher rates of women's descriptive representation will lead people to associate political institutions with more feminine and fewer masculine stereotypic qualities.

These gendered shifts may not occur evenly across all types of institutions. There are three ways past scholarship considers how stereotypes map onto different types of political institutions. First, there is the distinction between

Table 2.1 Key Predictions

Prediction	Empirical Test	Chapter
Gendered Shifts Prediction: Higher rates of women's descriptive representation will lead people to associate political institutions with more feminine and fewer masculine stereotypic qualities.	Experiments	Chapter 3
Institutional Type Prediction: The feminizing effects of women's descriptive representation are more likely to occur in a legislative (local-level) relative to an executive (state-level) political institution.	Experiments	Chapter 3
Partisan Differences Prediction: The feminizing effects of WDR will be stronger among Democrats relative to Republicans or Independents.	Experiments	Chapter 3 & Chapter 4
Raced-Gendered Prediction: Women of color's descriptive representation will weaken the white-masculine stereotypes associated with political institutions more so than the descriptive representation of White women and people of color more generally.	Experiments	Chapter 4
Linked Fate Prediction: Voters of color will be more likely to see institutions that descriptively represent women of color as more feminine and inclusive relative to white voters.	Experiments	Chapter 4
Political Engagement Prediction: Individuals, both women and men, will express more willingness to participate in politics when stereotyping institutions as more feminine relative to more masculine institutions.	Experiments	Chapter 5
Institutional Evaluation Prediction: Individuals will rate more feminine institutions more positively than masculine institutions.	Experiments	Chapter 5
Gendered Engagement Prediction: More feminine political institutions will lead to higher levels of engagement and more positive institutional evaluations among those who have more feminine traits over masculine traits.	Experiments	Chapter 5
Gendered Discourse Prediction: As the number of women in Congress increases, news coverage of political processes will reflect more feminine process frames compared to when there are lower levels of women in Congress.	Longitudinal content analysis of new coverage	Chapter 6
Gendered Source Prediction: Women's increased representation should lead the news media to rely on women political leaders as sources in news coverage.	Longitudinal content analysis of new coverage	Chapter 6

higher (federal) and lower levels of office (state and local). It is thought that as the prestige, power, and scope of an institution increases, the association with masculinity becomes stronger (Duerst-Lahti 2007; Conroy 2015).

The presidency is, arguably, considered to be most strongly associated with masculine stereotypes, but it is not clear if this association means lower offices are associated with feminine stereotypes or just less strongly associated with feminine stereotypes (Crowder-Meyer, Gadarian, and Trounstine 2015). The second way that past scholarship considers different types of institutions and their association with feminine or masculine stereotypes is through the issues associated with the office. Federal offices are associated with more masculine stereotypes because these offices prioritize policymaking around masculine issues (Holman et al. 2019) while state and local offices prioritize more feminine issues (Fox and Oxley 2003). By this logic, state and local offices should be seen as more feminine, however, past work shows that voters prefer candidates with masculinity even at these lower levels (Bauer 2020b; Conroy and Oliver 2020). The third way past work considers stereotypes across institutional types is through the activities or behaviors of the institutions. Executive institutions are thought to be more masculine because they involve a single actor holding a substantial amount of power, whereas a legislative institution involves a group of people who must work together (Dolan and Lynch 2016; Sweet-Cushman 2022). For practical reasons that I will detail in the following chapter, I consider differences in the feminizing of institutions across legislative and executive offices and then across state and local offices. Because I primarily test these feminizing effects at the state and local level, I cannot directly test how more women in Congress or a woman president might feminize those specific offices. The institutional type prediction details the feminizing differences I expect to find across offices.

Institutional Type Prediction: The feminizing effects of women's descriptive representation are more likely to occur in a legislative (local-level) relative to an executive (state-level) political institution.

A long-line of scholarship shows that people associate the Democratic Party as owning feminine issues, such as education or healthcare, and people associate the Republican Party as owning masculine issues, such as national security or crime (Petrocik, Benoit, and Hansen 2003). When it comes to gendered trait associations, the Democratic Party is more strongly associated with feminine traits while the Republican Party is associated with masculine traits such as aggression and assertiveness (Winter 2010, 2008; Hayes 2011; Hayes 2005). Moreover, the Democratic Party relative to the Republican Party has a reputation for recruiting and fielding women political candidates (Ondercin 2017). As such, I expect the feminizing effects predicted in my first hypothesis to occur most strongly among Democratic individuals. I still expect feminizing effects to occur among Republicans, but they just might not be as strong as they are for Democrats. The partisan differences prediction outlines these distinctions.

Partisan Differences Prediction: The feminizing effects of WDR will be stronger among Democrats relative to Republicans or Independents.

Women of color, I argue, are better positioned than men of color to change raced-gendered stereotypes than white women and men of color. I elaborate more on why women of color are well-positioned to change raced-gendered stereotypes of institutions in Chapter 4 but summarize my logic. Women of color frequently behave in ways that combine masculine stereotypes with feminine stereotypes of women as more communal and caring for others. White women often, though not always, behave in ways that prioritize their racial identities (Junn 2017). Men of color's descriptive representation is, of course, important for ensuring strong levels of group representation. But men of color will, I argue, not be able to shift both the raced and gendered stereotypes of political institutions. Stereotypes about men of color often reinforce masculine stereotypes (Schneider and Bos 2011) though masculine stereotypes applied to men of color do not convey the same meaning as they do in the context of white men (Dawson 2001). I argue that having more women of color in political institutions will lead people to see political institutions through an intersectional lens and not through a white-masculine lens. The raced-gendered prediction outlines the effects of women of color's descriptive representation.

Raced-Gendered Prediction: Women of color's descriptive representation will weaken the white-masculine stereotypes associated with political institutions more so than the descriptive representation of white women and people of color more generally.

Undoing the raced-gendered images of political institutions may occur more strongly among communities of color as opposed to white voters. The concept of linked fate defines the connection often perceived and felt between voters of color and representatives who share their minoritized ethnorace identity (Simien 2005; White, Laird, and Allen 2014). Voters of color may be more likely to observe and respond to increases in women of color's representation in ways that lead to a stronger weakening of white-masculine perceptions of political institutions compared to the perceptions held by white voters.

Linked Fate Prediction: Voters of color will be more likely to see institutions that descriptively represent women of color as more feminine and inclusive relative to white voters.

Pitkin (1967) argued that one of the effects of descriptive representation is that when political institutions mirror the people they represent along dimensions such as gender, the electorate will see the institution as more legitimate and this will increase political engagement. I argue that it is not necessarily *just* WDR that increases political engagement but the corresponding shift to seeing institutions through a feminine stereotypic lens. I expect these effects to occur for both women and men. The political engagement prediction outlines these effects below:

Political Engagement Prediction: Individuals, both women and men, will express more willingness to participate in politics when stereotyping institutions as more feminine relative to more masculine institutions.

Individuals hold negative views of legislative institutions (Hibbing and Theiss-Morse 2002) and see politics as rife with conflict and gridlock (Guttmann and Thompson 2012)—due in part to the news media's tendency to emphasize conflict and scandal over collaboration and compromise (Mutz 2015; Klar and Krupnikov 2016) which align with negative stereotypes associated with masculinity (Vinkenburg et al. 2011). The masculine, uncivil, and aggressive behaviors of Congress contribute to low levels of trust in political institutions (Mutz and Reeves 2005). While there is an extensive body of research tracing the negative impressions individuals hold of political institutions, there is less research measuring the factors that lead individuals to form more positive impressions of political institutions (for exceptions, see Bush and Zetterberg (2021); Clayton, O'Brien, and Piscopo (2019); (Kao et al. 2024)). I argue that more feminine institutions will improve evaluations of political institutions.

Institutional Evaluation Prediction: Individuals will rate more feminine institutions more positively than masculine institutions.

McDermott (2016) finds in her research that individuals who identify as having more feminine traits over masculine traits are those least likely to participate in the political system. Rather, the masculinity of politics attracts masculine citizens, both women and men, who are more likely to participate in politics and who are more likely to pursue political office (McDermott

2016; Bittner and Goodyear-Grant 2017; Conroy and Oliver 2020; Oliver and Conroy 2017). I argue that when women's increased descriptive representation leads to political offices being seen as more feminine, more individuals who identify as having feminine traits over masculine traits will be more likely to participate in politics and see political institutions in a more positive light. The gendered-engagement hypothesis below predicts these effects.

Gendered Engagement Prediction: More feminine political institutions will lead to higher levels of engagement and more positive institutional evaluations among those who have more feminine traits over masculine traits.

The news media are a key mechanism by which the public learns about politics and representation (Cook 1997; Patterson 1997; Schudson 1998). If the news media do not report on politics, it is much harder for people to learn about who represents them and how representation occurs. I argue that as WDR increases, the news media will start to change *how* they report on political processes to reflect more feminine stereotypes, or what I call *feminine process news,* and will rely less on conventional masculine stereotypes used to report on politics, or what I term *masculine process news.* I argue that feminine political process news is a critical mechanism by which the feminizing effects of WDR trickle down to the public.

Gendered Discourse Prediction: As the number of women in Congress increases, news coverage of political processes will reflect more feminine process frames compared to when there are lower levels of women in Congress.

Beyond the use of more feminine frames in political news coverage, more women in political office should also change whose voices appear in news coverage. More women in office should lead to the inclusion of more women's voices used as sources and experts in news coverage. Part of this effect should simply be motivated by the fact that more women in Congress means more available to quote and interview in news coverage. I expect that higher rates of women's representation should lead to differences in how journalists identify the stakeholders in passing legislation and who is affected by public policies in a way that leads them to include more women's voices.

Gendered Source Prediction: As the number of women in Congress increases, journalists will rely on women political leaders as sources in news coverage more frequently compared to when there are lower levels of women in Congress.

Chapters three through six work through testing of these predictions relying on several unique data collections including innovative survey experiments and an exhaustive content analysis of political news coverage. Before turning to the substantive tests of my institutional stereotype change theory, I conduct three analyses. First, I assess the state of WDR in American politics. Second, I offer an initial test of the visibility of WDR through post-election news coverage. Third, I consider whether people see political institutions, across different levels and types of office, as more masculine than feminine. There is an assumption that some political office, such as local offices, are seen as more feminine than masculine. I test this assumption.

The State of Women's Representation

Central to my theory of institutional stereotype change is the premise that women's representation is increasing. The current US Congress is the most gender and racially diverse. As of the summer of 2025, 151 women serve in the US House and US Senate, holding approximately 28 percent of seats.[11] Of these women lawmakers, sixty-one are women of color, which is just under 10 percent of the total seats between the House and the Senate. These rates of representation are the highest ever for women and women of color. At the close of the 2022 congressional term, Nancy Pelosi finished her second run as Speaker of the House, making her one of the most visible and high-ranking women in American politics. Since 2018, a group of women legislators dubbed "the squad" dominate political discourse in Congress, their districts, and on national platforms such as social media. Notable about the squad is that these women are women of color. This heightened visibility coupled with the growing ranks of women in Congress sets the stage on the federal level for the public to shift how they think about *who* serves in political office.

Women's presence in Congress certainly has the power to undo the white-masculine stereotypes of political institutions. But I argue and empirically test in later chapters the effect women's representation has on the stereotyping of political institutions at both the state and local level. Indeed, local and state governments are closest to home for many individuals. State and local offices are the political bodies that make decisions directly affecting people's lives such as trash collection, the quality of roads, and the accessibility of

---

[11] https://cawp.rutgers.edu/facts/levels-office/congress/women-us-congress-2023

health care facilities. Figure 2.1 plots the proportion of women state legislatures, combining upper and lower chambers, in each of the fifty states. There is considerable variation in women's representation in state legislatures, but some of the bodies that represent women at the highest rates are at the state legislative level. Across all state legislatures, as of 2025, there are 2469 women serving in the lower or upper house legislative chamber.[12] Nevada, New Mexico, and Arizona have majority-women state legislatures. Nevada's legislature became majority-women after the 2016 elections and Arizona's moves around a little bit as to whether women are just over or just under 50 percent. New Mexico's majority-women state legislature first hit this benchmark after the 2024 elections. Thirteen states ranging from Arizona to Washington have state legislatures that are at least 40 percent women. While 40 percent is not quite at gender parity, this is a considerably high rate of representation for women. Of course, the picture of women's descriptive representation is not always one of gains and progress as eight states do not even represent women at a rate of 25 percent.

Figure 2.2 records the percentage change in women's representation in each state legislature, upper and lower chambers combined, over the last

Figure 2.1 Proportion of women in state legislatures

---

[12] https://cawp.rutgers.edu/facts/levels-office/state-legislature/women-state-legislatures-2023

ten years. The states in light gray, almost pink color, are states where women lost seats, and these include West Virginia, Tennessee, and Arkansas. In most other states, women's presence increased, sometimes by just a few points such as the case of Montana and Minnesota. Almost half of the states had a 10 percent increase or more in women's representation. Other states like Nevada and New Mexico saw large and substantial gains in women's descriptive representation.

Figure 2.3 includes the percentage of women of color in state legislatures. Women of color are also making gains at the state legislative level. Out of roughly 7700 state legislative seats across the state legislatures in all fifty states, a total of about 720 identify as AAPI, Black, Latina, Native American, Middle Eastern, or multi-racial. The average number of women of color in state legislatures is around 10 percent.[13] But, as with women's overall representation, there is considerable variation. Across the states, the rates of women of color in state legislatures range from 30 percent in California and New Mexico to Idaho and New Hampshire where less than 1 percent of state legislators are women of color. Comparing the data on women's state-level representation for women, overall, and for women of color separately suggests that it is white women who drive many of the gains in women's representation at the state legislative level, but I argue that it is women of color who are at the best position to overturn the gendered and racialized stereotypes associated with political institutions.

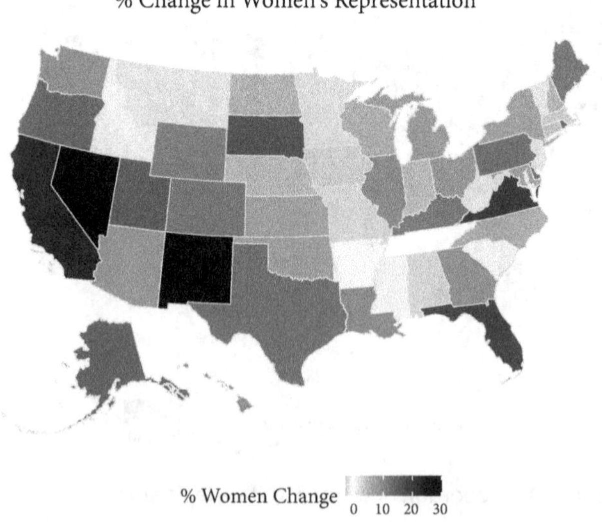

Figure 2.2 Percent change in women's representation in state legislatures, 2014–2024

[13] https://cawp.rutgers.edu/facts/levels-office/state-legislature/women-state-legislatures-2023

Women of Color in State Legislatures

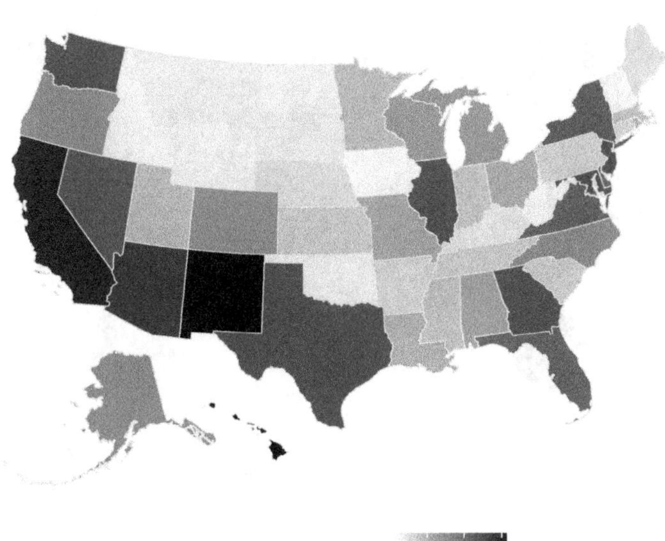

Figure 2.3   Women of color in state legislatures

Women's descriptive representation in Congress and throughout state legislatures will certainly affect how people stereotype political institutions. Many of the empirical tests I use in later chapters investigate the effects of women's descriptive representation at the local level. Local offices, such as city councils or county boards, are political institutions that are right in people's backyards. Local governments make decisions that directly affect the daily lives of individuals from the frequency of trash collection to the availability of hospitals and healthcare clinics. Despite the importance of local governments, little is known about *who* serves in these local institutions (Holman 2017). Recent work suggests that the diversity, in terms of gender and race, of local governments is on the rise (De Benedictis-Kessner et al. 2023; Filler and Lien 2023). To see how local governments might be setting the stage for the white-masculine stereotypes of political institutions to unravel, a team of student researchers collected data on the racial and gender diversity of 150 city and county governments in the US. Table A2.1 in Chapter 2 Appendix includes more details about this data collection. Briefly, we recorded who serves in the city and county governments of the 100 largest cities in the US and the largest city and/or state capitol of every state.

The data on women's local representation reveal some important trends, presented in the top panel of Figure 2.4. First, on average, women hold just

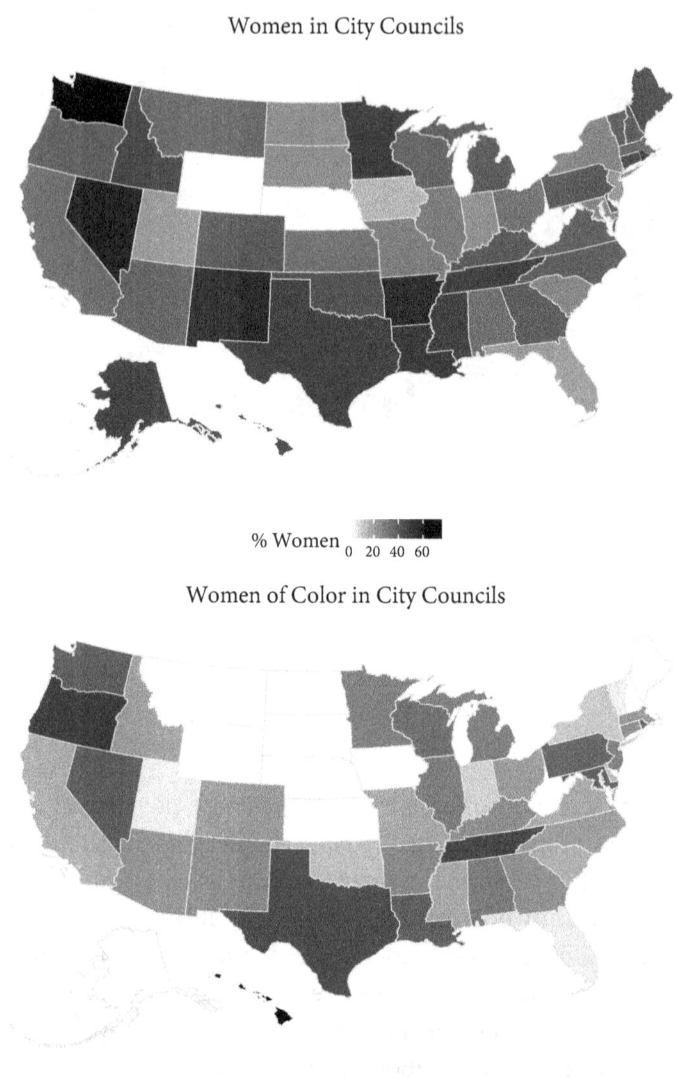

Figure 2.4 Women in city councils

under 40 percent of seats in local governments, and women of color hold 17 percent of local government seats. The representation for both women of color and women more generally at the local level often outpaces women's rates of representation in the federal legislature and many state governments. Second, the map for women's overall representation suggests that there are some cities where women do well in representation. For example,

Texas, a state not typically known for its strong descriptive representation of women, does well in several of its largest cities when it comes to women's representation.

The bottom map of Figure 2.4 charts the women of color on city councils and shows a striking disparity between women's rates of representation and women of color's rates of representation. Women of color are far less well-represented in local elected governments. The number of states with no shading means that there are no women of color serving in any of the city councils or county boards for which the research team recorded data. To be sure, some of these states include only a few cities in the dataset, but it is still striking that major cities in large swaths of the US lack representation for women of color. Important to remember is that even a level of WDR below parity can still lead to feminizing effects if this representation is visible.

WDR Visibility in Election News Coverage

My second test of WDR visibility is a short content analysis on the percentage of news stories published in local news outlets on the status of women's representation after the 2024 election cycle. This analysis uses the Access World News database, and I searched for "women and election" in the headline and lead paragraph of a news article, and I isolated the search to November 1, 2024, through January 31, 2025, to include coverage of the election results, and coverage of WDR that may occur when newly elected official take office. To understand how much space local outlets devote to coverage of WDR, I recorded the number of articles using just "election" in the headline and lead paragraph of an article. Each of these variables, the women-election variable and the election variable, are simply counts of the number of articles. I divide the two to create a variable recording the percentage of news articles about WDR. I searched for local outlets for each of the fifty states to include coverage about the presidential and congressional races as well as local and state elections (see West and Duell (2025) for a similar approach).

In this dataset, I also recorded the percentage of a state's congressional delegation that is women, whether the state has a woman governor, and the percentage of women in each state's legislature. My main outcome variable, the percentage of articles about WDR, ranges from 0, New Hampshire, to about 13 percent in New Mexico, Rhode Island, and Vermont. I estimate a model predicting whether the percentage of women in elected office predicts more news coverage. I do not find that any of the women's representation variables predict more coverage of women political candidates. However, descriptively, the results suggest that greater levels of WDR translate to more coverage. For example, in 2024, New Mexico's state legislature became majority-women, and this state has one of the highest levels of news coverage about WDR. Other states do not quite fit the expected pattern. For example, Vermont historically under-represents women but had a high level of WDR coverage. Some of this coverage is likely about women candidate's novelty status especially considering Vermont first elected a woman to Congress in 2022. New Hampshire, on the other hand, historically represents women well but I did not find any news articles about WDR. This is somewhat surprising as New Hampshire had an all-women gubernatorial race in 2024.

Are All Political Institutions Seen as Masculine?

A key tenet of my arguments around institutional stereotype change is that people's baseline impressions of political institutions are shaped by masculinity. There is a perception that not all political institutions are masculine and that some elected political bodies, such as city councils, may be seen as more feminine by the public. The logic is that city councils are less prestigious, and low prestige is associated with femininity (Crowder-Meyer and Smith 2015), but also that the policies and tasks of city councils fit into the stereotypic strengths of women (Rosenwasser and Dean 1989). Other work suggests that city councils are still masculine given that voters prefer candidates for city council who display masculine traits (Bauer 2020b) and many of those serving in elected political office identify themselves as having more masculine than feminine traits (Conroy and Oliver 2020; Oliver and Conroy 2017). A similar argument exists to suggest that gubernatorial offices might be more feminine than masculine given that the issues most pertinent to state government, such as education, fit into women's stereotypic issue strengths (Fox and Oxley 2003). The baseline image of political institutions as masculine bodies is a critical premise of my argument positing a stereotype change process away from masculinity to include more feminine qualities. I start by testing this assumption that political institutions are seen by the public as masculine institutions.

I conducted a short stereotyping test with $N = 792$ people recruited from the 2018 Cooperative Congressional Election Study. Participants rated the masculinity or femininity of different political offices including a city council, state legislature, governor, senator, and the president. Everybody rated each office with the office order randomized. The response options were "very feminine," "somewhat feminine," "somewhat masculine," and "very masculine." I refrained from including a neither feminine nor masculine option because a neither option could be a socially desirable safe option for those concerned about being seen as prejudiced toward women (Krupnikov, Piston, and Bauer 2016). The goal with this short empirical test is to affirm that individuals associate most levels of political office with masculinity.

To determine whether respondents identified a level of office as feminine or masculine, I followed an approach from Petrocik (1996) who determined that a political party "owned" an issue if at least 60 percent of individuals associated a particular issue with a particular party. In the same vein, if 60 percent of respondents associate an office as feminine, then I consider that a feminine political office. Conversely, if 60 percent of respondents associate an office as masculine, which I argue will most likely be the case, then I consider that a masculine political office. Table 2.2 displays the percentage of individuals who indicated that each level of office was very or somewhat feminine and masculine. I collapse the very and somewhat categories to see the major patterns of gender stereotyping more clearly. Higher percentages of respondents rated every level of office as more masculine relative to less feminine. Recall that respondents received no information about *who* served in the office. The likely assumption is that participants will assume that many officeholders are men given that most political officeholders across time and across space in the US are men.

Table 2.2 shows that as the level of office increases to become a higher executive level of office, it is seen as more distinctly masculine among respondents. For example, 63 percent of respondents rated city councils as very or somewhat masculine with about 37 percent seeing city councils as more feminine. Approximately just under 87 percent of people rated the presidency as masculine. The presidency is seen as much more masculine than city councils, but both institutions are still seen as dominantly masculine.[14]

Table 2.2 Feminine and Masculine Levels of Office

Political Institution	% Very or Somewhat Feminine	% Very or Somewhat Masculine
City council	36.56%	63.44%
State legislature	25.19%	74.81%
Senate	22.36%	77.46%
Governor	18.26%	81.74%
Presidency	13.12%	86.88%

[14] See Chapter 2 Appendix for more information on sample characteristics and additional analyses and comparisons.

This preliminary analysis confirms that people see political institutions as far more masculine than feminine.

Conclusion

Women's descriptive representation is on the rise with gains occurring at the state and local levels. I certainly do not want to overstate the gains made in women's political representation as the analyses on the status of women's representation clearly show both gender gains and gender disparities. There is still considerable room for improvement in Congress, across state legislatures, and in local governments. Indeed, few political institutions represent women at a rate that mirrors women's presence in the public. But it is not just women's numbers that are increasing but women's visibility is increasing as well. Heightened visibility coupled with the gains in women's descriptive representation sets the stage for a possible feminizing effect of political institutions. The next chapter turns to the first experimental tests of institutional stereotype change considering how women's rates of descriptive representation shift the stereotypic impressions people hold of these institutions.

3

Shifting the Gendered Lens

Long before Alan Turing developed the theoretical arguments that led to the creation of computers and the field of computer science, Ada Lovelace laid the groundwork for automated processing systems. Ada Lovelace, born in 1815, was the daughter of Lord Byron and his wife Annabella Milbank. In the mid-nineteenth century, Lovelace, working with Charles Babbage, developed the concept of the Analytical Engine. The proposed Engine was a device that could perform repetitive tasks through automation. While this machine was never quite fully developed in the nineteenth century, the theory behind the Analytical Engine contributed to the development of the first modern computers. Indeed, Lovelace is widely considered to be the first computer programmer and a founder of the field of computer science. The field of computer science was not only founded by a woman, but most computer scientists and programmers in the 1950s and 1960s were women. For example, the computer scientists at NASA engaged in calculating the complex mathematical equations needed to launch rockets and people into space were women, many of them Black women. The book and movie *Hidden Figures* documented the critical role of women computer scientists such as Katherine Johnson, Dorothy Vaughn, and Mary Jackson.

The dominance of women in the computer science industry at the midpoint of the twentieth century could lead to the presumption that computer science was a *feminine* profession, or a field designated as "women's work." Of course, nobody was conducting surveys at this time asking people to rate the femininity and masculinity of computer science, but the profession had a feminine bent to it. In more recent decades, few would argue that computer science is a feminine profession. Indeed, in 2025, nearly 200 years after Ada Lovelace articulated the theories that led to the development of the first computers, nearly 75 percent of computer scientists are men, and over 60 percent of those in computer science are white.[1] Computer science, in the present era, is a white-masculine profession. The shift from a diverse occupation dominated by women, including women of color, to an occupation dominated

---

[1] https://mindlab.cs.umd.edu/diversity-and-inclusion

Feminizing Political Institutions. Nichole M. Bauer, Oxford University Press. © Nichole M. Bauer (2026).
DOI: 10.1093/9780197841556.003.0003

by white men occurred as the importance and prestige of computer science grew as an industry. With this rise in prestige, more men flocked to the profession, and this left little room for women. As computer science became dominated by men, the profession also came to be associated with stereotypically masculine traits like intellectual rigor, mathematical skill, and lacking strong social skills and fewer feminine traits like being compassionate, kind, and having strong interpersonal skills.[2]

The shift from feminine to masculine in the field of computer science occurred in the opposite direction of what I predict will happen to political institutions under my theory of institutional stereotype change. Tracking the history of this profession illustrates how gender demographics shape gendered impressions of institutions and the conditions under which these impressions change. Shifts from masculine to feminine have occurred in other professions, such as teaching. Before mass compulsory public education, children often learned from men who served as tutors in the private homes of the elites, and, of course, most of these students were wealthy boys. The advent of compulsory public education opened more importunities for women to enter the profession. Today, in the United States, nearly 90 percent of elementary school teachers are women.[3] Teaching is widely characterized as a feminine field where traits like care, compassion, and kindness are considered essential to excelling in the profession. With both examples, computer science and teaching, the shifts in stereotypic perceptions occurred alongside the demographic changes in the profession. I argue that similar shifts will occur in the stereotypic perceptions people hold of political institutions based on changes in WDR.

Chapter 2 described how institutions became gendered through a masculine lens, and outlined the processes by which the gendered association of an institution can shift. I grounded this theory in social psychology and behavioral economics research documenting the characteristics and attributes of an institution that make it gendered in a masculine or a feminine way. I argue that the gendered associations of institutions come, first and foremost, from *who* serves in those institutions. Chapter 3 offers an answer, at least a partial answer, to the central question guiding this book: *Do individuals stereotype political institutions that are more diverse along racial and gender lines as less white and less masculine compared to institutions that under-represent*

---

[2] Of course, in practice, many women have these masculine qualities, and many men have these feminine qualities.

[3] https://www.pewresearch.org/short-reads/2024/09/24/key-facts-about-public-school-teachers-in-the-u-s/#:~:text=Most%20K%2D12%20public%20school%20teachers%20are%20women.&text=Thi s%20gender%20imbalance%20is%20especially, secondary%20or%20high%20school%20teachers.

women and people of color? To tackle this overarching question, I consider how stereotypes change in two parts. First, do individuals stereotype political institutions that have more women as less masculine compared to institutions that under-represent women and over-represent men? Second, do individuals stereotype political institutions that are more racially diverse and that have more women as more feminine and less white compared to institutions that under-represent women of color? I address part one of this question in the present chapter and consider part two, the gendered and racialized shifts in Chapter 4.

I start with the first half of this question in this chapter focusing on how women's presence, regardless of women's race or ethnicity, can shift the masculine perceptions of political institutions. If the racialized and gendered perceptions of institutions are going to shift to be more inclusive and feminine, this starts with a shift from masculine to feminine. If women's presence does not shift institutions from masculine to feminine, then women of color are going to be less likely to shift institutions to be both less white and less masculine. I start this chapter by reviewing the theoretical logic behind how this gendered shift should work in political institutions based on women's rates of political representation. I then outline the design of my first experimental tests, followed by the results. This chapter tests both the gendered shifts prediction, the institutional type prediction, and the partisan differences prediction.

Gendered Shifts in Institutions

Social psychology research identifies several factors that affect the classification of occupations as feminine or masculine: the ratio of women to men in a specific profession, the traits necessary to serve in a specific profession, and the observed behaviors of individuals in a specific occupation (Glick, Wilk, and Perreault 1995; Gottfredson 1981; Shinar 1975; Krefting, Berger, and Wallace 1978; Acker 1992, 1990). For example, being a firefighter is a stereotypically masculine occupation because there are more men than women working as firefighters, firefighters need stereotypically masculine traits for the work such as toughness, and firefighters engage in stereotypically masculine behaviors such as using physical force to protect people. These dynamics lead to the perception of firefighting as a masculine profession. Likewise, being a nurse is a stereotypically feminine occupation because there are more women than men working as nurses, nurses need stereotypically feminine traits for the work such as compassion, and nurses engage in stereotypically feminine behaviors such as caring for others—hence, nursing is a stereotypically feminine profession. The dominance of one gender over another in an institution leads people to associate gendered traits and behaviors with that institution.

My theory of institutional stereotype change argues that a change in the ratio of women to men in an institution is the first step that needs to occur before people will associate institutions with feminine stereotypes. I expect that higher rates of WDR will precipitate a shift in the gendered lens through which people view political institutions leading them to see majority-women institutions as more feminine than masculine. The gendered shifts prediction outlines this effect.

Gendered Shifts Prediction: Higher rates of women's descriptive representation will lead people to associate political institutions with more feminine and fewer masculine stereotypic qualities.

Observing the feminizing effects of women's descriptive representation will occur primarily through the traits that people apply to institutions. Majority-men institutions will be seen as having masculine traits such as being tough, assertive, or aggressive. These are traits that people expect to observe within the institution. I argue that when institutions move from majority-men to majority-women, people will expect to observe feminine traits in political institutions. Traits are closely connected to the way that individuals attribute stereotypes to occupations and organizations (Glick 1991). But when considering politics, there are other effects that can be observed as evidence of a stereotype shift such as the types of issues people think the institution will consider and prioritize. Masculine issues tend to be considered the *most important* political issues in any election cycle (Holman et al. 2019; Bauer and Santia 2023). I expect that people will see majority-women institutions as prioritizing more feminine issues such as education or healthcare. The gendered issue associations people form of women and men political leaders are based, in part, on the traits seen as necessary for being experts on these issues. Education is a feminine issue because it requires being caring, a feminine trait, and crime is a masculine issue because it requires being tough, a masculine trait (Huddy and Terkildsen 1993b). With shifts in issue perceptions, it will not necessarily be the case that masculine issues will fall off the radar—after all, masculine issues such as crime are important issues for nearly every level of office. I expect that feminine issues will rise in importance when people see institutions as more feminine.

The type of institutions in which women serve may affect whether the feminizing effects of WDR occur. I consider institutional differences in two ways: the difference between legislative and executive offices and the difference between state and local offices. The concept of increasing WDR or having majority-women institutions sets the stage for feminizing effects to occur in legislative institutions which are made up of multiple members. The effects of WDR may occur differently in legislative institutions rather than executive offices. While people identify both legislative and executive institutions as masculine, there are some differences in the size of the institutions and how those institutions operate (Gunderson et al. 2025). Legislative offices, for example, involve a *group* of elected leaders that must work together and where interpersonal communication skills, a feminine strength, are seen as valuable while executive offices involve a singular political actor occupying the role of a central decision-maker (Fox and Oxley 2003). Descriptive representation at the legislative level allows for women's collective representation to influence perceptions of the institution more broadly.

Executive offices, such as mayor, governor, or president, empower a single actor as the decision-maker, and this singularity may increase the masculinity of the institution over the characteristics of an officeholder in the institution (Sweet-Cushman 2022). Executive offices pose a challenge for women's entry into politics. Women have, at their height of their representation, never held more than 20 percent of gubernatorial seats in the US, and it is only in recent years that women won mayoral offices in major American cities. The presence of one woman occupying an executive office may not be strong enough to override the masculine perceptions of executive offices. Even when a woman is in an executive role, the office is still typified by a singular actor overseeing government and implementing policies, and this is a role that reinforces masculinity. Given these differences, I expect that the feminizing effects of WDR may occur more strongly in legislative over executive institutions.

In terms of differences between local and state offices, I expect that the feminizing effects of WDR may occur more prominently in local offices compared to state-level offices. Local offices, as Chapter 2 illustrated, are the level of office people associate least strongly with masculine stereotypes. Past work argues that women should have an advantage at the local level because the high level of constituent casework and types of issues and duties at this office fit into women's perceived stereotypic strengths (Huddy and Terkildsen 1993a; Crowder-Meyer, Gadarian, and Trounstine 2015). State-level offices are, however, considered somewhat more prestigious relative to local offices. Many of the state-level issues fit into both feminine and masculine stereotypes

(Fox and Oxley 2003), but state-level offices, because they are broader in scope, are likely to have a stronger association with masculine stereotypes relative to local offices. The institutional type prediction outlines these two points of difference that may come from WDR:

Institutional Type Prediction: The feminizing effects of women's descriptive representation are more likely to occur in a legislative (local) relative to an executive (state-level) political institution.

I next consider partisan differences. People see the Democratic Party as the party that embodies feminine traits and owns feminine issues while people see the Republican Party as the party that embodies masculine traits and owns masculine issues (Winter 2010; Petrocik, Benoit, and Hansen 2003; Hayes 2005). The issue associations that assign feminine issues to Democrats and masculine issues to Republicans are just one way that the parties reinforce gender stereotypes. The demographic make-up of officeholders also reinforces the feminine stereotypic impressions of the Democratic Party (Ondercin 2017). Indeed, Democratic women hold nearly twice as many seats in Congress relative to Republican women.[4] These partisan gaps in representation occur, in part, because of dynamics among partisan elites. The Democratic Party has a stronger record of recruiting, fielding, and funding women candidates relative to the Republican Party (Sanbonmatsu 2002b; Crowder-Meyer and Lauderdale 2014; Crowder-Meyer 2013; Crowder-Meyer and Cooperman 2018; Cooperman 2020). These partisan recruitment dynamics contribute to the perception that the Democratic Party is more feminine relative to the Republican Party.

In the latter half of the twentieth century, women increased their presence in higher education institutions and the workforce (BLS 2000). At the same time, issues affecting women began to emerge on the political agenda such as the Equal Rights Amendment (Mansbridge 1986, 1985) and the first set of equal pay laws (Connor and Fiske 2019). The political parties, at first, were not divided in their support of women's equity issues (Smith 2000; Wolbrecht 2002). As the parties began to ideologically divide in the 1970s, they took distinct positions on women's equity issues with the Democratic Party supporting these issues and the Republican Party taking a more limited government approach to solving gender equity problems (Wolbrecht 2000). This initial movement of the parties to stake out opposing positions on women's equity issues contributed to the association of the Democratic Party as stronger on stereotypically feminine issues and the Republican Party as

---

[4] https://cawp.rutgers.edu/facts/current-numbers

stronger on stereotypically masculine issues (Huddy and Terkildsen 1993b; Holman et al. 2019; Petrocik 1996).

The differences in the gender stereotypes associated with the political parties may lead to differences in how individual-level partisanship affects the extent to which feminizing effects occur. I expect feminizing effects to occur more strongly among Democratic individuals relative to Republican individuals. I still expect feminizing effects to occur among Republicans, but they just might not be as strong as they are for Democrats.

Partisan Differences Prediction: The feminizing effects of women's descriptive representation will be stronger among individuals identifying with the Democratic Party relative to those identifying with the Republican Party or Independents.

If the gendered shifts prediction is correct, then majority-women institutions should have more feminine traits relative to majority-men institutions. If the institutional type prediction holds, then majority-women legislative institutions should experience a stronger shift to feminine stereotypes than a woman holding an executive office; the feminizing effects should be stronger at the local rather than the state level. Finally, Democratic participants should see stronger shifts to feminine stereotypes when institutions become majority-women relative to Republicans.

Experimental Design

I start by examining how changes in WDR affect the stereotypic impressions individuals form of political institutions or the gendered shifts prediction. I use an experimental approach to test my predictions because the high level of internal validity allows me to isolate the causal mechanisms behind evaluations of candidate qualifications (Mutz 2011) and the balance of women and men elected to the institution, and because the appropriate observational data do not exist (Morton and Williams 2010). It would be ideal to find a city council that is majority-women or even all-women and to ask people living in these jurisdictions about the stereotypes they associate with these legislative institutions. Targeting individuals living in these cities can be cost prohibitive, and, as a researcher, I cannot control the other qualities of the institution such as the partisanship of the women, their race, or the actions of a city council. The inability to control for these confounds makes observational analyses difficult to use for this research. However, with an experiment, I can control key characteristics of institutions so that the only difference between them is whether a body is majority-women or majority-men. I manipulate the gender composition of institutions, majority-women or majority-men, and whether the institution is a legislative or an executive office as well as a state or a local office. Table 3.1 lists all the offices included in the study along with the treatment text.

Table 3.1 Experimental Conditions

Condition	Office	N	Treatment
Majority-women	City council	134	**City Council Election Results Bring in New Members** When the new city council takes over next year, the majority of its members will be women. Indeed, women will hold over 50% of seats in the city council. Residents are looking forward to seeing what new policies the majority-female city council puts into place next year.
Majority-men	City council	126	**City Council Election Results Bring in New Members** When the new city council takes over next year, the majority of its members will be men. Indeed, men will hold over 50% of seats in the city council. Residents are looking forward to seeing what new policies the majority-male city council puts into place next year.
Majority-women	State legislature	122	**State Legislative Election Results Bring in New Legislators** When the new state legislature takes over next year, the majority of its members will be women. Indeed, women will hold over 50% of seats in the state legislature. Residents are looking forward to seeing what new policies the majority-female state legislature puts into place next year.
Majority-men	State legislature	125	**State Legislative Election Results Bring in New Legislators** When the new state legislature takes over next year, the majority of its members will be men. Indeed, men will hold over 50% of seats in the state legislature. Residents are looking forward to seeing what new policies the majority-male state legislature puts into place next year.
Woman	Mayor	127	**New Mayor to be Sworn In** When the new mayor takes over in a few days, there will be a woman in the executive office. The mayor's inauguration will take place later this week, and she will start working on her policy agenda for the next year. The city is looking forward to having a woman in the city's top job.

Condition	Office	N	Treatment
Man	Mayor	123	**New Mayor to be Sworn In** The new mayor will take over in a few days. The mayor's inauguration will take place later this week, and he will start working on his policy agenda for the next year. The city is looking forward to having a new person in the city's top job.
Woman	Governor	122	**New Governor to be Sworn In** When the new governor takes over in a few days, there will be a woman in the executive office. The governor's inauguration will take place later this week, and she will start working on her policy agenda for the next year. The state is looking forward to having a woman in the state's top job.
Man	Governor	121	**New Governor to be Sworn In** The new governor will take over in a few days. The governor's inauguration will take place later this week, and he will start working on his policy agenda for the next year. The state is looking forward to having a new person in the state's top job.

The experimental treatment included a brief vignette that appeared as though it came from a newspaper headline announcing the results of a recent election. The vignette announced that most officeholders in the offices would either be women or men for the legislative offices. The manipulations differ in the executive office conditions to identify whether the new mayor or governor is a woman or a man. The text did not include any information about the ethnorace of the newly elected leaders or the partisan composition of the institutions. I test how the ethnorace and gender composition affect stereotyping patterns in Chapter 4. I left out the partisan information because some offices, e.g., city councils, tend be non-partisan but also because I did not want perceptions of partisan in-group favorability to affect the stereotypic impressions formed of the institutions (Bauer 2017).

Sample

The experiment was embedded in the Cooperative Election Study (CES) administered by YouGov in 2021. YouGov recruits samples that resemble the demographic characteristics of the adult population in the United States. The demographic characteristics of my YouGov sample recruited are in Chapter 3

Appendix, Table A3.1. The sample is 57 percent women and 67 percent white. The sample's partisan breakdown skews slightly more Democratic with 38.6 percent identifying with this party while 28.80 percent identify as Republicans. While these characteristics are not perfectly representative of the US population, they are comparable to the samples recruited in other online surveys. Moreover, the sample sizes for Democrats and Republicans, when broken down across the conditions, have just enough statistical power to test the partisan differences prediction.

Key Measures

I measure the stereotypic associations individuals have of political institutions through a measure that asks participants to rate the extent to which a series of feminine and masculine traits describes each institution but not the people serving in the institution (full question wording in Chapter 3 Appendix). This measure differs from the feminine–masculine scale used in Chapter 2. The feminine and masculine measures come from existing research on the extent to which gender stereotypes affect trait evaluations of women and men candidates (Huddy and Terkildsen 1993b; Bauer 2017). I use traits to test the way individuals stereotype institutions because the traits associated with organizations and occupations are, according to social psychology research, one of the primary ways that stereotypic impressions form (Shinar 1975; Glick, Wilk, and Perreault 1995). Additionally, scholarship finds that people place some value on feminine traits for political leaders (Bishin, Stevens, and Wilson 2006; Anzia and Bernhard 2022). Qualities like honesty and trustworthiness can advantage women entering masculine institutions (Fiske 2018) especially after an institution experiences a period of corruption (Barnes, Beaulieu, and Saxton 2020; Barnes and Beaulieu 2019; Barnes and Beaulieu 2014). My feminine trait measure allows me to track how feminine traits increase in importance based on levels of women's descriptive representation. The feminine traits included: warm, empathetic, and caring; the masculine traits included: assertive, tough, and aggressive. The final feminine and masculine measures average the trait attributions, and I recoded each measure to range from 0–1 and higher values indicate a stronger association with a specific stereotype.

I also used a battery of feminine and masculine issues. The issue items asked participants to rate how high of a priority they thought each issue would be in the institution with the response options including: "Very high priority,"

"Somewhat high priority," "Somewhat low priority," and "Very low priority." The complete feminine issue battery included the following items: education, healthcare, social welfare issues, and income inequality. The complete masculine issue battery included: infrastructure, economic development, and crime. I recoded the issue scales to range from 0 to 1 with higher values indicating the issue to be a higher institutional priority. I expect participants to rate the majority-women institutions as more likely to advocate on feminine issues relative to the majority-men institutions, but I do not expect majority-women institutions to be rated poorly on masculine issues.

Evidence of Feminized Political Institutions

I start by presenting the results of the shifts in stereotypes based on the gender composition of each institution included in the study: city councils, mayor, and state legislature.[5] I use a series of two-tailed t-tests to compare the stereotypic shifts in the majority-women to the majority-men institutions. Following this, I conduct comparisons across each level of office to see where the shifts in stereotypes are the largest and most pronounced. I plot the means in a series of figures to illustrate the differences across institutions and across feminine and masculine traits. In these figures, I use 84 percent confidence intervals as opposed to 95 percent confidence intervals so that any small differences between groups can be better seen on the plots. In my discussion of the results, I report full p-values and use a $p = 0.10$ minimum threshold for assessing statistical significance. In the subsequent chapters, Chapters 4 and 5, where I use t-tests to conduct group comparisons, I follow this same approach. I start with the trait scales to test the gendered shifts prediction and then I move onto tests with the gendered issue scales. I divide the analyses into the effects for legislative and then executive institutions before I compare more directly across institutions to test the institutional type prediction. The final section of the results compares heterogeneous effects based on participant partisanship.

Trait Shifts in Legislative Institutions

I start by looking at the stereotype shifts in city councils. Based on the descriptive data in Chapter 2, city councils are the least masculine elected political

---

[5] A manipulation check question asked respondents to indicate whether the institution they read about was majority-women or majority-men, 84 percent of respondents answered the question correctly.

institutions. Therefore, the shifts in stereotyping from majority-feminine to majority-masculine may not be as pronounced as other institutions. The left panel of Figure 3.1 displays the average stereotype ratings in the majority-women and majority-men conditions. The majority-women city council is rated as more feminine relative to the majority-men city council with a difference of 0.177 (SE = 0.029), or a 17.7% stronger association with feminine stereotypes across the gender composition of the council, $p < 0.001$. So far, this fits with my theoretical expectations. Comparing the feminine and masculine stereotype association within the majority-women condition shows no difference between the two. The feminine stereotypic association for the majority-women council is M = 0.593 (SD = 0.218) while the masculine stereotypic association is M = 0.577 (SD = 0.184), $p = 0.3809$. These patterns suggest that people see majority-women city councils as having *both* feminine and masculine stereotypes given that the majority-women institution does not lose on masculine stereotypes. The majority-men condition shows a marked difference in the feminine and masculine stereotyping patterns. The feminine stereotypic association in the majority-men city council is M = 0.415 (SD = 0.229) and the masculine stereotypic association is M = 0.569 (SD = 0.203), $p < 0.001$. The majority-men city council is definitively seen as more masculine than feminine. These findings fit with the gendered shifts prediction.

The right panel of Figure 3.1 displays the feminine and masculine stereotype shifts for state legislatures. The majority-women condition had a stronger feminine stereotype association, M = 0.569 (SE = 0.022), than the majority-men condition, M = 0.386 (SE = 0.019), $p < 0.001$. Participants

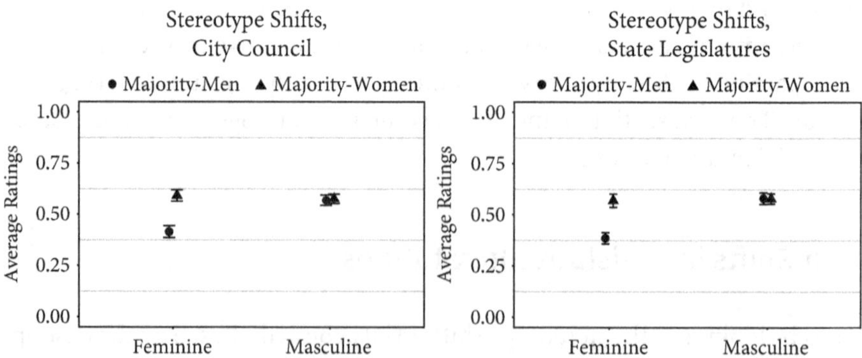

Figure 3.1 Stereotype shifts, legislative institutions

Note: 84 percent confidence intervals included. Full means and comparisons in Chapter 3 Appendix Table A3.3.

rated the majority-women institution equitably across feminine and masculine stereotypes, $p = 0.5390$, the same pattern found in the city council comparisons. In the majority-men institution, there is a statistically significant difference in the association between feminine stereotypes, M = 0.386, SD = 0.211, and masculine stereotypes, M = 0.580, SD = 0.202, with masculine stereotypes having the stronger association, $p < 0.001$.

I also tested differences across local and state institutions comparing, first, the majority-women city council condition to the majority-women state legislature condition; and second, the woman governor to the women mayor conditions. I find no statistically significant differences in the feminine and masculine trait attributions of institutions based on the local and state dimensions.

The state legislature and the city council results reinforce one another. Both majority-women institutions are seen as more feminine relative to the majority-men institutions, but the majority-women institutions are seen as having an even mix of feminine and masculine traits. This means that majority-women institutions do not lose on masculine traits, which are the traits most strongly associated with political leadership. The gendered shifts prediction originally posited that majority-women institutions would be seen as more feminine than masculine. However, what I find, thus far, is that people have a much more expansive view of the traits embodied by majority-women institution than I initially predicted.

Trait Shifts in Executive Institutions

The first set of analyses show that majority-women institutions lead to a stronger association with feminine stereotypes without losing on stereotypically masculine qualitites. How do these shifts occur across executive institutions? I examine the effects for executive offices using a mayoral office and governor.

Figure 3.2 shows the stereotyping levels of mayoral offices (left panel) and gubernatorial offices (right panel). The level of feminine stereotyping when the mayor is a woman is M = 0.579 (SD = 0.537) but when a man holds the office, feminine stereotyping is at a level of M = 0.486 (SD = 0.257), and this is a significant difference, $p = 0.0043$. These comparisons show the same pattern I found in the legislative institutions. Comparing levels of masculine stereotyping shows a significant difference between when a woman holds the office and when a man holds the office. A woman mayor leads to a masculine stereotyping association of M = 0.558 (SD = 0.228) but in the man mayoral condition, masculine stereotyping is lower: M = 0.482 (SD = 0. 257), p = 0.0138. These comparisons on masculine traits are interesting as I did not expect a woman as mayor to be seen as more masculine than a man as mayor. This masculine boost for the woman mayoral condition could reflect the expectation that women who get into executive offices must work harder to prove their qualifications relative to men (Bauer 2020a). As with the legislative institutions, I find that the woman mayoral condition was seen as having both feminine and masculine stereotypes, p = 0.2374. There are also no differences in feminine and masculine stereotyping in the man mayoral condition, p = 0.7572; but, recall, the woman mayoral condition had higher levels of feminine and masculine stereotypes compared to the majority-man conditions.

The right panel of Figure 3.2 shows the stereotyping patterns for gubernatorial offices held by a woman relative to a man. The governor's office is rated a feminine stereotyping level of M = 0.561 (SD = 0.261) when a woman holds the office, but feminine stereotyping for the man gubernatorial condition is M = 0.498, (SD = 0.239), p = 0.0451. These differences suggest that when a woman serves as governor, there is a shift in feminine stereotyping in line with my expectations. I also compared the level of feminine and masculine stereotyping for the woman governor condition and the man governor condition. There are no differneces in the levels of masculine stereotyping of the woman and the man gubernatorial conditions, p = 0.6348—suggesting that having a woman in office does not mean that the office loses on masucline traits. Comparing the feminine and masculine stereotyping levels for the woman governor condition shows a significant difference. The gubernatorial office held by a woman is seen as 0.0538 points, or 5.38%, more feminine than

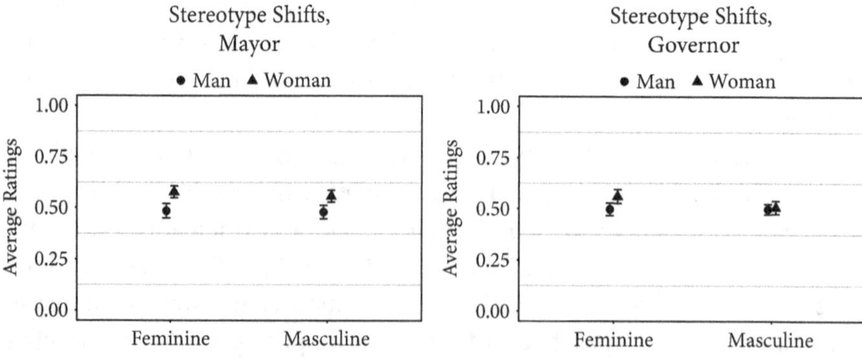

Figure 3.2 Stereotype shifts, executive institutions

Note: 84 percent confidence intervals included. Full means and comparisons in Chapter 3 Appendix Table A3.3

masculine, $p = 0.0035$. This differs from the patterns found in the previous analyses which found that majority-women had both feminine and masculine stereotypes. Here, the majority-woman governor is seen as significantly more feminine than masculine. The gubernatorial office held by a man is seen just as feminine as it is masculine, $p = 0.999$.

These results suggest that people see all institutions where women hold a majority of seats or there is a woman as the sole officeholder as having more feminine qualities than institutions with men holding the majorities of seats. I tested whether there are differences in these gendered trait associations based on participant gender. These full comparisons are in Chapter 3 Appendix, Tables A3.5–A3.8. Overall, the findings show no major differences between women and men seeing majority-women institutions as more feminine. The lone exception where women participants differed from men participants is in the woman governor condition, $p = 0.0761$. The results at the executive office level support my gendered shifts prediction.

Trait Shifts across Institutional Types

The institutional type prediction argued that the shift from feminine to masculine traits associated with majority-women institutions would occur more prominently in legislative relative to executive institutions and more prominently in state relative to local institutions. The first set of results showed no differences across legislative offices; as such, I pool across institutional types for these analyses. I then test whether the feminine stereotyping effects occur differently across majority-women legislative institutions relative to majority-women executive institutions, and then conduct similar comparisons for state and local institutions. I include these full comparisons in Chapter 3 Appendix Table A3.4 and summarize the key findings here.

Feminine stereotyping of majority-women institutions occurs equitably across legislative and executive institutions. The majority-women legislative institutions had a mean feminine stereotype rating of M = 0.5811 (SD = 0.2387) and the feminine stereotyping for executive institutions was M = 0.5718 (SD = 0.2466), and these values do not differ, $p = 0.6687$. These patterns shift somewhat on the masculine trait measures. The mean masculine trait rating of majority-women legislative institutions was M = 0.5789 (SD = 0.2000) but for executive institutions, the mean for majority-women institutions was M = 0.5361 (SD = 0.2403), $p = 0.0320$. This first set of comparisons suggests a slightly higher masculine trait association for majority-women legislative relative to majority-women executive institutions.

I also conducted comparisons across the state and local levels within legislative institutions (city council vs. state legislatures) to see if the shifts in stereotyping based on women's representation move more among city councils or state legislatures. I compare majority-women city councils to majority-women state legislatures. I find no differences in the levels of feminine stereotyping across these two institutions, $p = 0.4440$, and no differences in masculine stereotyping levels, $p = 0.9143$.[6] This first test of the gendered shifts prediction follows my theoretical expectations. I also examined differences in the feminine and masculine stereotyping of mayoral offices and gubernatorial offices with a woman officeholder. As with the legislative institution analyses, there are no differences in feminine stereotyping levels of the mayoral and gubernatorial offices when a woman serves in those roles, $p = 0.5837$, and there are no differences in levels of masculine stereotyping, $p = 0.1402$.

Executive institutions are long thought to be the more masculine institutions (Huddy and Terkildsen 1993a; Rosenwasser and Dean 1989), and executive offices pose higher barriers for women's entry into politics (Windett 2011; Fox and Oxley 2003). People may see an institution with a woman as the only officeholder to be a more extreme shift in who holds power in that institution. A woman mayor means there is not a man serving as mayor in a particular city. In the legislative conditions, the gender composition is either majority-women or majority-men but never no women or no men. There is always some gender representation in legislative institutions, but this is not the case moving from a man-only to a woman-only executive. These feminizing effects of women-only executive institutions presented here may be a conservative estimate of such effects as the experiments do not disclose whether the woman in the executive office is breaking new ground as a "female first" (Schwindt-Bayer and Reyes-Householder 2017). Many women officeholders are often the "first" to hold that position given the long-standing dominance of men in executive offices. When a woman is the first to hold a particular executive office, I would expect an even stronger shift from masculine to feminine stereotypes.

---

[6] The question of *how many women* is enough to shift gender stereotypes and change institutions more broadly sparks considerable debate about in the literature. Some scholars interpret Kanter's (1977a) work as setting a 15 percent threshold of women's presence in an institution to have a meaningful effect. Subsequent work on gender and representation argues against the 15 percent threshold (Childs and Krook 2006). See Chapter 3 Appendix for an experimental test showing whether the proportion of women in majority-women institutions affects these stereotyping shifts. There are no substantive differences in stereotyping patterns of an all-women city council relative to a majority-women city council (Table A3.13–Table A3.15 for full results).

Partisan Differences in Trait Shifts

The partisan differences prediction argues that the feminizing effects of WDR will be stronger among Democrats rather than Republicans. Important to note is that this prediction only focuses on partisan differences based on the partisan identification of participants in the experiment and not on differences based on the partisanship of women. To test for partisan differences, I conduct comparisons across participant partisanship within the experimental conditions to examine differences between Democrats and Republicans. If the partisan differences prediction holds, then Democratic participants in the majority-women conditions should have higher feminine trait ratings relative to Republican participants.

Figure 3.3 displays the feminine trait ratings for Democrats and Republicans in each of the experimental conditions (Table A3.8 includes full means, standard deviations, and comparisons across conditions). I find that

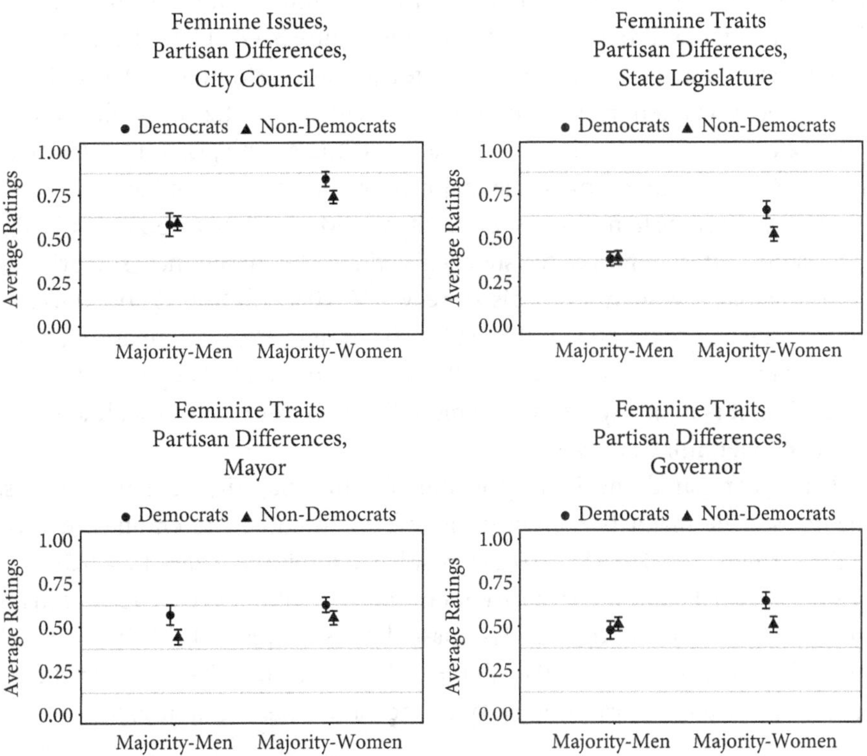

Figure 3.3 Partisan differences in feminine trait attributions

Note: 84 percent confidence intervals included.

Democrats are more likely to see majority-women institutions, across all four types, as more feminine than Republicans, $p < 0.10$.[7] These patterns, thus far, show support for the partisan differences prediction. Democrats see both executive and legislative institutions that are majority-women as more feminine relative to Republicans.

The partisan differences prediction did not have any direct hypotheses about whether non-Democrats, or Republicans, would be more likely to see majority-men institutions as more masculine given the associations between the Republican Party and masculinity. I do not find that Republicans see majority-men institutions, or majority-women institutions, as more masculine relative to Republicans. Table A3.8 reports the full means, standard deviations, and p-values.

Issue Priorities of Legislative Institutions

I start with the perceived issue priorities of legislative institutions, and here I, again, use two-tailed t-tests for comparisons within institutions on gendered issue priorities and then across institutions. Figure 3.4 displays the mean ratings for city councils (left panel) and state legislatures (right panel). People see the majority-women institutions as more likely to prioritize masculine issues over feminine issues in the city council and the state legislature. The masculine issue priority rating in the majority-women city council was M = 0.97 (SD = 0.23) but the feminine issue priority was M = 0.78 (SD = 0.17), $p < 0.001$. The same pattern emerges for state legislature. The masculine issue priority in the majority-women state legislature was M = 0.97 (SD = 0.23) but the feminine issue priority was M = 0.78 (SD = 0.14), $p < 0.001$. Comparing across institutions shows no significant differences, $p = 0.9989$. People see the city council that is majority-women as more likely to prioritize masculine issues relative to feminine issues.

I also compared the issue priorities for the majority-men institutions. People see the majority-men city council as more likely to emphasize masculine issues, M = 0.96 (SD = 0.21), relative to feminine issues, M = 0.59 (SD = 0.20), $p < 0.001$. In the majority-men state legislature, people see the institution as more likely to prioritize masculine issues, M = 0.94, (SD = 0.22) than feminine issues, M = 0.6 (SD = 0.19), $p < 0.001$. There are no differences across the majority-men city council and state legislature, $p = 0.4590$.

---

[7] I also find that Democrats see the majority-men mayoral condition as more feminine than Republicans, but Democrats still see the majority-women mayoral condition as more feminine than masculine. See Table A3.7 in the Appendix.

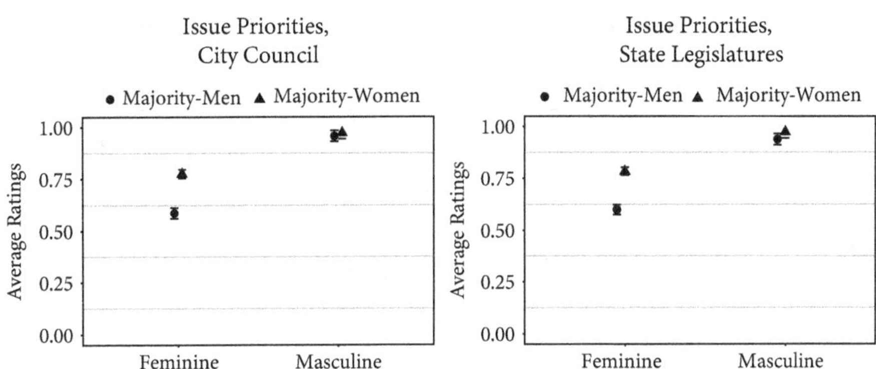

Figure 3.4 Issue priorities of legislative institutions

Note: 84 percent confidence intervals included. Full comparisons in Chapter 3 Appendix Table A3.9.

Masculine issue priorities persist even with the gendered trait shifts shown in the first analyses of this chapter.

I also compared the majority-women and majority-men institutions to one another. There are no differences in the masculine issue priorities of the majority-women relative to the majority-men city council, $p = 5835$, and state legislature, $p = 0.2238$. I find that the majority-women city council, $p < 0.001$, and state legislature, $p < 0.001$, are both perceived as more likely to prioritize feminine issues relative to the majority-men institutions. This finding is consistent with my expectations in the gendered shifts prediction. But all the legislative institutions are seen as more likely to prioritize masculine relative to feminine issues. This finding suggests some limits to feminizing effects. These perceptions could come from the high priority that people often place on masculine issues regardless of who is in office. Another possibility is that women in elected office often work very hard to fill in the masculine issue deficit in their perceived qualifications and people are drawing on seeing women prioritize masculine issues outside the experimental setting to form these assessments.

Issue Priorities of Executive Institutions

The pattern in the executive institution analyses mirrors those of the legislative institutions. Figure 3.5 shows the gendered issue priorities for executive institutions. People see the woman mayor and woman governor as, again, more likely to emphasize masculine issues relative to feminine issues. The masculine issue score for the woman mayor was M = 0.97 (SD = 0.23) and

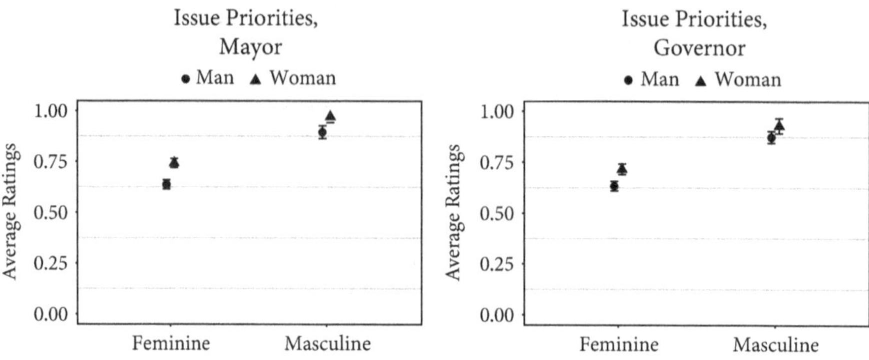

Figure 3.5 Issue priorities, executive institutions

Note: 84 percent confidence intervals included. Full comparisons in Chapter 3 Appendix Table A3.9.

the feminine issue score was M = 0.74 (SD = 0.17), $p < 0.001$. The masculine issue priority score for the woman governor was M = 0.93 (SD = 0.29) and the feminine priority score was M = 0.72 (0.21), $p < 0.001$. Comparing the woman mayor's and the woman governor's issue priorities shows no differences in masculine issues, $p = 0.2136$, and feminine issue priorities, $p = 0.2744$. These findings, thus far, mirror the patterns found in the legislative analyses.

As with the legislative analyses, people rate the man mayor higher on masculine issues, M = 0.89 (SD = 0.24), relative to feminine issues M = 0.64 (SD = 0.18), $p < 0.001$; the masculine issue priority with the man as governor was M = 0.87 (SD = 0.23) and the feminine issue priority level was M = 0.63 (SD = 0.19), $p < 0.001$. Comparing the woman mayor to the man mayor's issue priorities shows that people see the woman mayor as more likely to prioritize masculine issues, $p = 0.0115$, and more likely to prioritize feminine issues, $p < 0.001$. These patterns appear in the gubernatorial analyses. People see the woman governor as more likely to prioritize masculine issues, though this is only marginally significant, $p = 0.0952$, and more likely to prioritize feminine issues, $p = 0.0012$, compared to the condition with the man as governor.[8]

Issue Priorities across Institutional Types

Are there differences in the issue priorities of majority-women legislative relative to executive institutions with a woman holding office? I use the same

---

[8] See Chapter 3 Appendix Tables A3.11 and A3.12 for issue comparisons broken down by party and gender.

analytical approach from the trait analyses and compare across the pooled institutional types. The full results are in Chapter 3 Appendix Table A3.10. I find that majority-women legislative institutions (M = 0.7798, SD = 0.1592) are seen as more likely to prioritize feminine issues relative to majority-women executive institutions (M = 0.7302, SD = 0.1902), p = 0.0016. This perception that majority-women legislative institutions will be more likely to prioritize feminine issues compared to similarly situated executive institutions with a woman holding office, this finding fits with the idea of legislative institutions as more feminine institutions. Comparing the masculine issue priorities across institutional types shows no significant differences, p = 0.3240.

The results show that when there are more women in political institutions, people see those institutions as having more feminine traits and these feminizing effects occur among both legislative institutions and executive institutions. However, people do not see majority-women institutions as more likely to emphasize feminine issues over masculine issues. These results are striking because research suggests that women in political office do, in fact, prioritize feminine issues (Swers 1998; Kaslovsky and Rogoswki 2022; Bratton and Haynie 1999). However, people still see all levels of local and state offices as being far more likely to prioritize masculine issues over feminine issues, even if women dominate those bodies.

Partisan Differences in Issue Prioritizes

Finally, I test for partisan differences among participants in the perceptions of issue priorities across feminine and masculine institutions. As with the feminine trait attributions, I expect that Democratic participants may be more likely to see majority-women institutions as more likely to prioritize feminine issues relative to Republicans and Independents. Figure 3.6 displays the comparisons in feminine issue priorities for each institution with the results broken down by Democrats and Republicans (see Table A3.11 for the full means for feminine and masculine issue priorities). Across all four majority-women institutions, Democrats think that these institutions will prioritize feminine issues relative to Republicans and Independents.

The results in Table A3.11 in Appendix also include the comparisons for masculine issues. Democratic participants are more likely than Republican and Independent participants to see majority-women institutions as placing a high priority on masculine issues. Both Democrats and Republicans rate the majority-women institutions as likely to prioritize feminine issues relative to

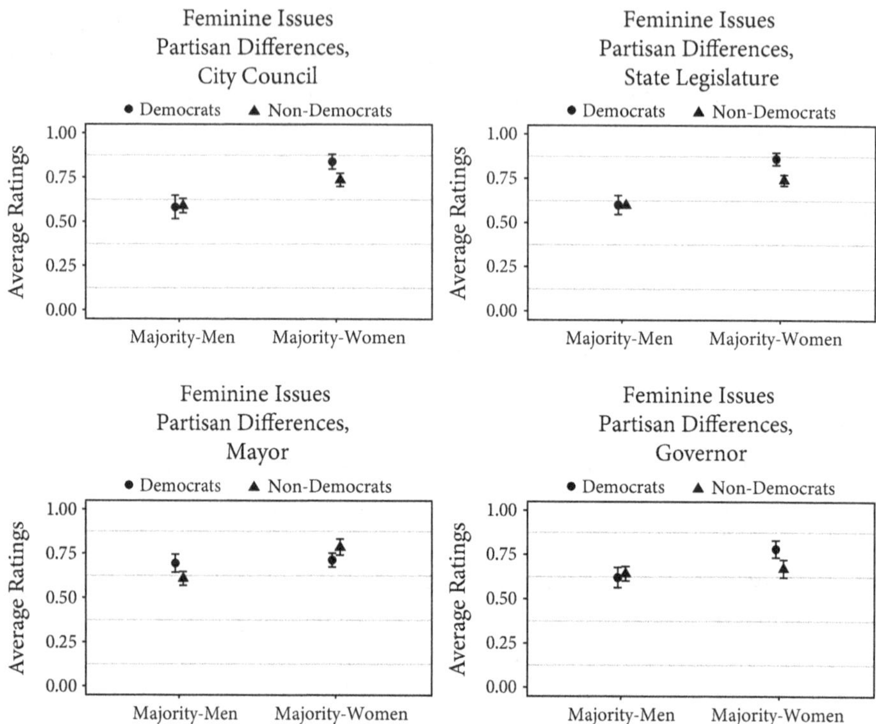

Figure 3.6 Partisan differences in feminine issue priorities

Note: 84 percent confidence intervals included. Table A3.11 in Chapter 3 Appendix include the full means.

masculine issues. It appears that Democrats, on all the issue metrics, simply see majority-women and majority-men institutions as more likely to emphasize issues, regardless of the gendered nature of the issues. This difference could be less about the stereotypic perceptions of the issue priorities of the political parties and may be better explained by ideological differences in the role of government. Republicans and conservatives often advocate for a less active and smaller government relative to Democrats. The partisan differences on issue priorities may simply be due to different ideological beliefs in the proper scope of government.

Results Summary

This chapter found support for the gendered shifts and partisan differences predictions but did not find the expected differences in the institutional type prediction. Majority-women institutions are seen as more feminine than majority-men institutions. These gendered shifts occur across all four institutions tested: a city council, state legislature, mayor, and governor. Moreover, majority-women institutions do not lose on masculine traits. People view majority-men institutions through a much narrower lens relative to majority-women institutions tending to see these institutions strictly through masculinity. Important to note is that these feminizing effects were stronger for the trait measures than for the issue measures. Masculine issues still top the expected priorities of institutions, and this is not surprising as the issues that dominate most election cycles are masculine issues (Bauer and Santia 2023). Nevertheless, participants rated majority-women institutions as more likely to prioritize feminine issues relative to majority-men institutions. Just as with the traits, people see majority-women institutions as more likely to handle both feminine and masculine issues, whereas people see majority-men institutions as much more likely to prioritize masculine issues.

Discussion and Conclusion

I turn back to the central question addressed in this chapter: *Do individuals stereotype political institutions that have more women as less masculine compared to institutions that under-represent women and over-represent men?* The results presented here suggest that, yes, individuals do, in fact, see political institutions with more women as more feminine but not necessarily as less masculine than majority-men institutions. There has long existed an assumption that the impressions and opinions people hold of political institutions are unlikely to change. I show that the gendered lens through which people see political institutions is not static. People update their perceptions based on levels of descriptive representation. This is an important finding about how people view political institutions. The experimental results show that people see majority-women institutions as having *both* feminine and masculine traits. My original gendered shifts prediction argued that feminine traits would be the most dominant traits in majority-women institutions. That people see majority-women institutions as having both feminine and masculine traits is certainly striking but also mirrors patterns of behavior of women in politics outside the experimental setting.

This chapter only examined gendered shifts and not raced shifts. Nevertheless, the findings in this chapter set the stage for examining whether women of color can change the whiteness of political institutions along with feminizing effects. The next chapter turns to testing how the raced and gendered perceptions of institutions shift based on women of color's presence in institutions. I argue that women of color are best positioned legislator to undo the whiteness and masculinity of political institutions because of the unique experiences women of color have navigating political institutions. Chapter 4 builds on my findings in this chapter to test how majority-women of color institutions lead people to see institutions as more feminine and more inclusive.

4

Women of Color's Descriptive Representation

In 2021, the Los Angeles County Board of Supervisors became, for the first time, all women. The County Board of Supervisors, often referred to as the "five little kings" long reigned as a bastion of local political power for men, primarily white men, in Los Angeles. Certainly, five women holding what many argue to be one of the most powerful political offices in Los Angeles is notable, but the racial diversity and range of experiences these women brought to their positions are also striking. The Board included Hilda Solis, who is Latina, a former congresswoman, and the former Secretary of Labor under the Obama administration, as well as Holly Mitchell, a Black woman elected to the board in 2020. Also elected to the Board was Sheila Kuhl, the first openly LGBTQ woman elected to a local office in Los Angeles. The County Board's all-women slate of supervisors, in and of itself, is notable. As of 2025, the County Board of Supervisors is still all women with two of the five women being women of color. To round out the successes of women at the local level in Los Angeles was the 2022 election of Karen Bass as the city's mayor. Bass became the first woman mayor of Los Angeles, and she is a Black woman who served in Congress for about a decade before her successful mayoral bid. These political gains made by women of color are not isolated to California. In 2023, Cherelle Parker became the first woman and the first Black woman mayor of Philadelphia, and in St. Paul, Minnesota, the city elected an all-women and majority-women of color city council.

Preceding these recent victories for women of color were the 2018 midterm elections. In 2018's "Pink Wave" election some 600 women of color ran for political office at the local, state, or federal level, whether in a primary or a general election (Ford Dowe 2020). The "Pink Wave" moniker obfuscates the fact that many of women's gains in this election cycle came from women of color's victories. Since the 2018-midterms, women of color have become more visible and prominent leaders in American politics. To be sure, women of color have a long history of leadership in American politics, but their leadership contributions are not always acknowledged. In 2018, Ayanna Pressley

Feminizing Political Institutions. Nichole M. Bauer, Oxford University Press. © Nichole M. Bauer (2026).
DOI: 10.1093/9780197841556.003.0004

became the first Black woman elected from the state of Massachusetts, and Alexandria Ocasio-Cortez, a Latina from New York, also took office that same year among record numbers of Black women, Latinas, Asian American women, and Native American women. The women of color who won election in 2018 quickly became assertive, vocal, and outspoken members of Congress. The aggressive, some might say masculine style, of these women attracted, and still attracts, ample media attention, leading commentators to collectively, and sometimes derisively, refer to these women as "the squad." These women embrace an arguably masculine style of leadership, but the squad are not always advancing masculine goals in Congress. Rather, the squad uses their masculine styles of leadership to advance goals that frequently align with feminine stereotypes. These women advocate for paid family leave, national strategies to reduce the high maternal mortality rates among Black women, and aid to families aimed at reducing child poverty. These are all issues that fit into women's perceived stereotypic strengths (Osborn 2012; Schneider 2014). If these women advanced masculine goals in Congress, they would, perhaps, be less focused on policy and more focused on advancing their personal power (Schneider et al. 2016). The blending of a masculine style of leadership with goals that match feminine stereotypes exemplifies my theoretical arguments around how women of color are best positioned to overturn the white-masculine stereotypes associated with political leadership.

This chapter turns to the second half of that first question posed in Chapter 1: *Do individuals stereotype political institutions that are more diverse along racial and gender lines as less masculine and less white compared to institutions that under-represent women and people of color?* Chapter 3 tracked how majority-women institutions change the gendered stereotypes people associate with political institutions. This chapter documented how women's descriptive representation leads people to associate political institutions with both feminine and masculine stereotypes, whereas majority-men institutions are seen as just masculine. These initial tests do not show whether the racialized perceptions of institutions change. I consider how women of color's rates of descriptive representation can change *both* the gendered and racialized stereotypes of political institutions, testing the raced-gendered and linked fate prediction in this chapter.

Women of color, I argue, are best positioned to erode the white-masculine stereotypes of political institutions so that people see institutions as more feminine and inclusive bodies. I focus on women of color specifically, as opposed to people of color or men of color (i.e., Black or Latino men), because women of color are uniquely positioned to undo both the raced and gendered stereotypes people have of political institutions. Men of color have the potential to undo the raced perceptions of institutions, but it is less likely that they will alter the masculine perceptions of political institutions. Stereotypes about men of color in political leadership, for the most part, reinforce masculine traits and behaviors and include little content from feminine stereotypes (Schneider and Bos 2011). Women of color will be able to undo the white-masculine stereotypes because of their experiences entering the political pipeline, the type of representation they provide, and the mixed stereotype content applied to this group.

I start this chapter by outlining the existing research on the experiences of women of color in politics, especially how women of color navigate raced-gendered institutions. Then I move on to identifying how women of color will shift the raced-gendered perceptions of institutions. In this section, I also contrast the experiences of women of color in politics with those of similarly situated men to better develop my argument around why it is women of color's descriptive representation, rather than men of color's, that will weaken the masculine stereotypes associated with political institutions. I use several experiments to test the raced-gendered and linked fate predictions. The results show that women of color's descriptive representation leads to a much stronger shift in the feminine stereotypes associated with political institutions compared to institutions that are just majority-women. People also see majority-women of color institutions as representing a broader range of minoritized group interests.

Intersectionality and Women of Color in American Politics

I apply my theory of institutional stereotype change to ascertain the effect of *women of color's* increased descriptive representation on the raced-gendered perceptions of political institutions. Theories of intersectionality argue that the stereotypes people associate with women of color do not have an additive effect that simply combines racial/ethnic stereotypes with gender stereotypes (Crenshaw 1991). People see, experience, and evaluate women of color based on *both* their gender and their perceived ethnorace simultaneously (Hancock 2007). Intersectional identities and their associated stereotypes come from the unique sets of traits and attributes that people apply specifically to Black women, Latinas, or Asian American women (Gershon et al. 2019; Cargile 2023; Santia and Bauer 2023; Qi, Kim, and Bauer 2023). Stereotypes about men of color tend to be additive rather than intersectional. Moreover stereotypes about men of color are largely dominated by the broad stereotypes around minoritized ethnoracial groups, i.e., Black stereotypes, Latino stereotypes, etc. (Katz and Braly 1933; Dawson 2001; Lee and Fiske 2006). The additive rather than intersectional nature of these stereotypes means that the increased representation of men of color will not have the effect of both feminizing and diversifying political institutions. I use the intersectionality framework to consider how the experiences of women of color in politics best position this particular group to undo the raced-gendered perceptions of political institutions.

I start with the research on the political ambition of women of color. Women of color's political ambition differs from the ambition of white women (Frederick 2013; Scott et al. 2021). Ford Dowe (2020) describes three forces that influence whether Black women, specifically, run for office: (1) Radical imagination, (2) Ambition, and (3) Marginalization. Radical imagination refers to a social vision that positions Black women as agents of social change. Black women must see themselves in roles where there are few Black women, and Black women must think of themselves as individuals who can uplift not just Black women but their communities. Ambition for Black women is motivated by their participation in Black women's organizations (Brown and Lemi 2021; Bejarano and Smooth 2022). These organizations, such as Black women sororities, socialize Black women to think of themselves as leaders but also provide valuable networking to mobilize support for Black women's candidacies (Brown and Lemi 2021). The role of Black women sororities reflects the relationally embedded model articulated by Carroll and Sanbonmatsu (2013), where women seek support from multiple stakeholders, including community groups, before pursuing political office. Organizations that mobilize women of color into the pipeline are critical because mainstream party organizations or groups organized around race tend to overlook women of color candidates (Bejarano and Smooth 2022). Finally, Black women push against marginalization. Black women often face marginalization based on both their race and gender (Brown and Lemi 2021). This marginalization can come from within their own racial community, where Black men's leadership roles frequently take priority over those of Black women (Philpot and Walton 2007). Holman and Schneider (2018) find that Black women, Latinas, and Asian women are more likely to run for political office when they receive messages emphasizing the structural barriers that limit women of color's ability to run for political office, such as pointing out that parties are less likely to support the candidacies of women of color. This motivation to pursue political office reflects both the ambition and marginalization components of Ford-Dowe's model of Black women's political ambition.

This model of ambition for Black women can apply to other women of color groups, such as Latinas, who also face marginalization because of their ethnicity and gender (Cargile 2016; Cargile 2023; Cargile, Merolla, and Schroedel 2016). Latinas, like Black women, run for office because they see themselves as agents of social change who want to uplift both their ethnic communities, but also other marginalized groups (Fraga et al. 2006; Bejarano 2013) and Latinas often base their political engagement in grassroots activism (Takash 1993). Latinas also run for political office based on their collectivist identities as both Latino and women, which fosters a sense of group consciousness that extends to other marginalized groups (Jaramillo 2010). These collectivist identities for Latinas mirror Ford Dowe's (2020) concepts of radical imagination and marginalization. Latinas focus on the marginalization of their group in their motivations to pursue political office and the type of representation they bring to politics. But to get into political office, Latinas, like Black women, must overcome the perception of politics as a white-masculine domain.

Once making the decision to run for political office, women of color face a complex set of gendered-racialized hurdles. These hurdles differ based on the specific ethnorace of a woman. In other words, Black women do not face the same challenges as Latinas, and neither Black women nor Latinas face the same challenges as Asian American women (Gonzalez and Bauer 2022; Lien and Filler 2022). Black women, in particular, face scrutiny based on their physical appearance from the darkness of their skin (Johnson Carew 2016) to the way they wear their hair (Lemi 2019; Orey and Zhang 2019). Black women face pressure to dress in ways that downplay their race, their Afrocentric facial features, and to straighten their wear as opposed to wearing their hair natural or curly (Brown and Lemi 2021). These pressures can come from those with whom Black women share a racial identity and from white voters as well (Brown and Lemi 2021).

Latinas and Asian American women do not face the same type of scrutiny and criticism over their hair and facial features as Black women, but they still face a layered set of challenges based on the stereotypic perceptions that people form of these women. People stereotype Latinas as lacking the masculine traits and qualities that voters look for in political candidates (Cargile 2016) and see these candidates as being more compassionate than Latino men but lacking strength, especially compared to Latino men (Cargile 2023). These negative stereotypic impressions of Latinas can come from voters with whom they share an ethnic identity and from white voters (Cargile 2016; Cargile, Merolla, and Schroedel 2016; Santia and Bauer 2023).

Asian American women also face a set of stereotypic obstacles stemming from the unique stereotypes attributed to them based on their gender and ethnorace. Overall, Asian American women face a set of negative stereotypes that characterize them as deferential to authority, lacking ambition, being hard workers, and lacking strong interpersonal communication skills (Kawahara 2007a, 2007b; Lien and Filler 2022; Qi, Kim, and Bauer 2023). Based on this contradictory and negative set of stereotypes, Asian women often downplay their ethnorace identities in their strategic communication while playing up their gender identities (Qi, Kim, and Bauer 2023).

The experiences women of color have navigating the white-masculinity of the candidate entry and campaign process lay the groundwork for the more transformative effects I predict. Women of color who win elections to political office have already learned how to successfully manage white-masculine expectations. Once in political institutions, women of color often engage in behaviors that differ from those of other women (Bauer and Cargile 2023). Women of color in Congress are more likely to respond to constituent service requests (Lowande, Ritchie, and Lauterbach 2019); and women of color often promote and support legislation that reflect the issue priorities of their racial and ethnic communities but also the issue priorities of women, more generally, and other marginalized groups (Bratton and Haynie 1999; Fraga et al. 2006; Bratton, Haynie, and Reingold 2007; Brown 2014a; Brown and Banks 2014). Patterns of bill sponsorship among Black women, for example, show that these legislators have different policy agendas relative to white women, white men, and Black men (Bratton, Haynie, and Reingold 2007). Women of color often achieve policy successes that focus on intersectional issues through coalitions built with men of color, white men, and white women to advance their policy interests (Brown 2014a; Brown and Banks 2014). These relationships allow women of color to successfully pass legislation that improves the lives of their communities and secure their success in re-election. Women of color's focus on caring and providing for their communities embodies a communal vision of representation that fits with feminine stereotypes.

Men of color in elected political office certainly engage in the substantive representation of their ethnoracial group. Black men and Latino men in state legislatures sponsor more bills focused on issues that disproportionately affect their ethnoracial groups, including policies on policing, criminal justice, and the distribution of social welfare benefits (Haynie 2001; Fraga et al. 2006). The substantive representation men of color provide in state legislatures for their ethnoracial group is certainly important to ensuring that minoritized groups receive adequate representation (Clark 2019). It is reasonable to expect that the representational behaviors of men of color could certainly lead to the public seeing political institutions as more inclusive and diverse. I argue that the increased descriptive representation of men of color is unlikely to change the *masculine* perceptions held of political institutions. This limited effect of the descriptive representation of men of color comes, in part, from the often single-axis policy agenda adopted by Black and Latino men in political office (Owens 2005; Clark 2019).

Women of color legislate and serve their communities in distinct ways that stand out from the behaviors of white women, white men, and men of color. I argue that the intersectional experiences of women of color on the campaign trail and in political office will lead people to perceive political institutions in distinctly different ways from how they perceive institutions dominated by men and institutions dominated by white women. The way that women of color engage in the task of representation and legislating is one that breaks down the white-masculine norms that shape the perceptions people have of political institutions.

Undoing Raced-Gendered Stereotypes of Political Institutions

The stereotypic impressions others hold of women of color position these political actors to undo the white-masculinity of politics (Cassese 2019). Stereotypes about Black women can be grouped into three central tropes: The mammy stereotype, the Jezebel stereotype, and the Sapphire stereotype (Harris-Perry 2013). These three stereotypic tropes come from the roles historically performed by Black women. The mammy stereotype characterizes Black women as caregivers, and stems from the caregiving roles performed by Black women frequently in white households (Reynolds-Dobbs, Thomas, and Harrison 2008). The Jezebel stereotype characterizes Black women through a hyper-sexualized lens and positions Black women as objects of sexual desire to both Black men and white men (Givens and Monahan 2005). The Sapphire stereotype reflects the angry Black woman stereotype and comes from the roles of Black women as heads of households or economic providers (Brown 2014b). None of these stereotypes accurately reflects the lived experiences of Black women in the United States. These stereotypic tropes reflect how stereotypes about Black women are uniquely shaped by the perceptions others have of this group.

The stereotype content of Black women frequently includes both feminine and masculine content. However, feminine stereotypes in the context of a Black woman do not lead to the same associations as feminine stereotypes in the context of a white woman. These feminine stereotypes combine with masculine stereotypes to project an image of a Black woman who fiercely defends and cares for her community and family. For Black women, feminine stereotypes do not create an image of weakness but one of strength, but for white women feminine stereotypes often lead others to see them as weak. For example, Brown (2014a) shows that Black women in the Maryland state legislature embrace and demonstrate positive feminine stereotypes, such as care and compassion, as well as masculine stereotypes that align with leadership stereotypes, such as strength and toughness. Black women also display these dual stereotypes in their campaign messages (Bauer, Lee-Johnson, and Qi 2025). The dual feminine and masculine stereotype content about Black women contrasts with the stereotypes about Black men that largely include masculine traits and behaviors (Staples 1978; Katz and Braly 1933).

Scholarship by Cargile (2016, 2023) lends insight into the stereotypes that people hold about Latinas and Latinos. Stereotypes about Latinas in politics are also shaped by whether a voter shares a Latino identity with the woman (Cargile 2023). Non-Latino voters see Latina political candidates as lacking the expertise needed to advocate on masculine stereotypic issues, such as crime or the military (Cargile 2016), but non-Latino voters also see Latinas as lacking feminine stereotypic traits, such as care and compassion, and lacking masculine traits such as strength and authority (Cargile 2023). Latino voters, on the other hand, tend to see Latina candidates as having both feminine and masculine traits (Cargile 2023). For Latino men, both non-Latino and Latino voters see these candidates as having few masculine traits, especially compared to the traits associated with white men. Scholarship on how Latina political leaders advocate for their communities reinforces the notion that Latinas have both feminine and masculine qualities that they bring to leadership roles (Bejarano 2013). While there are distinct differences between the stereotypes of Latinas and Latinos men, it is also the case that stereotypes about Latino men, or Latinos in general, include more feminine traits relative to the stereotypes of white men (Sigelman et al. 1995; Cargile, Merolla, and Schroedel 2016). This stereotype content is striking given that many Latino cultures have a strong patriarchal norm with a prevailing sense of machismo (Lavariega Monforti 2017).

The stereotypes of Asian American women are less clearly defined compared to women of other minoritized ethnoracial groups due to large gaps in research on this topic (for exceptions, see Filler and Lien 2016; Lien and Filler 2022; Qi, Kim, and Bauer 2023).[1] The gap in research on Asian American women is striking, given that the first woman of color to hold a seat in the US Congress was an Asian American woman, Patsy Mink, a member of the

---

[1] Research often groups Asian American and Pacific Islander women together as there is some overlap between the two groups, few studies consider the differences in the ethnicity of AAPI women political leaders (Lien and Filler 2022).

House representing Hawaii who won election in 1964.[2] To theorize on the stereotypes applied to Asian American women, I draw on a small but theoretically rich body of scholarship in political science and social psychology. Asian American women are perceived as lacking many positive feminine attributes, like warmth, along with agentic attributes, such as assertiveness (Mukkamala and Suyemoto 2018). Rather, Asian American women and men are often cast in deferential roles where they cede power to others and work in supportive social roles (Kawahara 2007a), and are stereotyped as lacking strong interpersonal skills (Keum et al. 2018).

Asian American women, and men, often must contend with the model minority stereotype that casts them as quiet, hardworking, and diligent (Lien and Filler 2022). These model minority stereotypes appear to have positive connotations for Asian American women and Asian American men, as many in politics want representatives who are both hardworking and diligent. It is important to remember that even stereotypes that seem positive are still harmful as they constrain the behaviors of people to these stereotypic expectations, and the model minority stereotypes still cast Asian Americans as deferential to authority and lacking strong people skills (Li 2014). The masculine stereotypes embodied by Asian American women still present a challenge to the *whiteness* of the masculine stereotypes that define political leadership.

I argue that both the stereotype content that people apply to women of color and the experiences and behaviors of women of color in politics provide a direct challenge to the white-masculine stereotypes that dominate views of the political institution. Stereotypes about Black women, for example, encompass both feminine and masculine traits, and this is also true of many stereotypes about Asian American women leaders. This dual stereotype content for many women of color does not mean that women of color will simply reinforce the masculine traits people already associate with political institutions, but how women of color exercise power and display these masculine traits will lead to a more feminine perception of political institutions. Women of color often fulfill communal goals through a masculine style when they are on the campaign trail and in political office. It is the way that Black women, Latinas, or Asian women exercise power and display gendered traits that will undo the white-masculine stereotypes of political institutions. These feminizing and diversifying effects will, I argue, occur more strongly in the context

---

[2] Two years after Mink was elected Shirley Chisholm became the first Black woman to hold a seat in the US Congress. Both Mink and Chisholm ran for the presidency in 1972, and Chisholm stayed in the race up to the Democratic convention, making both women the first women of color to pursue the presidency. No woman of color would hold a seat in the US Senate until 1992 when Carol Mosley Braun won in Illinois. In 2012, Mazie Hirono became the first Asian American woman elected to the Senate.

of women of color's descriptive representation. Stereotypes about men of color do not include the dual feminine and masculine stereotype content, and this limits the ability of this group to undo both the raced and gendered perceptions of institutions. This brings me to the raced-gendered prediction:

Raced-Gendered Prediction: Women of color's descriptive representation will weaken the white-masculine stereotypes associates with political institutions more so than the descriptive representation of White women and people of color more generally.

Candidates of color, especially Black and Latino candidates, tend to run for office in majority-minority districts. Majority-minority districts are districts created to ensure that the interests of minority voters are not diluted but that these voters can select a candidate that will best represent them (Tate 2003). These types of districts emerged out of the Voting Rights Act of the 1960s, which sought to undo the weakening of Black voting power in the South, where districts were created to divide communities of color and guarantee that white voters made up majorities in all congressional districts. Many, though not all, candidates of color for Congress or state legislative districts come from these majority-minority districts.

Majority-minority districts rest on the premise that descriptive representation can lead to substantive representation, and this link between these two forms of representation for voters of color can manifest in a sentiment called linked fate. Political leaders who share a minoritized ethnoracial identity with their constituents are better positioned to draw on their own shared experiences to substantively represent these groups (Bejarano et al. 2021). Much of the scholarship on linked fate focuses on the relationship between Black voters and Black candidates, with an implicit focus on Black men candidates (White, Laird, and Allen 2014). This concept of shared experiences, often steeped in experiences of marginalization, underlies theories of linked fate where people of color share common electoral interests (Simien 2005; Campi and Junn 2019; Bejarano et al. 2021). Linked fate, in other words, works because voters of color believe that candidates and legislators of color will substantively represent their interests based on their shared experience of belonging to a minoritized ethnoracial group. Scholarship on women of color candidates finds a linked fate bond with women of color voters (Gay and Tate 1998; Simien 2005). This bond between women of color voters and candidates does not generally extend to white women voters (Matos, Greene, and Sanbonmatsu 2020) or men of color voters (Matos and Sanbonmatsu 2024). I argue that linked fate will lead voters of color to be more responsible for updating their gendered and raced impressions of political institutions when women of color's descriptive representation increases. The linked fate prediction delineates these effects below:

Linked Fate Prediction: Voters of color will be more likely to see institutions that descriptively represent women of color as more feminine and inclusive relative to white voters.

This chapter extends my theory of institutional stereotype change to consider how women of color's descriptive representation shifts *both* the white stereotypes and masculine stereotypes associated with political institutions. When women of color's descriptive representation is high, people will form more feminine and more inclusive perceptions of political institutions (raced-gendered prediction), and these effects will be especially pronounced among voters of color (linked fate prediction).

Experimental Design

I conducted three experiments to test the raced-gendered and linked fate predictions. The design of these studies is adapted from the experiments presented in Chapter 3. I used a city council in two of the experiments because I want the experimental participants to believe that a city council could be majority-women of color. The third experiment uses a mayoral office to test the dynamics of women of color's representation at the executive office level.

The first study, the Women of Color City Council Experiment (WOC City Council Experiment) includes two conditions: A majority-women of color city council and a city council with no race or gender information provided. These two conditions test how people evaluate majority-women of color institutions relative to a control condition. The Diversified City Council Experiment (the Diversified CC Experiment) includes three conditions: A city council where women of color hold a majority of seats (majority-women of color), where people of color (no gender or ethnorace information provided) hold a majority of seats, and a city council where women hold a majority of seats (majority-women). In this second study, I can compare how women of color relative to just women or people of color are uniquely positioned to shift the raced-gendered stereotypes of political institutions. The third experiment examines women of color's representation at the executive level, focusing on a mayoral race. The WOC Mayoral Experiment includes just two conditions: A woman of color elected to be mayor and a man of color elected to be mayor. This study's manipulation allows me to further drill down into how people perceive the descriptive representation of women of color differently from men of color. The WOC mayoral experiment experiment does not specify the exact ethnorace identity of the new mayor (i.e., Black, Latino); however, the experiment asks participants what they think the ethnorace of the mayor is in a post-treatment question. The full treatment texts are included in the Chapter 4 Appendix and in Table 4.1.

Table 4.1 Experimental Conditions

Condition	Office	N	Treatment
Women of Color (WOC) City Council Experiment, N = 256			
Majority-Women of Color	City Council	119	**New City Council Elected** When the new city council takes over next year, the majority of its members will be women of color. Indeed, women of color will hold over 50% of seats in the city council. Residents are looking forward to seeing what new policies the majority-women of color city council puts into place next year.
Control	City Council	137	**New City Council Elected** A new city council takes over next year. Residents are looking forward to seeing the new policies the city council puts into place next year.
Diversified City Council Experiment, N = 295			
Majority-Women	City Council	100	**City Council Election Results** When the new city council takes over next year, the majority of its members will be women. Indeed, women will hold over 50% of seats in the city council. Residents are looking forward to seeing what new policies the majority-women city council puts into place next year.
Majority-Women of Color	City Council	101	**City Council Election Results** When the new city council takes over next year, the majority of its members will be women of color. Indeed, women of color will hold over 50% of seats in the city council. Residents are looking forward to seeing what new policies the majority-women of color city council puts into place next year.
Majority-People of Color	City Council	95	**City Council Election Results** When the new city council takes over next year, the majority of its members will be people of color. Indeed, people of color will hold over 50% of seats in the city council. Residents are looking forward to seeing what new policies the majority-people of color city council puts into place next year.

Condition	Office	N	Treatment
WOC Mayoral Experiment, $N = 203$			
WOC	Mayor	107	**New Mayor Elected** When the new mayor takes over in a few days, there will be a woman of color in the executive office. The mayor's inauguration will take place later this week, and she will start working on her policy agenda for the next year. The city is looking forward to having a woman of color in the city's top job.
Man of Color	Mayor	96	**New Mayor Elected** When the new mayor takes over in a few days, there will be a man of color in the executive office. The mayor's inauguration will take place later this week, and he will start working on his policy agenda for the next year. The city is looking forward to having a man of color in the city's top job.

Note: Table A4.3 displays the breakdown for the Women of Color CC Experiment by participant race/ethnicity.

Sample

I recruited an experimental sample from Amazon's Mechanical Turk (mTurk) for the WOC City Council Experiment, and two separate Prolific samples in the Diversified CC Experiment and the WOC Mayoral Experiment. The mTurk sample recruited balanced numbers of minoritized ethnoracial group members and white people. This over-sampling is necessary so that I have adequate statistical power to test the linked fate prediction. The Prolific sample for the Diversified City Council Experiment includes just non-white participants, and the sample for the Mayoral Experiment includes both white and non-white participants. The Chapter 4 Appendix, in Table A4.1 displays the demographic characteristics of these samples.

Key Measures

I measure the raced-gendered associations people formed of the city councils in several ways. First, I use an expanded version of the feminine and masculine trait measures from Chapter 3, and include the full suite of traits in the Chapter 4 Appendix. I use these measures in all three experiments in this chapter. These measures allow me to compare how women of color institutions are perceived relative to institutions where the ethnorace of women in office is not provided. There are several possibilities for how these trait measures will lend evidence that majority-women of color institutions undo both the raced and gendered perceptions of political institutions. Stereotypes about women of color frequently attribute them with both masculine and feminine qualities, and people may see a majority-women of color city council as having both gendered traits. This effect would not be that different from what I found in Chapter 3, where people saw the majority-women institutions as having both feminine and masculine traits. Another outcome may be that people see majority-women of color institutions as more feminine than masculine, with a clearer separation in the gendered traits associated with the institutions. Women of color frequently run for political office to fulfill communal goals, even if these women use masculinity to fulfill these goals. The communal focus motivating women of color's candidacies may lead people to see these institutions as more feminine than masculine, rather than having both sets of gendered traits. Either outcome, I argue, indicates a raced-gendered shift in the perceptions people hold of majority-women of color institutions.

The Diversified CC Experiment asked participants to rate whether the institution would make a set of issues a "high priority," "medium priority," or "low priority." For the issue priorities, I created several issue scales. First, I replicated the feminine issue scale from Chapter 3. These issues include education, childcare, and healthcare. Second, I created an issue scale that captures issues that disproportionately affect communities of color. This race-focused issue scale includes housing, immigration, minimum wage, and criminal justice reform. Ideally, I would have a scale that includes issues that disproportionately affect women of color, but many of these issues are also considered feminine issues (Santia and Bauer 2023). The feminine issue scale reflects issues that, in the context of a majority-women of color city council, people are likely to see as intersectional issues, whereas in the context of just a majority-women city council, these feminine issues are likely to be seen through a single-axis lens of gender. I expect that people will see the majority-women of color institutions as more likely to prioritize feminine issues relative to a majority-people of color institution, but not necessarily more likely to consider feminine issues than the majority-women city council. I also expect that majority-women of color city council to be seen as more likely to address race-focused issues compared to the majority-women city council, but not necessarily more so than the majority-persons of color city council. Each issue scale is the average rating of how high a priority respondents expect the city council to place the issues, and each scale ranges from 0 to 1, with higher values indicating a higher priority.

I asked one additional set of questions in the Diversified CC Experiment to track perceptions of which types of groups the city council is likely to represent. I asked participants to rate how well the city councils would represent different groups. People indicated how well the city council they read about would represent Black Americans, Latinos, Black Women, Latinas, People of Color, Asian American & Pacific Islander (AAPI) Women, Working Class Voters, and the Wealthy. The response options included "very well," "somewhat well," "somewhat unwell, and "very unwell." I rescaled the responses to range from 0 to 1 with values closer to 1 indicating a more positive evaluation. I expect participants will have higher expectations that the majority-women of color city council will represent minoritized ethnoracial groups and women of color equally well. These comparisons can show whether people see majority-women of color institutions as more racially inclusive institutions relative to just majority-women institutions in terms of the groups represented.

Women of Color City Council Results

I start with the findings on the feminine and masculine trait measures in the WOC City Council Experiment. I compare the majority-women of color institution to the control condition on the ratings for feminine and masculine traits, and then I compare differences between participants of color and white participants. I use a series of two-tailed t-tests to conduct comparisons both within the experimental conditions and across the experimental conditions. The figures all use 84 percent confidence intervals to better illustrate smaller but substantive differences between groups. The raced-gendered prediction argues that women's descriptive representation will lead people to see majority-women of color institutions as more feminine than masculine. The linked fate prediction builds on this expectation to argue that the shifts in the gendered and racialized perceptions will be strongest among voters of color relative to white voters.[3]

Figure 4.1 displays the average feminine stereotype and masculine stereotype ratings across the experimental conditions, and the full comparisons are

---

[3] The manipulation check question asked respondents whether the institution they read about was mostly women or mostly men, 95 percent of respondents correctly recalled that the women of color condition was mostly women.

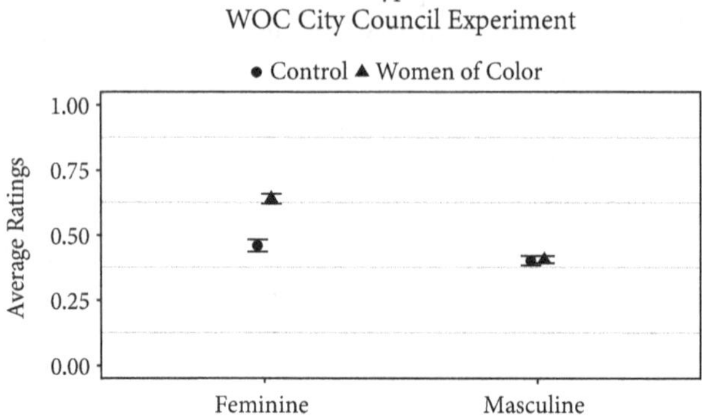

Figure 4.1 Stereotype shifts, women of color city council
Note: 84 percent confidence intervals included. Full means in Table A4.4.

in Table A4.4 in the Chapter 4 Appendix. Support for the raced-gendered prediction is indicated by a stronger feminine than masculine stereotype association for the majority-women of color institutions. The feminine stereotype rating for the majority-women of color condition is 0.63 ($SD = 0.153$), and this is significantly higher than the masculine stereotype rating 0.405 ($SD = 0.113$), $p < 0.001$. This finding differs slightly from the initial findings of Chapter 3, which found that majority-women institutions are seen as having *both* feminine and masculine traits. I find that majority-women of color institutions are seen as having mostly feminine traits. This finding is striking because stereotypes about women of color, especially Black women, often include a mix of feminine and masculine traits. I also find in the control condition that people associate the city council as having more feminine, $M = 0.460$ ($SD = 0.135$), relative to masculine, $M = 0.401$ ($SD = 0.135$), $p < 0.001$. Comparing across the conditions shows that the majority-women of color condition is associated with more feminine traits than the control condition, $p < 0.001$, but there are no differences in the masculine trait associations across the two conditions, $p = 0.8039$.

The linked fate prediction argues that the shift from masculine to feminine stereotypes may be more pronounced among members of minoritized ethnoracial groups. Support for the linked fate prediction is confirmed if voters of color see majority-women of color institutions as more feminine than white voters. Figure 4.2 displays the mean ratings for each condition based on participant ethnorace for feminine and masculine traits, and these full results are also in Table A4.4. I find that non-white participants rate the majority-women

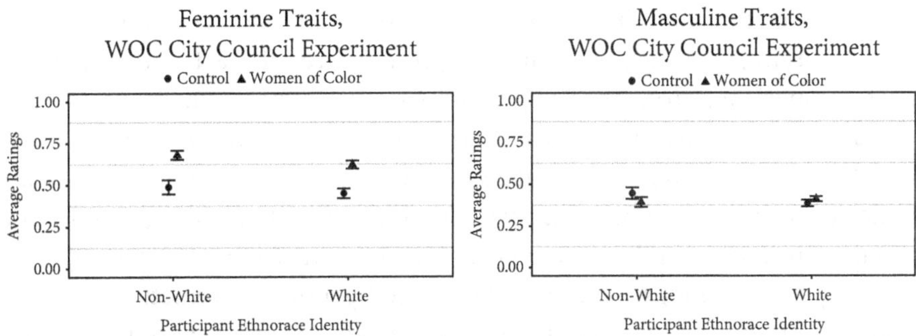

Figure 4.2 Feminine and masculine traits by participant ethnorace identity
Note: 84 percent confidence intervals included. Full means in Table A4.4.

of color city council higher, by 0.059-points (*SE* = 0.028), on feminine traits compared to white participants, p = 0.0383. There are no differences on feminine traits and participant ethnorace in the control conditions, p = 0.3186. These patterns suggest that non-white participants are more likely to identify majority-women of color city councils as having more feminine traits relative to white people, and this is in line with my expectations.

I also compared across participant ethnorace on masculine traits (see right panel Figure 4.2). There are no differences in the masculine trait associations in the majority-women of color condition across participant ethnorace, p = 0.4256. I find that non-white participants rate the city council in the control condition higher on masculine traits relative to white participants, p = 0.0356. Together, these comparisons suggest that when there are majority-women of color institutions, people will associate those institutions with more feminine relative to masculine traits, and these effects are particularly strong among non-white individuals. This first study suggests support for my raced-gendered prediction and the linked fate prediction.

Diversified City Council Experiment

The Diversified CC Experiment builds on the WOC City Councils Experiment in several ways. First, the Diversified CC Experiment digs a bit more into how people of color think the type of representation provided by a more diverse institution can change. Second, the Diversified CC Experiment includes a majority-women condition so that I can compare majority-women to majority-women of color institutions. Third, this second study can also conduct comparisons between institutions that are majority-women of color and institutions that are majority-persons of color institutions without specifying the gender of those representatives. I start with the same trait comparisons from the WOC City Council Experiment, then I move on to using the issue priorities and group representation questions to track how both the gendered and racialized perceptions shift when institutions are majority-women of color. I again use two-tailed t-tests to conduct the relevant group comparisons and display 84 percent confidence intervals in the figures. This experiment focuses on testing the raced-gendered prediction more so than the linked fate prediction, as this experimental sample only includes participants who identified as belonging to a minoritized ethnoracial group.[4]

Trait Shifts in Diversified City Councils

Figure 4.3 displays the mean feminine and masculine trait ratings for the three experimental conditions. The majority-women of color city council is rated as having more feminine than masculine traits, $p = 0.001$. I find that people also rated the majority-women city council as more feminine than masculine, $p = 0.002$. I compared the feminine and masculine trait patterns in the majority-people of color condition and found no differences, $p = 0.8623$. These patterns fit with the expectations for the raced-gendered prediction.

I found no differences in this study between the majority-women and majority-women of color institutions on feminine traits, $p = 0.6723$.

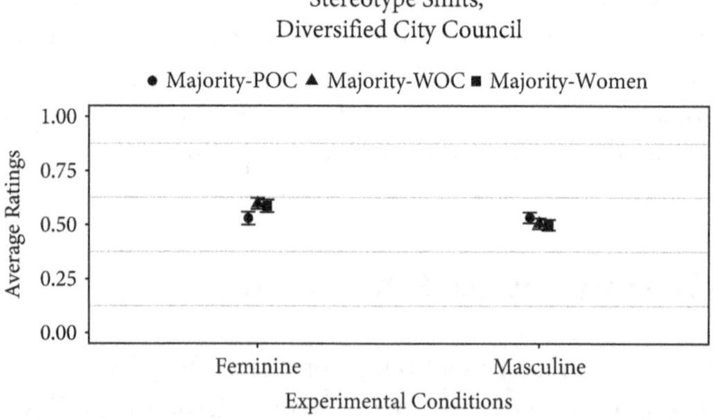

Figure 4.3 Stereotype shifts, women of color city councils, diversified city council experiment

Note: 84 percent confidence intervals included. Full results are in Table A.7 in Chapter 4 Appendix.

[4] About 85 percent of respondents correctly identified the ethnorace and/or gender composition of the city council they read about.

This deviates somewhat from my raced-gendered prediction, which argued for more pronounced differences between majority-women of color and majority-women institutions. Participants rated the majority-women of color institution as more feminine than the majority-people of color institution, $p = 0.0166$. This pattern suggests that participants likely assume that the majority-people of color city council may still be majority-men, though I did not directly test this expectation in the experiment. I also compared the attribution of masculine traits across the three conditions, but there were no differences.

I tested differences across participant party and gender. I include these full comparisons in Tables A4.8 and A4.9 in the Chapter 4 Appendix. Democratic participants rate the majority-women of color institution as more feminine relative to Republicans. The partisan differences on feminizing effects are not statistically significant for the majority-women and majority-people of color conditions. For masculine stereotypes, Democrats, again, rate the majority-women of color along with the majority-women conditions as more masculine relative to Republicans. Pairing these partisan differences with the findings in Chapter 3 suggests that the feminizing effects of WDR appear to occur more strongly among Democrats.

Diversified Issue Priorities

I examine how the racialized perceptions of political institutions shift the types of issues people think that majority-women of color city councils will be most likely to prioritize. I expect that majority-women of color institutions will be seen as more likely to advocate for feminine issues than the majority-people of color city council and more likely to advocate for race-focused issues than the majority-women city council (Enders and Scott 2019).

Figure 4.4 displays the issue priorities for the three experimental conditions, and Appendix Table A4.10 includes the full comparisons. Several key patterns emerge. First, respondents expect the majority-women of color city council to be more likely to prioritize feminine issues relative to the majority-people of color city council, $p = 0.0007$; but people expect the majority-women of color and majority-women institutions to be equally likely to prioritize feminine issues, $p = 0.9676$. These patterns fit with my general expectations.

The second main finding from Figure 4.4 is the results on race-focused issues. Here, I find no differences in the priority ratings of these issues across the three experimental conditions. This is somewhat unexpected given that legislators of color prioritize these types of issues more than white legislators

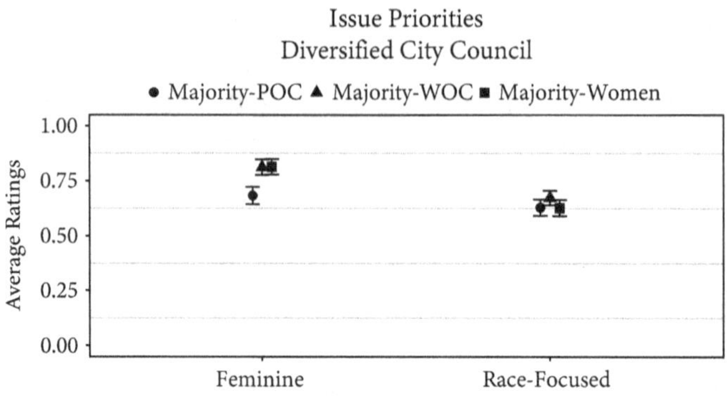

Issue Priorities
Diversified City Council

● Majority-POC ▲ Majority-WOC ■ Majority-Women

Figure 4.4 Issue priorities across demographic compositions of legislatures
Note: 84 percent confidence intervals included. Full results are in Table A4.10.

(Grose 2010). While I did not expect differences between the majority-people of color and majority-women of color city councils, I expected differences between the majority-women of color and majority-women conditions.

I also tested partisan and gender differences on issue priorities. These results are in Tables A4.11 and A4.12. Democrats see all the institutions in this study as more likely to prioritize feminine issues relative to Republicans. Democrats also majority-women of color and majority-people of color institutions as more likely to prioritize issues on race relative to Republicans.

Perceptions of Group Representation

For the group-representation questions, I expect people to see majority-women of color institutions as more inclusive relative to majority-women institutions. Figure 4.5 displays the mean group representation ratings for each condition, and the full results are in Table A4.13. Comparing the majority-women of color to the majority-women condition shows that participants think the majority-women of color city council will be more likely to represent Blacks, Latinos, Black women, people of color, and the working class, $p < 0.10$. There were no differences in the group representation ratings between the majority-women of color and majority-women conditions on representing Latinas and Asian American women. Participants indicated that they expected the majority-women city council to represent the wealthy better than women of color. Women of color are thought to do a better job representing a broader range of minoritized ethnoracial groups compared to city councils that lack ethnorace diversity in women's representation.

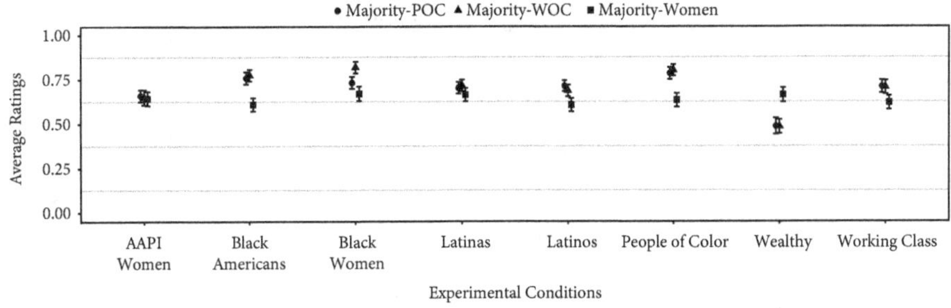

Figure 4.5 Group representation across demographic compositions of legislatures
Note: 84 percent confidence intervals included. Full results are in Table A4.13.

I also compared the majority-women of color to the majority-people of color conditions and found that participants expect the majority-women of color city council to better represent Blacks and Black women, $p < 0.10$, with no differences for the other groups. This specific finding reinforces my expectation that women of color, more so than men of color, are better positioned to undo the racialized and gendered stereotypes people hold of political institutions.

I tested partisan and gender differences in perceptions of group representation, see Tables A4.14–A4.17. Democrats rate the majority-people of color institution as more likely to represent all groups except for the wealthy, whereas Republicans are more likely than Democrats to see majority-people of color institutions as likely to represent the wealthy. The fact that partisan differences only strongly emerge on perceptions of group representation for the majority-people of color institution is certainly curious. The majority-people of color condition did not specify if the institution was majority-women or majority-men; however, it is likely that participants assume that there are some women and some men in the majority-people of color condition. Together, the results on the trait shifts and the more expansive forms of group representation suggest that women of color can undo the raced-gendered perceptions of institutions.

Woman of Color Mayor Results

This final experiment tests whether the diversifying and feminizing effects of women of color's descriptive representation extend to executive offices. I start by examining the trait shifts across the mayoral offices, then I turn to the

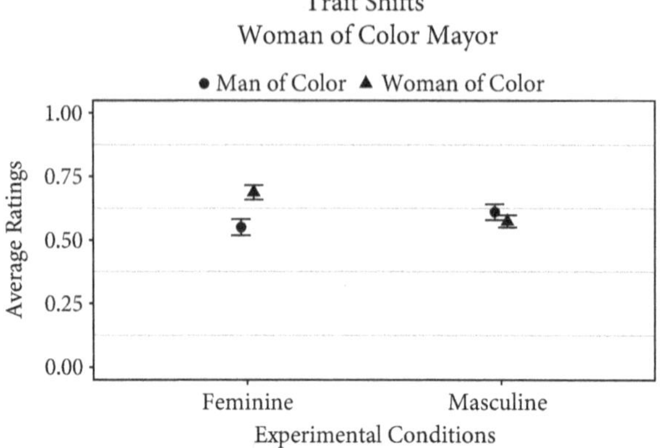

Figure 4.6 Trait shifts, woman of color mayor

Note: 84 percent confidence intervals included. Full means in Table A4.20.

results on issue priorities and patterns of group representation. I expect that the effects of a woman of color mayor should lead to the mayoral office as being seen as more feminine than the man of color mayor, and will prioritize a more diverse range of issues.[5]

Figure 4.6 plots the mean ratings on the feminine and masculine stereotype scales across the two experimental conditions, see Table A4.20 in the Chapter 4 Appendix. Participants rated the woman of color mayor as having more feminine traits, $M = 0.6910$ ($SD = 0.1987$), relative to masculine traits $M = 0.5734$ ($SD = 0.1741$), $p < 0.001$. In the man of color condition, the results are in the opposite pattern. Participants rated the man of color mayor as having more masculine traits, $M = 0.6123$ ($SD = 0.2045$), relative to feminine traits, $M = 0.5487$ ($SD = 0.2165$), $p = 0.0033$. As a next step, I compared across the experimental conditions on the two trait measures. There are no statistically significant differences on masculine traits in the two conditions, $p = 0.1845$; but the woman of color mayor is rated as having more feminine traits than the man of color mayor, $p < 0.001$. Partisan and gender comparisons across participants are in Tables A4.21 and A4.22 and show no significant differences based on participant characteristics.

Thus far, these results fit my expectations around the first part of the raced-gendered prediction. The masculine stereotypes of institutions weaken when

---

[5] A manipulation check question asked participants to recall the gender of the mayor they read about. 93 percent of participants in the woman of color mayor condition correctly recalled the gender, and 79 percent in the man of color condition correctly recalled the gender. This study also asked people their perceptions of the ethnorace identity and partisanship of the mayor. 70.44 percent of people identified the mayor as Black and 63.55 percent identified the mayor as Democratic.

women of color's descriptive representation increases in an executive office. One of the goals of this third experiment was to further parse out the differences that come from women of color's descriptive representation compared to men of color's descriptive representation. The results shown in Figure 4.6 provide further confirmation that the feminizing effects of women of color are unique to this group.

I also analyzed the perceived issue priorities based on the gender of the mayor, and I include these results in the appendices. These results show that there are no differences in the feminine-focused and race-focused issue priorities of mayors based on whether it is a woman or a man in office. There are also no differences based on participant party or gender. These full results are in the Chapter 4 Appendix, Tables A4.43–A4.25. This third study did not ask about group representation.

Results Summary

This chapter finds support for the raced-gendered and linked fate predictions. The results from the series of experiments presented in this chapter show that people associate majority-women of color institutions with more feminine than masculine stereotypes. I show that these gendered shifts occur among all study participants, though these effects are stronger among communities of color. Majority-women of color institutions are seen as representing the interests of women, women of color, and minoritized ethnoracial groups more broadly. The final experiment in this chapter offers an initial test of the feminizing and diversifying effects of women of color in office at the level of a local executive office. The effects of women of color's descriptive representation differ from the effects of men of color's descriptive representation. Together, the set of results in this chapter confirms the raced-gendered and linked fate prediction.

Conclusion

This chapter investigated how women of color's descriptive representation affects the raced-gendered perceptions people have of political institutions. I find evidence of these feminizing and diversifying effects. I focused on women of color's descriptive representation because the intersectional identities of these women, coupled with their experiences navigating the raced-gendered campaign processes, should lead people to form a more feminine-inclusive perspective of political institutions. Ample research documents the importance of descriptive representation for minoritized communities (Bejarano et al. 2021; Reingold, Haynie, and Widner 2021), as such representation can lead to substantive representation (Fraga et al. 2006; Brown 2014a). Important to note is that women of color are not a monolithic group. The extent to which people see women of minoritized ethnoracial backgrounds as having feminine traits is not entirely clear in the extant scholarship (Gonzalez and Bauer 2022). My findings in this chapter may not follow the same pattern if a city council is filled with majority-Black women or majority-Latinas as the specific stereotypes of these groups will start to differ from overall stereotypes about women of color more generally.

Together, the analyses in Chapters 3 and 4 provide support for the central tenets behind my theory of institutional stereotype change. WDR leads people to see institutions as more feminine, and these effects are especially strong when women of color's representation are high. Chapter 5 turns to the downstream effects. It is long assumed that how people think about political institutions is "sticky," or simply unlikely to change. While it seems a stretch to argue that simply electing more women can reverse this half-century decline in public opinion, it is possible that people might think more favorably of majority-women institutions because of the feminine stereotypes people apply to such institutions. Chapter 5 turns to these very dynamics.

5

Downstream Effects of Women's Descriptive Representation

In the wake of the 2016 presidential election, women began organizing protests, signing up to run for political office, and mobilizing voters (Conroy and Green 2020; Dolan and Shah 2020). This rise of women in politics culminated in the 2018-midterm elections which saw record numbers of women running for and winning political office (Mechkova and Wilson 2021). One major motivation for women's heightened political activity was Hillary Clinton's somewhat unexpected presidential loss (Castle et al. 2020). Clinton's loss of the presidency drew attention to the continued exclusion of women from the highest political office in the country; her loss to a candidate marred with accusations of sexual assault and harassment did nothing to soften the blow for many women. Other events leading up to the 2018-midterm elections contributed to a spike in women running for political office including the #MeToo movement and the hearings for Brett Kavanaugh's nomination to the Supreme Court (Wright, Clark, and Evans 2021). The Kavanaugh hearings were a particularly resonant moment for many women that called back to the 1991 hearings for then Supreme Court nominee Clarence Thomas. It appears that in the time between Clinton's presidential loss and the 2018-midterm elections, attention to women's political exclusion motivated women's political participation.

Certainly, women's exclusion from politics can spur many women, and some men, to increase their political participation. For example, Oden et al. (2024) found that women's political discussion increased after the 2016 election and during the height of the #MeToo movement compared to a pre-2016 period when gender was not a highly salient political issue. Recent experimental research documents this positive effect of exclusion. Clayton, O'Brien, and Piscopo (2023b) conducted an experiment where they presented participants with a decision a city council made about abortion policy and this city council either included or excluded women in the decision-making process. The authors found that reports about women's exclusion increased women's nascent levels of political ambition. When women read about institutions that

Feminizing Political Institutions. Nichole M. Bauer, Oxford University Press. © Nichole M. Bauer (2026).
DOI: 10.1093/9780197841556.003.0005

lacked women, women felt a need to fix these gender gaps in representation to transform politics into places that include more women (Holman and Schneider 2018). I turn this question around by investigating how women's inclusion can lead to more political engagement from voters. This chapter extends my theory of institutional stereotype change to investigate the full implications for gains in WDR.

Witnessing the exclusion or marginalization of women in politics can certainly mobilize voters (Mechkova and Wilson 2021) and potential political candidates (Clayton, O'Brien, and Piscopo 2023a). This notion of political exclusion leading to greater political engagement is a long-standing organizing principle in communities of color, especially Black communities. Black women are active political players in mobilizing Black communities to turn out and vote (Barnett 1993) but these women also perform the immense work organizing and supporting the Democratic Party (Brown 2014b). Black women's mobilizing efforts certainly came to the fore in the 2017 Alabama Senate special election to fill the vacancy left when Senator Jeff Sessions became attorney general. The special election featured Democratic nominee Doug Jones who gained some attention decades prior when he led the successful prosecution of the 16th Street church bombing of perpetrators in Birmingham, Alabama. This act of domestic terrorism in 1963 left four young Black girls dead. The Republican nominee was Roy Moore. Moore was the twice removed Chief Justice of the Alabama state Supreme Court. Moore was removed from the office two times after being found guilty of ethics violations by the state's ethics oversight board. During the 2017 campaign, it also came to light that Moore appeared to pursue romantic and sexual relationships with teenage girls as young as 14 years when he was in his 30s.[1] The thought of electing a man who thought it appropriate for a grown adult man to pursue sexual relationships with children over a prosecutor with a strong record on civil rights was a mobilizing force. Black women organized at the community level throughout the state which spurred high levels of voter turnout, especially considering this was an off-year special election, and delivered the election for Doug Jones. Black women voted for Jones at a rate of 98 percent in this election.[2]

In this chapter, I center on the second major question guiding this book: *How does changing the stereotypic perceptions the public holds of political institutions change the way women and men engage in political participation and evaluate political institutions?* I test three downstream effects: (1) increased

---

[1] https://www.bbc.com/news/world-us-canada-42054780
[2] https://www.vox.com/identities/2017/12/13/16772012/alabama-election-black-women

political engagement, (2) improved opinions of political institutions, and (3) the heterogeneity of these effects across gendered characteristics of individuals. Pitkin (1967) argued that when political institutions mirror the people they represent along dimensions such as gender, the electorate will see the institution as more legitimate. Past scholarship offers mixed support on this point (Fridkin and Kenney 2014; Hinojosa and Kittilson 2020; Atkeson 2003; Kim 2022; Kim 2019; Arnesen and Peters 2018). I argue that a necessary condition for WDR to activate increased political participation is a stereotypic shift in the perceptions of political institutions as masculine to feminine. When people see institutions as more feminine, they will see these institutions as more inclusive and a place that will be more receptive to the voices of regular people.

The second downstream effect I test is how WDR changes the generally negative evaluations people have of political institutions. As the earlier chapters briefly reviewed, people see political institutions negatively, and what people say they dislike about political institutions are behaviors and activities that reinforce masculine stereotypes. For example, people hate the gridlock and grandstanding of political institutions (Hetherington 1998; Hibbing and Theiss-Morse 2002), and these are behaviors that fit into masculine stereotypes (Koenig et al. 2011). While there is an extensive body of research on the public opinion of American political institutions (Ansolabehere and Kuriwaki 2022; Kaslovsky and Rogoswki 2022; Ansolabehere and Jones 2010; Mayhew 1974), this work implicitly assumes that these negative sentiments are unlikely to change in a positive direction. People, according to my argument, will see feminine institutions as more likely to embody the types of behaviors people want to see in political institutions such as more compromise (Wolak 2020a), and compromise is a behavior that fits into feminine stereotypes (Heilman 2001). I consider how these gains in political engagement and institutional perceptions occur based on rates of women's representation as well as women of color's rates of representation.

The third effect I test addresses the question of *who* will be more engaged and think more positively about more feminine political institutions. I consider the role of gender among participants in two ways. First, I look for gender differences in people who see themselves as having feminine traits and people who see themselves as having masculine traits. Past work documents that those most likely to participate in politics at every level are people with masculine traits (McDermott 2016; Conroy and Oliver 2020; Oliver and Conroy 2017; Kanthak and Woon 2015; Stoddard and Preece 2015). Thereby, people who see themselves as having feminine traits are implicitly excluded from the political system. I argue that this gendered trait gap will close under feminine institutions. Second, I look for differences between women and men. Some past work indicates that women will be more engaged than men when women run for political office (Atkeson 2003) and other work finds that women's increased descriptive representation leads to more engagement from both women and men (Wolak 2020c; Hinojosa and Kittilson 2020). Second, I test these three downstream effects using questions asked post-treatment from the experiments described in Chapters 3 and 4. Before testing my key predictions around engagement, institutional evaluations, and heterogenous treatment effects, I start by developing the logic behind these expectations in more detail. This theoretical development builds on the logic of dismantling institutional stereotypes presented in Chapter 2. After outlining the theoretical logic, I turn to the empirical tests.

Political Engagement

Past work offers inconsistent conclusions on whether WDR leads women, and men, to become more engaged in politics with some research arguing for positive effects (Clayton, O'Brien, and Piscopo 2019; Fridkin and Kenney 2014; Hinojosa and Kittilson 2020; Schwindt-Bayer 2010; Barnes and Taylor-Robinson 2018; Karp and Banducci 2008; Verge, Wisehomeier, and Espirito-Santo 2020; Kao et al. 2024) and other work finding a null or conditional effect (Wolak 2020c; Atkeson 2003; Wolak 2015; Broockman 2014; Dolan 2006; Lawless 2004; Huber and Gunderson 2023). I argue that WDR will be more likely to affect levels of political engagement when people see these institutions as more feminine. Political engagement stemming from high levels of WDR will only happen if the masculine stereotypes associated with political instructions change from masculine to feminine. The feminizing effect is part of how visibility shapes people's responses to institutions with high levels of WDR. Institutional stereotype change is a necessary condition for WDR to improve political engagement among the public. In this section, I outline the conditions under which WDR can increase political engagement.

The literature on descriptive representation in bureaucracies offers a useful starting point. This scholarship finds that WDR in bureaucracies can have positive effects on those who interact with the bureaucracy (Keiser et al. 2002; Keiser and Wilkins 2004; Keiser 2010). Other work finds that having women present in an institution, whether bureaucratic or elected institutions, increases the responsiveness of institutions to *women's* concerns (Schwindt-Bayer and Mishler 2005). This shift in who receives representation suggests that people see institutions with women as a place for women. Applying this research to my theory suggests that when WDR leads people to see political institutions as less masculine and more feminine, individual levels of political engagement will increase.

I also expect a unique increase in political engagement based on women of color's rates of representation. I do not necessarily predict that majority-women of color institutions will lead to more engagement than majority-women institutions, but there may be differences in *who* is engaged based on women of color's rates of representation. Majority-women of color institutions should be able to mobilize voters of color more powerfully than majority-women institutions. The causal process is similar to the effects of majority-women institutions, but majority-women of color institutions will not only signal that politics is more feminine, but that politics is more inclusive in who it represents. As such, I expect a unique engagement effect between majority-women of color institutions and voters of color.

I argue that a missing link behind understanding whether political engagement increases in conjunction with women's gains in descriptive representation is whether institutional stereotypes change. It is not necessarily *just* WDR that increases political engagement but the corresponding increase in feminine stereotypes associated with the institution that can increase political engagement. Feminine stereotypes include forming consensus, listening to others, and building strong relationships across diverse groups (Eagly and Carli 2003b). These positive qualities associated with feminine stereotypes will lead to an increase in political engagement. Innovative research by Stauffer (2021) tracks a connection between the perceptions people have about WDR and people's levels of political efficacy. This work shows that high levels of WDR lead to a rise in people's feelings of political efficacy and the efficacy bump occurs even when people over-estimate women's levels of representation in political institutions. People will see feminine political institutions as places where their political preferences are more likely to be heard and responded to by elected officials. The political engagement prediction outlines these effects below:

Political Engagement Prediction: Individuals, both women and men, will express more willingness to participate in politics when stereotyping institutions as more feminine relative to more masculine institutions.

When people see political institutions through the lens of feminine stereotypes, people will see those institutions as more responsive to constituents and communities. It is this shift in stereotypic perceptions that can prompt an increase in political engagement.

Institutional Evaluations

People do not like political institutions. Indeed, public opinion polls asking people to rate their approval of Congress show steady declines in institutional approval over the last half-century (Hibbing and Theiss-Morse 2002). As of the summer of 2025, just 26 percent of people approve of the job Congress is doing.[3] These negative perceptions of political institutions extend even to the Supreme Court, which long boasted relatively high approval ratings even while approval of Congress and the presidency declined. In the summer of 2025, nearly 60 percent of people disapproved of the Supreme Court.[4] Growing levels of political polarization coupled with increasing levels of negative partisanship certainly contribute to the growing distrust and dislike of institutions (Layman and Carsey 2002; Levendusky and Malhotra 2016). Many of the facets of Congress and politics that people say they dislike are behaviors and traits that fit squarely into masculine stereotypes. Masculine stereotypes include behaviors such as fighting, being quick to anger, and acting only in one's own self-interest as opposed to looking out for others (Vinkenburg et al. 2011). People not only report disliking the behaviors of Congress that fit into masculinity, but people also report that they want to see more behaviors such as compromise (Wolak 2020a).[5] Compromise is a quality that fits squarely into feminine stereotypes and studies show that women in leadership roles regularly promote and engage in more compromise compared to their men counterparts (Eagly and Carli 2003a). Women in Congress who fail to compromise on legislation when they have an opportunity to do so frequently receive more negative ratings among out-partisan voters than men who also fail to compromise (Bauer, Yong Harbridge, and Krupnikov 2017; Vraga 2017). Women receive this negative punishment because they are breaking with feminine norms.

I argue that increased levels of WDR can lead to improved ratings of political institutions. Chapter 3 showed that people see majority-women institutions as more feminine relative to majority-men institutions, and I argue that this perception should lead people to see majority-women institutions in a more positive light relative to majority-men institutions which people see through a distinctly masculine lens. While there is an extensive body of research tracking the negative impressions individuals hold of political

---

[3] https://news.gallup.com/poll/1600/congress-public.aspx

[4] https://www.nbcnews.com/meet-the-press/meetthepressblog/new-poll-shows-approval-supreme-court-dipping-rcna86014

[5] There is some debate about whether people want bipartisan compromise or if they just want the other political party to adopt its position (Wolak 2020a; Bauer, Yong Harbridge, and Krupnikov 2017).

institutions, there is less research measuring the factors that lead individuals to form more positive impressions of political institutions (for exceptions, see Bush and Zetterberg (2021); Clayton, O'Brien, and Piscopo (2019)). Some preliminary work shows that increased representation for women increases trust in government among women but not men (Ulbig 2007). But other work does not find as strong a relationship between institutions and women's representation (Shortell and Valdini 2022; Schwindt-Bayer 2010). Missing from this scholarship is an investigation of how *masculinity* affects the impressions people form of political institutions. Recent research on the effects of Nevada's majority-women state legislature suggests a link between women's increased representation and a change to relying on more feminine norms of legislating, such as brokering compromise on legislation (Sweet-Cushman, Gill, and Zorn 2025). Consequently, Nevadans have more confidence in government when there are more women in the institution (Gill, Sweet-Cushman, and Zorn 2024). I expect that as WDR increases, people will see institutions engaging in more feminine norms of behavior and these changes will lead to improve evaluations of political institutions.

The improved evaluations will occur across both majority-women and majority-women of color institutions. Women of color in political office engage in feminine norms of lawmaking through their support and advocacy for issues that disproportionately and negatively affect minoritized groups (Bratton and Haynie 1999; Bratton, Haynie, and Reingold 2007; Bratton 2006). Achieving policy goals for minoritized communities requires women of color in legislatures to forge collaborative relationships with other women in institutions as well as across party lines (Brown 2014a). These collaborative behaviors exemplify the feminine norms and expectations that people will attach to majority-women and majority-women of color institutions. Beyond the promotion of compromise and consensus-building, women of color in legislative institutions are more responsive than other legislators to constituent communication (Lowande, Ritchie, and Lauterbach 2019), a behavior exhibiting care and concern for constituents, and this is in line with feminine stereotypes. People will expect majority-women institutions to engage in feminine behaviors such as building consensus and compromise, and these are activities that the public reports wanting to see more of in political institutions (Wolak 2020a). The next prediction outlines these effects.

Institutional Evaluation Prediction: Individuals will rate more feminine institutions more positively along dimensions such as trust and fairness in decision-making compared to more masculine institutions.

Majority-women institutions, by virtue of being seen as more feminine than majority-men institutions, will receive more positive evaluations. These positive evaluations will come from the increase in feminine stereotyping of majority-women institutions. In the next section, I turn to explaining which people will evaluate political institutions more positively, and which people will be more likely to participate in politics when institutions are majority-women.

Whose Engagement Increases?

Much of the work identifying the effects of WDR centers on the effects among women in the electorate. The logic is that more women in office, or even just running for office, will have an engagement effect among women more generally (Fridkin and Kenney 2014). Certainly, tracking the political engagement of women is important to understanding who participates in democratic institutions. A burgeoning body of scholarship suggests that differences between women and men are not the critical and important gaps in politics. Rather, a feminine gap exists in political participation where the people more likely to engage in politics are individuals who see themselves as having more masculine than feminine traits (Bittner and Goodyear-Grant 2017). I argue that feminine political institutions will close this feminine–masculine gap in political participation. I outline how past scholars use the theory of gender-typing, derived from social psychology research, to understand gaps in political participation, and I then move onto explaining how feminine institutions can close the feminine–masculine participation gap.

I argue that majority-women institutions will increase political engagement among individuals who have more feminine relative to masculine attributes. The sex-typing literature in social psychology pioneered by Sandra Bem (1981) argues that everybody is made up of some masculine traits and some feminine traits that define who they are as individuals. These gendered traits emerge in both women and men (Bittner and Goodyear-Grant 2017), and for some people, one set of gendered traits might be more dominant than the other. For example, people who are highly empathetic are likely high on other feminine traits like being compassionate but are also likely a bit lower on masculine traits like being aggressive. The opposite can also hold true. Some individuals may have aggression as a dominant trait along with other masculine traits such as being assertive, but these same people may be lower on compassion or empathy. While one set of gendered traits can be more dominant than the other, everyone has both feminine and masculine traits that define who they are to some degree, and some individuals will have feminine and masculine traits in equal measure.

Recent work finds that a gendered-trait gap, rather than a gender gap between women and men, more aptly explains who participates in politics (Conroy and Oliver 2020; McDermott 2016). People for whom feminine traits are their dominant characteristics are turned off by the masculine language and behaviors that typify politics (Conroy and Green 2020; Schneider et al. 2016). Indeed, McDermott (2016) found that people who were feminine-trait-dominant were less likely than people with more masculine-dominant traits to engage in a variety of political behaviors from political discussion to the basic act of voting. Other research finds that conflict, in general, turns people away from politics (Groenendyk and Krupnikov 2021). The masculinity of politics excludes people from participating in the most basic forms of political activities. The exclusionary effects of masculinity flow upward to more elite political activities such as running for political office and serving in elected office (Conroy and Oliver 2020; Oliver and Conroy 2017; Dynes et al. 2021). The result is that the political preferences of only a select group of people are actively expressed, and this slant toward masculinity can have deleterious effects on democratic norms.

Eroding the masculinity that defines political institutions can, I argue, lead to more inclusive political participation among those who have dominant feminine and dominant masculine traits. If it is masculinity in politics that attracts like-minded individuals, then, it stands to reason, that more femininity in politics should attract more feminine people. I expect that people with dominantly feminine traits will increase their political engagement under majority-women institutions relative to majority-men institutions. This effect of majority-women institutions will come from the association of these institutions with more feminine traits. I also expect that majority-women institutions will be rated more positively by people with feminine traits. People will see feminine political institutions as more inclusive places that are likely to be more responsive to the public's needs. The gendered engagement prediction outlines the effects of majority-women institutions on people who have more feminine traits over masculine traits as their dominant trait characteristics.

Gendered Engagement Prediction: More feminine political institutions will lead to higher levels of engagement and more positive institutional evaluations among those who have more feminine traits over masculine traits.

Important to note is that this prediction argues for an effect of majority-women institutions on people with dominantly feminine traits, but this does not mean that majority-women institutions will shut out people with dominant masculine traits. Rather, I argue that the gendered gap in politics will close when there are majority-women institutions. Recall from Chapter 3 that majority-women institutions had *both* feminine and masculine traits, but majority-men institutions have just masculine traits. Thus, majority-women institutions will not necessarily exclude those with masculine traits from the political system. I argue that institutions with high levels of WDR will attract both feminine and masculine people.

In total, I test three predictions in this chapter: the political engagement, institutional evaluation, and gendered engagement predictions. First, people will be more willing to participate in politics. Second, people will form more positive evaluations of majority-women political institutions. Third, people with feminine traits will be more likely to participate in politics and will evaluate institutions more positively when those institutions are majority-women. I also test for partisan differences in this chapter. The previous chapters found that Democratic respondents had higher feminizing effects relative to Republicans. It stands to reason then that Democrats might have higher levels of engagement and more favorable evaluations of institutions relative to Democrats.

Key Measures and Analytical Plan

I use data from the experiments in Chapters 3 and 4. Recall that the Chapter 3 experiment presented people with majority-women or majority-men institutions for a city council, state legislature, mayoral office, and gubernatorial seat. The results showed, across all institutions, that people see majority-women institutions as more feminine than majority-men institutions, but majority-women institutions do not lose on masculine traits. People see majority-women institutions as having both feminine and masculine traits. The experiment included questions about levels of political engagement, institutional evaluations, and an adapted personal attributes questionnaire (PAQ) to test the three predictions that undergird this chapter. These questions were all asked as post-treatment outcomes. Chapter 5 Appendix includes the full question wording and response options for all the outcomes.

To test the political engagement prediction, I asked participants how likely it is they would contact an elected representative, talk about politics with a friend, and run for political office. The response options for each of these questions were as follows: "very likely," "somewhat likely," "somewhat unlikely," and "very unlikely." I ask about how likely people are to contact their elected representative because this is a very low-cost and accessible form of political participation. People do not need to have access to elite networks of political power players to contact their elected representative

(Lowande, Ritchie, and Lauterbach 2019). People often contact their elected representative when there is a problem with accessing government benefits, such as social security, and many of government-run social service programs are used by women (Davis, Livermore, and Lim 2011; Keiser and Wilkins 2004). Thus, being able to contact an elected official is especially pivotal for women.

I use talking about politics and running for office as behaviors that women are less likely to engage in relative to men (Morehouse Mendez and Osborn 2010; Herring et al. 2022; Thomsen and King 2020; Bos et al. 2022). Indeed, the political discussion literature finds that women just do not discuss politics as much as men (Mendelberg and Karpowitz 2016), in part, because political discussion exemplifies conflict (Van Duyn, Peacock, and Stroud 2019) and women tend to be conflict-avoidant (Wolak 2020b). I expect that when political institutions are associated with more feminine stereotypic traits, women, and men, will be more willing to engage in political discussion. In short, when the perception of politics as conflictual falls away, people will be more willing to talk about politics.

When it comes to political ambition, a long line of research shows that women are just less willing to run for political office relative to men (Thomsen and King 2020; Bernhard, Shames, and Teele 2021), in part, because of the strong masculine orientation of politics (Crowder-Meyer 2020; Dittmar 2015; Schneider et al. 2016). However, when the masculinity of politics erodes, I expect that women and men may express more interest in pursuing political office. Measuring political ambition as a post-treatment question in an experiment may present a tough bar for finding effects as most people simply have no interest in running for political office (Shames 2019). However, including this outcome in my engagement battery can allow me to track general patterns in nascent political ambition across majority-women and majority-men institutions. My last two engagement measures are activities that, historically, men are more likely to do relative to women—this is an intentional choice. Part of my argument surrounding the downstream effects of WDR is that more women will not only engage more people in politics, but will increase women's participation in activities that tend to be dominated by men.

The institutional evaluation questions asked people to rate how much trust they have in the newly elected institution with the following response options: a great deal, a lot, a moderate amount, a little, none. I ask about institutional trust because this is a metric where individuals tend to rate existing political institutions poorly (Chanley, Rudolph, and Rahn 2000; Hetherington and Husser 2012), and these poor ratings come, in part, from dissatisfaction with the masculine behaviors of the legislators in these institutions, such as gridlock and grandstanding (Guttmann and Thompson 2012; Harbridge and Malhotra 2011). I argue that majority-women institutions can improve these perceptions because women tend to engage in behaviors that reinforce feminine stereotypes such as building compromise and consensus (Volden, Wiseman, and Wittmer 2013) and trust is a metric where women tend to fare better than men (Alexander and Anderson 1993).

The second question I ask is about institutional productivity with the response options including: "very productive," "somewhat productive," "somewhat unproductive," and "very unproductive." Again, individuals tend to dislike the lack of productivity in current institutions where women are not well-represented (Wolak 2020a). Women legislators have a record of being much more productive than men in political office (Anzia and Berry 2011), as such, this is a metric where majority-women institutions should fare better than majority-men institutions. I rescaled all the outcome questions to range from 0 to 1.

To test the final prediction in this chapter, I use a short version of the PAQ which is often used in political science research (Conroy and Oliver 2020; Oliver and Conroy 2017; McDermott 2016). This scale was adapted from the Bem Sex Role Inventory which was originally developed to identify the extent to which people have feminine-dominant or masculine-dominant traits (Bem 1981). I expect that majority-women institutions will engage feminine-dominant individuals in the political process more than majority-men institutions. The PAQ inventory asked people to indicate the extent to which the following phrases described them: "can make decisions easily," "competitive," "stands up well under pressure," "devotes self to others," "aware of feelings of others," and "kind." The first three items reflect masculinity and the latter three femininity. The response options included "very well," "somewhat well," "somewhat unwell," and "not well at all." The final PAQ measure is the difference between the feminine trait and the masculine trait ratings. More positive values indicate that a person is feminine-dominant, negative values indicate that a person is masculine-dominant, and values of zero indicate that a person has even levels of feminine and masculine traits.

Political Engagement Effects

The political engagement prediction argues that people will be more engaged in politics when people see those institutions as more feminine rather than masculine. I start with the three political engagement outcomes: contacting an elected official, talking about politics, and running for political office.

For these analyses, I use a series of two-tailed t-tests to examine differences across majority-women and majority-men institutions. I examine the downstream effects for political engagement within each institution starting with city councils then moving onto state legislatures, mayors, and governors, and I group these findings together as opposed to parsing out the separate effects of executive and legislative institutions as I did in Chapter 3.

Figure 5.1 displays the political engagement results for majority-women city councils and majority-men institutions in each of the four panels. The full results are in Table A5.1. Starting with city councils, shown in the top left panel of Figure 5.1, there are two key findings. First, the results on city council institutions show that people report being more willing to contact an elected official when the institution is majority-women relative to majority-men, $p = 0.0003$. The difference in people's expressed willingness to contact their elected official is sizable, a 0.1147 difference, or 11.47%, between the majority-women and majority-men institution. People also report being more willing to talk about politics when there is a majority-women relative to a majority-man city council, $p = 0.0431$. The results for measuring people's

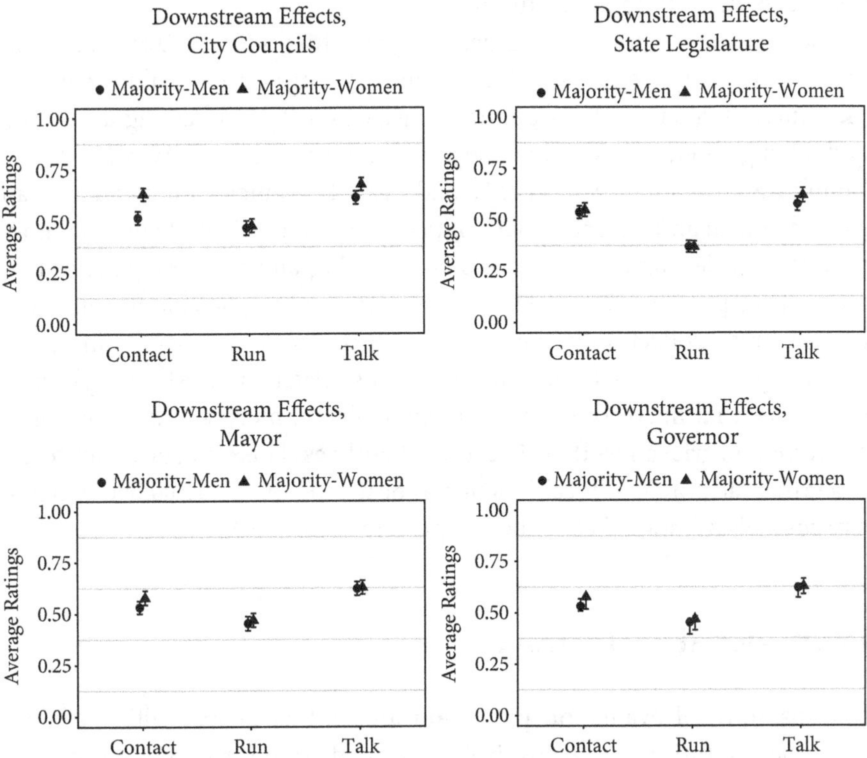

Figure 5.1 Political engagement in majority-women institutions

Note: 84 percent confidence intervals included. The full results are in Table A5.1.

intentions for running for political office are not statistically significant between the majority-women and the majority-men institutions—though measuring political ambition in a survey experiment among everyday women and men is a very tough bar for finding effects given the generally low levels of ambition among the public (Crowder-Meyer 2020; Shames 2019).

Measuring political behaviors through post-treatment questions in an experiment may be a tough bar to find significant effects, especially for questions about political ambition. Including a measure of political ambition, even nascent ambition especially in an experiment, is, well, ambitious, for lack of a better word. Most people do not have an interest in pursuing political office, and it is possible this measure produces floor effects. People start out at very low levels of political ambition, and any increase in political ambition might not be captured well in a survey question. Looking at the means displayed in Figure 5.1 suggests that floor effects may not be a problem. The mean values on this measure range from 0.36 to 0.47, which fall in the middle quartile of the measure's distribution given that it ranges from 0 to 1. Thus, this does not appear to be a case of floor effects. Rather, people, overall, are just not likely to be moved to run for political office under majority-women institutions relative to majority-men institutions.

The tests for the political engagement prediction offer a mixed picture on whether majority-women institutions increase engagement. I find that people express higher levels of political engagement for contacting an official and talking about politics when there is a majority-women city council. The significant effects for city councils, and just city councils, on contacting an elected official and talking about politics may be a particularly unique function of the role that city councils play in setting and enacting policies that often affect people's daily lives. City councils are responsible for ensuring efficient trash collection in communities, access to local health clinics, and regulating the flow of traffic on local roads (Peterson 1981). People may simply see that majority-women city councils are more willing to listen to concerns and grievances that affect their daily lives. This effect tags back to the adage that "all politics is local," and it may be that people find majority-women city councils as more likely to be receptive to their needs.

Institutional Evaluations

The institutional evaluation prediction argues that people will rate more feminine institutions more positively. This prediction is based on the consistent finding that people hate political institutions, most political institutions are dominated by men, and most institutions are typified by undesirable masculine behaviors, such as engaging in political grandstanding. People will see more feminine institutions as more communal, responsive to the public's needs, and more trustworthy. My two outcomes are institutional trust and productivity. I use the same analytical approach from the previous section with a series of two-tailed t-tests and compare majority-women to majority-men institutions within each level of office. Figure 5.2 displays the institutional evaluation outcomes for each of the four institutions I tested, and I again group the findings for all the institutions together.

I start with the productivity measure. I expect a significant and positive effect for majority-women institutions given that women elected officials are, in fact, more productive than their men counterparts (Anzia and Berry 2011); their higher levels of productivity come from engaging in feminine stereotypic behaviors such as building compromise and promoting collaboration (Barnes 2016; Holman and Mahoney 2019). The results, shown in Figure 5.2, are insignificant across every level of office. People do not expect majority-women institutions to be any more productive than majority-men institutions.

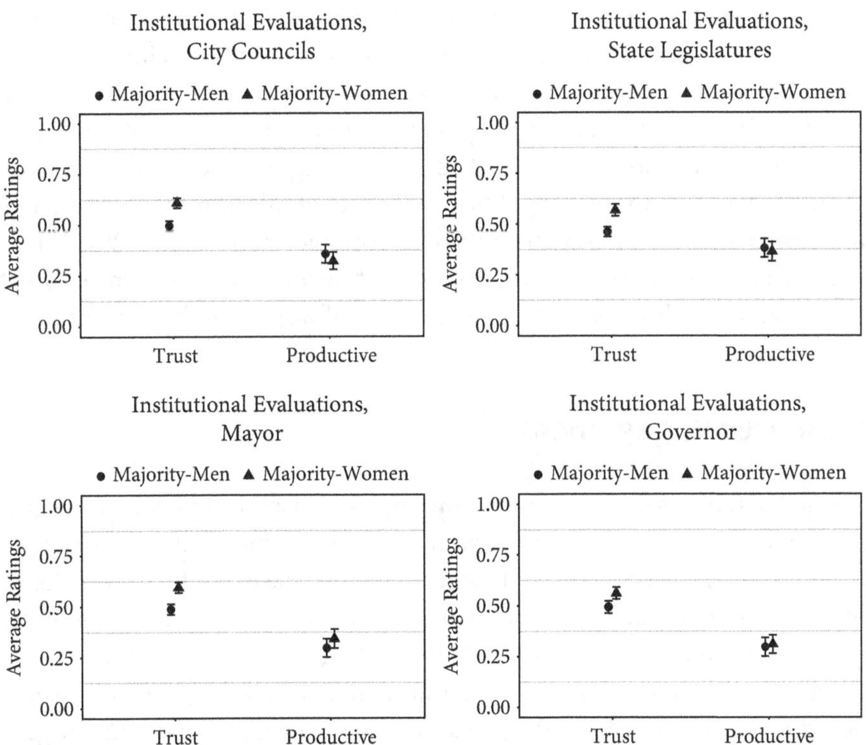

Figure 5.2 Institutional evaluations in majority-women institutions
Note: 84 percent confidence intervals included. Full results in Table A5.1.

Figure 5.2 also displays the results for institutional trust for each level of office, full results in Table A5.1. The effects are consistent across each level of office, and these effects are in line with the institutional evaluation prediction. People rate majority-women institutions higher on trust relative to majority-men institutions. The effects are quite substantial. People's levels of trust in majority-women city councils relative to majority-men city councils is 0.1121, or 11.21 percent higher (top-left panel of Figure 5.2); for state legislatures, the size of the effect is 0.1065 points, or 10.65 percent higher (top-right panel of Figure 5.2); people's levels of trust when a woman is mayor are 0.1075 points, or 10.75 percent higher than when a man is mayor (bottom-left panel of Figure 5.2); and, for governors, the effect is such that people rate gubernatorial offices held by women 0.068 points, or 6.8 percent higher than gubernatorial offices held by a man (bottom-right panel of Figure 5.2). These effects are all in line with the institutional evaluation prediction, and fit with existing work showing the positive benefits of women's descriptive representation (Stauffer 2021). Thus far, these results strongly support for the institutional evaluation prediction on trust though the findings were insignificant on productivity.

Taken together, the findings on the two outcomes for institutional evaluations suggest mixed support for this prediction. People, as expected, rate majority-women institutions higher on trust, a quality that reinforces feminine stereotypes. But people do not expect majority-women institutions to be any more productive than majority-men institutions. The lack of significant differences on the productivity metric is surprising considering that research shows that women in elected political office are significantly more productive than men (Anzia and Berry 2011; Volden, Wiseman, and Wittmer 2013). This may be a case where people's expectations of institutions do not match what empirical research shows about the influence of women in these institutions.

Gendered Engagement

The gendered engagement prediction argues that majority-women institutions will attract feminine-trait-dominant people more than majority-men institutions. Past work finds that for most people, masculinity is more dominant as a trait characteristic than femininity, and that masculine-dominant people participate in politics much more than feminine-dominant people (Bittner and Goodyear-Grant 2017). I start off this section by providing some descriptive statistics of the PAQ measure used to gauge the dominant gendered trait characteristics for the experimental sample. The average masculine attribute rating was M = 0.3592 (SD = 0.2120) and for feminine attributes, the mean was M = 0.2721 (SD = 0.1988). Comparing these means with a two-tailed t-test shows that masculinity was a more dominant set of attribute than femininity, p = 0.001, and this fits with past work (Bittner and Goodyear-Grant 2017). I created an overall PAQ measure that is the difference in the average number of feminine traits relative to masculine traits for each person. With this measure, positive values indicate that feminine traits are more dominant than masculine traits, and negative values indicate that masculine traits are more dominant than feminine traits. Figure 5.3 displays the distribution of the PAQ measure. The average PAQ difference in the combined measure was M = −0.0863 (SD = 0.2281), and the measure ranges from −0.8889 to 0.6667.

I analyze whether majority-women institutions increase engagement and improve institutional evaluations among people with feminine-dominant, masculine-dominant, and neutral gendered traits, or having equal parts of feminine and masculine traits. I use the same engagement and institutional measures used earlier in this chapter. For these analyses, I treat the PAQ measure as a moderating variable, and the main results discussed in this chapter present the marginal effects of majority-women institutions. I estimate Ordinary Least Squares (OLS) regression models to examine how the PAQ measure moderates people's levels of engagement in majority-women and majority-men institutions. Each model includes a three-way interaction

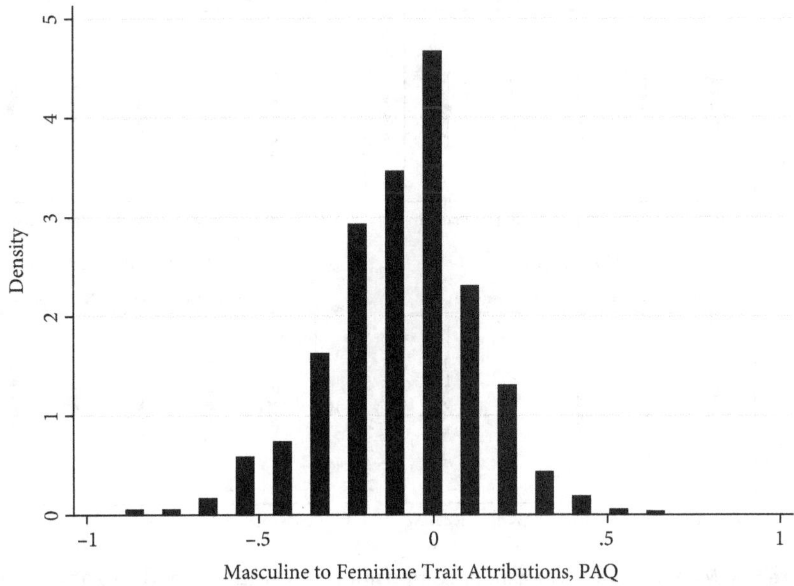

Figure 5.3 Distribution of PAQ among experimental subjects

between the PAQ measure, the majority-women conditions, and the type of institution, city council, state legislature, mayor, or governor. I include a dummy variable for each level of office not included in the interaction term, and exclude the gubernatorial condition in the city council, state legislature, and mayoral models. In the gubernatorial model, I exclude the mayoral condition. I also include a host of controls for participant gender, party, and socio-economic characteristics among individuals. I expect that, at the very least, the two-way interaction between the PAQ measure and the majority-women condition will be significant and positive; but there may be differences across the types of offices included, i.e., city council versus state legislature, and the three-way interactions may also indicate a significant and positive effect. I have included the full set of models in Chapter 5 Appendix Tables A5.6–A5.9.

I graphed the marginal effect of the PAQ measure with majority-women institutions for each outcome, and included the full downstream outcomes in Figure 5.4. Each point on the figure is the difference in the level of engagement when institutions are majority-women relative to majority-men. Positive values indicate more engagement under majority-women institutions. The key test of the gendered engagement prediction is whether feminine-typed people

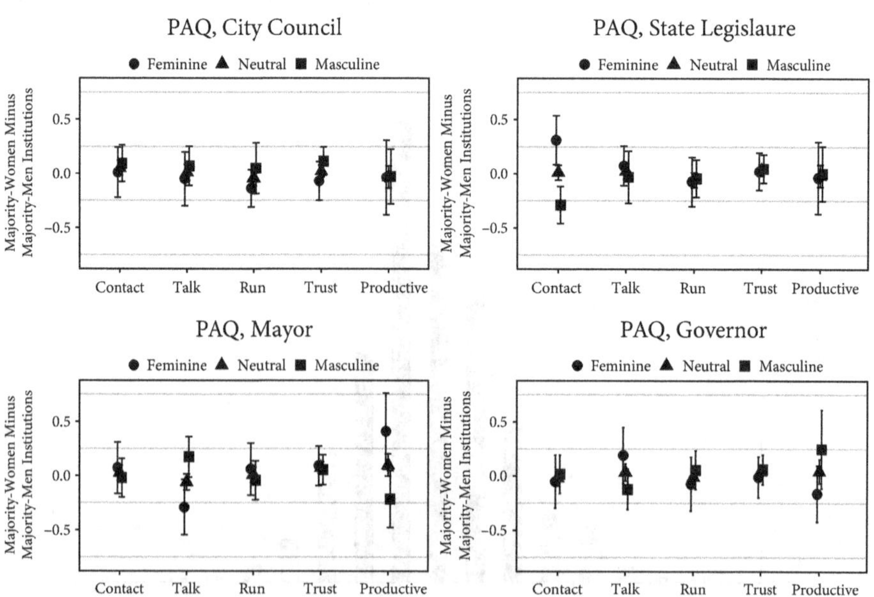

Figure 5.4 Marginal effects of gender composition of institutions and PAQ attributes on political engagement
Note: 95 percent confidence intervals included. Full results in Table A5.6–A5.9.

are more likely to participate or see institutions more positively when institutions are majority-women relative to majority-men. The circles for each panel of Figure 5.4 are the difference for feminine-typed people, and these should be positive values where the confidence interval does not cross zero if the gendered engagement prediction is confirmed. A positive value for feminine-typed people indicates that they are more engaged and evaluate institutions more positively when those institutions are majority-women relative to majority-men.

There are few differences in feminine-typed people's willingness to participate in politics or see institutions more positively under majority-women to majority-men institutions. The biggest effects for feminine-typed individuals are for state legislatures on the contact an elected official outcome. Feminine-typed people are significantly more likely, by 31.17 percent, to contact a state legislator when the institution is majority-women relative to majority-men, $p = 0.007$. This finding fits with my gendered engagement prediction, but this is the only significant finding based on the gender-typing of individuals. The rest of the results are insignificant.

It is striking that feminine-typed people are not all that much likely to participate in politics when WDR is high. It may be that the gendered differences are captured more strongly by gender, whether a person identifies as a woman or a man, rather than gendered attributes measured through the PAQ. As a next step, I assess gender differences in engagement among women and men. These full comparisons are in Tables A5.4 and A5.5. For these comparisons, I use t-tests and compare differences between women and men within each condition. I find no differences in engagement levels between women and men in majority-women conditions for all four institutions I tested. The absence of gender differences on engagement outcomes fits with past work which often finds few differences in the effects of WDR (Hinojosa and Kittilson 2020; Wolak 2020c). For the institutional evaluations, I find a few gender differences, but these differences are not consistent along the evaluation outcomes and institutions. I find that women rate majority-women state legislatures higher on productivity relative to men and that women trust majority-women city councils more than men.

Partisan Differences in Downstream Effects

Chapters 3 and 4 found that the feminizing effects of WDR are somewhat higher among Democrats relative to Republicans. In this section, I test whether these partisan differences extend to the downstream effects.

In other words: *Are Democrats more engaged than Republicans by WDR? Do Democrats rate more feminine institutions more positively than Republicans?* I break down the results on the engagement and institutional evaluation measures to test partisan differences within each experimental condition—this follows the same approach I used in Chapters 3 and 4. Tables A5.2 and A5.3 include the full partisan differences, and I summarize the key patterns in this section.

I start with partisan differences in the engagement outcomes. For the most part, there are no differences in levels of engagement among Democrats and Republicans exposed to majority-women institution on our contact and run for office measures. Democratic participants indicate that they are more likely to talk about politics relative to Republicans when exposed to a majority-women city council and the woman mayoral condition. These effects on two local offices among Democrats are certainly curious, especially given that the main results show stronger effects at the local level. This suggests that, for some individuals, women's increased representation at the local level may be particularly more likely to fuel increased political engagement.

Next, I turn to the institutional evaluation outcomes to assess partisan differences. The differences across participant partisanship are insignificant on the productivity outcome. On trust, the results show some significant effects of participant partisanship. Democrats rate all majority-women institutions higher on trust relative to Republicans. Moreover, Republicans rate majority-women and majority-men institutions, except for the woman mayoral condition, similarly on trust. These patterns on trust suggest that participant partisanship affects the extent to which the public view majority-women institutions as more trustworthy relative to majority-men institutions. This partisan difference may be based on the ideological differences between Democrats and Republicans in how they view the scope and role of government, as I discussed in Chapter 3. Democrats may just have higher baseline levels of government trust relative to Republicans. Another possibility for what drives these partisan differences may be that Democrats assume that the majority-women institutions are composed of mostly Democratic women.

Women of Color and Downstream Effects

The earlier results in this chapter found that majority-women city councils sparked an increase in political engagement at the city council level, and majority-women institutions received more positive trust evaluations than majority-men institutions. I did not develop direct predictions about whether majority-women and majority-women of color institutions would lead similarly to these downstream effects. Nevertheless, it is reasonable to expect that women of color's descriptive representation might lead to strong engagement effects and improved institutional evaluations among non-white voters—this expectation is based on the linked fate prediction positing that voters of color would be most likely to adjust their stereotypic expectations for political institutions. For these analyses, I use the outcome questions in the Diversified City Council Experiment from Chapter 4 that match the engagement and institutional evaluation questions used in the earlier analyses of this chapter. The engagement questions asked people to indicate whether they would contact a city council member, vote in the next election, and run for political office to test the political engagement prediction. The institutional engagement questions include levels of trust and productivity. Both sets of outcomes are coded to range from 0 to 1 and higher values indicate more positive evaluations. The main comparison in these analyses is the difference between women of color institutions and majority-women institutions. Recall that this experiment only sampled voters of color, so I cannot compare between white voters and non-white voters, but I can compare how voters of color shift their engagement and institutional evaluations based on the gender and racial composition of the political institution.[6]

I display the main results and comparisons in Figure 5.5, and Table A5.10 includes the full comparisons across all the groups. I find no significant differences in engagement between the majority-women of color institutions and the majority-women institutions on any of the engagement outcome. I find few differences between the majority-women of color and majority-people of color institutions. On the institutional evaluation outcomes, I again find few differences between the majority-women of color and the majority-women institutions. People rate both institutions high on trust and productivity. I find that people expect that the majority-women of color city council will be more productive than the majority-people of color, but this is the only difference, $p < 0.10$. These analyses suggest that majority-women of color institutions may not lead to the expected downstream effects of more political engagement and more positive impressions of political institutions.

---

[6] I also include the downstream effects from women of color's representation from the Women of Color Mayoral Experiment; these results are in Table A5.11 for Chapter 5 Appendix. These results show no significant differences between the woman of color and man of color conditions.

Figure 5.5 Downstream effects in women of color institutions
Note: 84 percent confidence intervals included. See Table A5.10 for full results.

Results Summary

This chapter tested how majority-women institutions affect political engage-ment, institutional evaluations, and who is most likely to increase political engagement. The results suggest that majority-women *city councils* have the largest effect on political engagement. The institutional evaluation tests sug-gest that people see majority-women institutions as more trustworthy on all four political offices, but people do not see majority-women institutions as any more productive than majority-men institutions. Finally, the results sug-gest some support for my prediction that majority-women institutions would engage feminine-dominant people. Overall, the findings suggest mixed sup-port for all three predictions. I find no strong differences in engagement and institutional evaluations between the majority-women and majority-women of color institutions. In the concluding discussion, I speculate about why the analyses lead to mixed support for my predictions, and I outline some directions for future research.

Conclusion

I started this chapter with the question: *Does women's increased descriptive representation lead to increased political engagement among the public and improve evaluations of political institutions?* Past research points to mixed results on the political engagement effects of higher rates of WDR, and the link between WDR and improved institutional evaluations is ambiguous in existing scholarship. My theory of institutional stereotype change argued that a missing link between descriptive representation and political engagement was whether stereotypes of institutions shifted from masculine to femi-nine. While Chapters 3 and 4 documented this stereotype shift, Chapter 5 suggests that those shifts do not always lead to increased political engagement. I find that majority-women institutions increase political engagement when that institution is a city council. Chapter 3 revealed that people see majority-women institutions councils as more feminine than majority-men institutions, and I found even stronger feminizing effects on the women of color experiments from Chapter 4.

It is not entirely clear why the engagement effects only occur for city councils and not the other offices. I speculated in the main findings that the local nature of city councils in conjunction with the gender composition of the city council may lead to these increased engagement effects. But mayoral offices are also local offices that form and implement policies on the same types of issues as city councils. In many cities, mayors are also more visible than city council members. One factor that may affect these differences is that city councils are legislative bodies composed of small groups of individuals. A mayoral office is held by a singular entity. While people in the previous chapter still saw the woman mayoral office as more feminine than masculine, the nature of executive offices may limit the engagement effects. It may be that increased engagement is most likely to occur from local legislative bodies that are majority-women.

An important caveat is in order regarding the findings and tests for the political engagement prediction. I relied on post-treatment questions about intentions to engage in politics and not actual political behaviors. Indicating on a survey question that a person would contact their elected representative is very different from measuring whether people participate in politics based on levels of WDR—though existing work finds that constituents contact their women representatives more than men representatives (Butler, Naurin, and Öhberg 2022). A next step for future scholarship is to connect "real world" levels of WDR to measurable forms of political participation such as voter turnout or constituent service requests. While an approach that connects political participation to levels of WDR cannot pinpoint whether women's representation *caused* an increase in voter turnout, such an approach could connect my experimental findings to the political world outside the experimental lab.

A striking finding from this chapter is that experimental subjects do not expect majority-women institutions to be more productive than majority-men institutions though people do see these institutions as more trustworthy than majority-men institutions. Women in elected political office are, in fact, more productive than men (Anzia and Berry 2011). Women's high levels of productivity come from, in part, their willingness to form policies by engaging in stereotypically feminine behaviors like forging compromise

(Volden, Wiseman, and Wittmer 2013; Barnes 2016; Holman, Mahoney, and Hurler 2022; Holman and Mahoney 2019). The null effects found may indicate a high level of cynicism among the public about productivity in politics, and not even majority-women institutions can overcome this level of cynicism. A natural question that arises from these findings is whether people know women are highly productive legislators. The average voter may simply lack the baseline knowledge that women are super productive. This question about voter awareness of women's behaviors in elected office is an excellent question to study in follow-up research. Another factor that could contribute to the null effects on productivity is how the news media report on political processes. The news media may simply be more willing to report on the conflict and contention that surrounds the policy-making process rather than the collaboration and consensus-building that often occurs when legislation successfully becomes law. The role of the news media in shaping the feminine views people hold of majority-women political institutions is addressed, in part, in Chapter 6.

6

Gendered Political Discourse in the Media

After the 1992 and 2018 elections ushered in record rates of women in the House and Senate, the news media reported on the "Year of the Woman" and "Pink Wave" in each election year. A very basic search of US-based news coverage in the aftermath of 1992 shows that 696 news articles in the US used the term "Year of the Woman."[1] This appears to be a substantial number of articles reporting on the record-setting rates of women in political office. In 2018, eighty-seven articles used the phrase "Pink Wave" and 357 articles used the phrase "Year of the Woman" in the first year after the midterm elections.[2] While this appears to be a bit less coverage compared to the first "Year of the Woman," it is still, again, a fairly substantial number of news stories reporting on changes in women's descriptive representation. Headlines after the 1992 election declared "Election '93—Women In A Boy's Game";[3] "Female Caucus Works for Another Year of the Woman";[4] and the more dark, Is 'Year Of The Woman' Over?"[5] Some of the more notable headlines after the 2018 "Pink Wave" include "Boss Ladies";[6] "'See Jane Win': A riveting political deconstruction of 2018";[7] and "Girl Power: Record number of women serving in Ohio House."[8] The news media, in the aftermath of these two landmark elections for women's representation, suggests that journalists reported on the changes in WDR.

Past scholarship consistently finds that people do not know much about just how many women serve in elected political office at any given time

[1] I used Access World News Database to search for articles using the phrase "Year of the Woman" in the headline, lead, or first paragraph of news articles in the US between November 1, 1992, through December 31, 1993. I use the same parameters for 2018 searching for "Pink Wave" or "Year of the Woman" in the headline, lead, or first paragraph of news articles in the US between November 1, 2018, through December 31, 2019.

[2] The second search for news discussion of WDR in 2018 shows that there are far fewer articles compared to 1992. The differences are, likely, due to the decline of local news outlets that occurred in the 26 years between the two elections.

[3] *The Atlanta Journal & Constitution*, November 5, 1993.

[4] *The San Francisco Chronicle*, July 9, 1993.

[5] *Daily Press (Newport News, VA)*, November 1, 1993.

[6] *Reno News & Review* October 23, 2019.

[7] *The Monitor* (Boston, MA) September 3, 2019.

[8] NBC 4, WCMH, Columbus, Ohio, January 18, 2019.

Feminizing Political Institutions. Nichole M. Bauer, Oxford University Press. © Nichole M. Bauer (2026).
DOI: 10.1093/9780197841556.003.0006

(Dolan and Sanbonmatsu 2009) though people tend to over-estimate women's rates of descriptive representation (Stauffer 2021). The lack of precise knowledge on the proportion of women in a political institution is not surprising as the public generally have low levels of this type of factual political knowledge (Delli Carpini and Keeter 1996), though most Americans can, likely, find information on the numbers of women in office if they need to know this precise information (Lupia and McCubbins 1998). Even if people do not know exact rates of WDR, there are still ways that the public can learn this information, including through news coverage. I argue in this chapter that the feminizing effects of WDR will occur, in part, through indirect channels of information the public receives about political processes. More specifically, when there are more women in office, the news media will rely more frequently on feminine themes and behaviors in their reporting on political processes. My logic is that when there is a higher level of WDR, the news media will rely on more feminine stereotypes in reporting on political processes, such as passing a budget, and this feminine process news will, in part, contribute to the feminizing effects of WDR. The increase of feminine process news roughly follows a mediated process grounded in past scholarship on the effects of the news media on how the public think about government (McCombs and Shaw 1972; Krosnick and Brannon 1993; Iyengar and Kinder 1987).

In this chapter, I address a critical question underlying my arguments about the feminizing effects of WDR: *How do the public learn about the feminizing effects of women's descriptive representation?* I argue that as WDR increases, the news media will start to change *how* they report on political processes to reflect more feminine stereotypes, or what I call *feminine process news*, and will rely less on conventional masculine stereotypes used to report on politics, or what I term *masculine process news*. The news media are a key mechanism by which the public learns about politics and representation (Cook 1997; Patterson 1997; Schudson 1998). If the news media do not report on politics, it is much harder for people to learn about who represents them and how representation occurs. Information about who is in political office and political processes can be difficult for the most educated members of the public to understand. My approach in this chapter builds on the recent scholarship by Barnes, Kerevel, and Saxton (2024) who argue that news media coverage can increase the visibility of group representation, and they examine this dynamic for working call representation.

I test two ways that news media coverage of politics contributes to the feminizing effects of WDR: (1). relying on more feminine stereotypic behaviors of institutional processes and (2) relying on more women as sources in political news stories. First, I expect higher rates of women's descriptive representation will lead to less masculine and more feminine political discourse (*the gendered discourse prediction*). I argue that higher rates of WDR will lead to the use of more feminine process frames in news coverage. Briefly, feminine process frames will draw on core leadership behaviors that fit into broader feminine stereotypes and reflect the types of legislative activities, such as compromise, that women legislators are more likely to engage in relative to men (Volden, Wiseman, and Wittmer 2013). Masculine process frames, in contrast, are frames that fit into broader masculine stereotypes and reflect the types of legislative activities, such as grandstanding or holding up legislation, that men are more likely to engage in relative to women. Feminine process frames provide a signal to the public that political institutions embody more feminine qualities.

The second way the news media will contribute to institutional stereotype change is through changes in *who* journalists rely on as sources in political news coverage (*the gendered source prediction*). I argue that as WDR increases, journalists will be more likely to use women as sources in their political process news coverage. Part of this increase in gendered sources comes from the fact that there are simply just more women leaders available when WDR is high. However, when WDR is high and reporters are turning toward more feminine process frames, they will be primed to consider women sources in their reporting.

I start this chapter with a review of how gender, as a social construct and as a characteristic of people, affects how the news media cover politics. Following this review, I turn to defining gendered political process frames. The results show that higher rates of WDR do not, as I predicted, lead to more feminine process frames. I find that higher rates of WDR lead to more women political leaders and expert sources in news coverage, and I find that women of color's descriptive representation has a particularly large effect on the use of women as sources.

News Media Influence on Institutional Stereotype Change

A long line of scholarship establishes that the news media play a critical role in informing the public about political processes, shaping public opinions, and framing the major political issues of the day (Graber 1988; Druckman 2001; McCombs and Shaw 1972; Iyengar and Kinder 1987). The news media can be especially influential in institutional stereotype change when reporting on political processes in Congress, at the presidential level, or through the coverage of local and state political institutions. Political processes, such as the passage of major legislation, can be complex, technical, and fast-moving for the average person to follow without guidance from the news media (Graber 1988). I argue that the way the news media cover political processes will change based on the rates of WDR. As more women enter political institutions, the news media will report on the more feminine behaviors that women bring to political processes. In this way, the news media, itself, should use more feminine process frames over masculine process frames in news coverage.

In the absence of a high level of WDR, masculinity is likely to dominate political process news coverage. Classic news values are a set of criteria that journalists, editors, and other gatekeepers use to decide what exactly constitutes a newsworthy event (Gans 1980; Galtung and Ruge 1965). Newsworthy stories have a common set of elements in which they frequently highlight conflict, scandal, and drama (Harcup and O'Neill 2017)—these are all values that align with conventional notions of masculinity. Masculinity is deeply embedded in how the news media identify stories and events worthy of coverage. The media tend to position white men as the key actors in political stories (Baitinger 2015), men are more likely to be quoted in news stories (Armstrong 2004), journalists tend to rely on white men over women and men of color as experts (Searles et al. 2023; Katsuo et al. 2009; Sui et al. 2018), and masculine issues dominate the issue agenda (Bauer and Santia 2023). Masculine news values emerge in how the media characterize relationships between Democrats and Republicans and the relationships between different branches of government. These masculine news norms and values are evident in political news coverage where stories about political process highlight conflict and gamesmanship, rely on sports narratives about battles, duels, and clashes, and the media construct dramatic narratives (Krupnikov and Ryan 2022; Klar and Krupnikov 2016; Groenendyk and Krupnikov 2021; Dunaway and Lawrence 2015; Cappella and Jamieson 1996; Hibbing and Theiss-Morse 2002; Levendusky and Malhotra 2016; Hitt and Searles 2018).

The masculinity of the news media is exemplified in the reporting on women and men political candidates. Some work finds that there is less bias in the coverage of women political candidates in the present compared to the coverage in the past when women were more of a political novelty (Hayes and Lawless 2016). Other work finds that media bias is still prominent in how the media discuss women and men running for political office (Meeks 2012; Bligh et al. 2012; van der Pas and Aaldering 2020). Existing scholarship finds gender biases in coverage based on superficial characteristics (i.e., clothing and hair) (Heldman, Carroll, and Olson 2005; Aday and Devitt 2001), personal qualities (i.e., families) (Bystrom et al. 2005), issue coverage and gendered traits (Dunaway et al. 2013), qualifications (Bauer 2024b), and horse race coverage (Kahn 1996; Lawrence and Rose 2010). This research illustrates that women are characterized as not fitting into the masculine norms that characterize not just how the media report on politics but also how voters think about political leadership.

When it comes to the creation of the news, men dominate the news creation processes. Most journalists, especially journalists reporting on politics, are men (Usher, Holcomb, and Littman 2018; Usher 2014; Weaver 1997; Bauer 2024b; Bauer et al. 2024). Even though women journalists have similar views, attitudes, and interests as men in the profession, they are assigned to write more soft news stories and fewer hard news stories (North 2016a, b; Hanitzch and Hanuch 2012; Armstrong and Boyle 2011; Armstrong 2004; Rodgers and Thorson 2003). Gendered patterns of story assignment reflect stereotypical beliefs about the skills and interests of women and men. Masculine stereotypes characterize men as more tough, stronger, and more authoritative (Koenig et al. 2011) and these stereotypes lead editors to assign men to write stories that reflect these qualities (Shor et al. 2015). Feminine stereotypes characterize women as more soft, compassionate, and warm (Prentice and Carranza 2002), and this perception, in turn, can lead editors to assign women to write stories that reflect these qualities (Rodgers and Thorson 2003).

This preference toward masculinity as a news value comes, in part, from the dominance of men in journalism (Weaver 1997) and from the market pressures that drive news organizations (Dunaway 2008). News organizations need readers and subscribers to attract advertisers (Usher 2014), and that advertising revenue allows news organizations to stay in business (Darr, Hitt, and Dunaway 2021). People are attracted to dramatic narratives that frame politics as an us versus them competition (Mutz 2015), even though such frames can have deleterious effects on democracy (Cappella and Jamieson 1996). The market pressures of journalism as a business contribute to the news media's dominant use of masculinity in its coverage of politics. This extensive body of research on news norms and processes has yet to consider when the media shifts from using masculinity to more femininity in political news coverage.

Feminine and Masculine Political Process Frames

I develop a framework for identifying gendered political process frames in routine political news coverage and I argue that WDR can shift the media from using masculine process frames to feminine process frames. I start by defining what I mean by political process frames, and then, I move onto explaining the characteristics and differences of masculine and feminine process frames. Process frames refer to news coverage of routine political processes including the consideration of bills, passing bills into law, and the relationships between key political actors and institutions in political processes. I analyze news coverage of routine political processes rather than campaign news coverage not only because the use of masculinity in process frames is relatively understudied, but also because WDR has the potential to shift how legislatures engage in lawmaking.

The key predictions I test in this chapter are the *gendered discourse prediction* and the *gendered source prediction*. The gendered discourse prediction argues that as the number of women in Congress increases, news coverage of political processes will reflect feminine process frames over masculine process frames. The gendered sourcing prediction posits that news coverage will include more women's voices as sources as WDR increases. Changes in both gendered discourse and gendered sourcing are two critical ways that news coverage of political processes can affect the process of institutional stereotype change.

Women's Descriptive Representation and Gendered Discourse in the News

Masculine process frames are likely to be the default frames that the news media rely on in the coverage of political processes. The previous section outlined how factors such as polarization and increasing market pressures on news outlets lead to the use of conflict frames (Levendusky and Malhotra 2016; Dunaway 2008). The media's dominant orientation to politics centers on masculinity in its coverage. I argue that the use of masculine frames should decline, and the use of feminine process frames should become more prominent as WDR increases. This shift from masculine to feminine process frames will occur for two reasons: first, when there are more women involved in politics, especially in leadership roles, the media will be more likely to turn to corresponding feminine stereotypes; second, women in politics are more likely to engage in feminine stereotypic behaviors when engaged in the task of lawmaking, and this will lead the media to shift the frames for their coverage accordingly.

A force that affects how the news media report on political processes is the fact that, for most of American history, the key actors in politics are men. Only one woman served as Speaker of the House, Nancy Pelosi, no woman served as a majority or minority leader in the US Senate, and no woman has won election to the presidency. I argue that as more women win seats in Congress, there should be a shift in not just whose voices the news media include in political coverage, but also the type of language the media use to report on politics.

The second reason I expect a shift from masculine to feminine process frames when women's representation increases is that women in political office regularly engage in stereotypically feminine behaviors when creating and passing laws. Women leaders, outside of politics, are known to bring a transformational style of leadership to political office (Vinkenburg et al. 2011; Burris et al. 2013; Fine 2009). A masculine style of leadership is one that emphasizes maintaining hierarchies, represents a command-and-control relationship with employees, and where the leader gets to claim credit for organizational successes (Heilman and Okimoto 2007; Heilman et al. 2004). Women are more likely to forge collaborative relationships in legislatures and build consensus among political actors with diverse sets of interest (Barnes 2016; Holman and Mahoney 2019), and these are all behaviors that fit into feminine stereotypes (Prentice and Carranza 2002), and especially stereotypes about women in leadership roles (Eagly and Carli 2003a; Grant 1988; Hegelsen 1990; Fine 2009). This style of leadership differs from the dominant masculine style used by men in that it breaks down hierarchies, builds consensus across political actors, and shares credit for successes across different groups (Fine 2009).

Women run for office to accomplish policy goals (Schneider et al. 2016) and women legislators' high rates of productivity relative to men reflect the fulfillment of policy goals (Anzia and Berry 2011). Women's high levels of productivity come, also, from the gendered vulnerability women feel (Lazarus and Steigerwalt 2018) and from the feminine activities, such as compromise, women use to pass legislation (Volden, Wiseman, and Wittmer 2013). Women are more likely than men to pass legislation through collaboration, compromise, and bipartisanship (Barnes 2016). In fact, women who fail to compromise when faced with an opportunity to do so can face a punishment among some voters (Bauer, Yong Harbridge, and Krupnikov

2017). Women forge these collaborative relationships across partisan lines (Volden, Wiseman, and Wittmer 2013) and women collaborate with other women (Barnes 2016; Holman, Mahoney, and Hurler 2022; Holman and Mahoney 2019; Mahoney 2018). One way that women legislators facilitate these collaborative relationships is through women's caucuses in state legislatures (Mahoney 2018). These caucuses allow women legislators to identify common interests, even across partisan lines, and develop strategies for passing legislation that addresses their shared goals. More women engaged in lawmaking means that it is more likely that these women will engage in feminine activities to push through legislation, such as compromise, and reporting on these processes will lead the media to rely on feminine process frames. This leads to the first prediction I test in this chapter:

Gendered Discourse Prediction: As the number of women in Congress increases, news coverage of political processes will reflect more feminine process frames compared to when there are lower levels of women in Congress.

The increase of women in politics coupled with women's engagement in feminine behaviors can prompt the media to use what I term as feminine process frames in news coverage of legislative processes. I do not necessarily expect that masculine process frames will disappear, but I expect a discernible shift in the gendered frames the media rely on when covering political processes.

Women Descriptive Representation and Gendered Sourcing Patterns

More women in Congress not only means the use of more feminine process frames, but also means that women should be quoted and referenced in political news coverage more frequently. Political news coverage highlights men as the main political actors in shaping the passage of legislation and as having more at stake in the passage of legislation (Usher, Holcomb, and Littman 2018; Padgett, Dunaway, and Darr 2019). This trend reflects the dominance of masculinity in politics and in the news media. When there are more women in Congress, especially women in key leadership roles, the news media should quote these women and use them as sources more frequently. Part of this dynamic may simply be a numbers effect. When there are more women in the pool of political leaders available to quote from, the media should use these women as sources more frequently. This effect should be especially strong as the period in which I test the gendered dynamics of news coverage occurs during Nancy Pelosi's two tenures as Speaker of the House.

It is not just that WDR will increase the presence of women in political process news stories, but also that WDR will lead to an increase in the women's presence in news stories more generally. Women, overall, are not well-represented as sources in news coverage (Searles et al. 2023). Women in media leadership positions use their positions to open the door for more women to enter stereotypically masculine domains (Rodgers and Thorson 2003). Existing work shows that women in editorial roles lead to changes in newsroom routines, and the output of news coverage (Splichal and Garrison 2000; Splichal and Garrison 1995). Women editors prioritize covering issues that disproportionately affect women, such as reproductive rights, and how a politician's personal life, versus their public life, should be covered (Splichal and Garrison 2000; Splichal and Garrison 1995). Women journalists are more likely to use and cite other women as expert or non-expert voices in news stories (Katsuo et al. 2009; Grabe et al. 2011; Zoch and Turk 1998) and women journalists cover women political candidates differently from what men do (van der Pas and Aaldering 2020; Bauer 2024b; Meeks 2013). Women in media leadership roles shift the way journalists report on the news by including more women's voices. I expect that women in political leadership roles will have a spillover effect that will lead journalists to think more about women *not in politics* as sources and/or experts about political policies and political processes. I argue that simply seeing women in high-profile political leadership roles will, implicitly, lead journalists to seek out women's voices to fill out their stories. The gendered sourcing prediction outlines this effect:

Gendered Source Prediction: As the number of women in Congress increases, journalists will rely on women political leaders as sources in news coverage more frequently compared to when there are lower levels of women in Congress

In short, I test two ways that WDR can alter the way the news media report on politics. First, more women in Congress should lead to more feminine process frames compared to when there are fewer women in Congress. Second, the news media should rely on women as sources and key political actors more frequently as women's representation increases.

Data Collection

The gendered discourse dataset includes a sample of articles published in the *New York Times* about politics from 2007 through the end of 2020. I start with 2007 because this is when Nancy Pelosi became Speaker of the House, the first woman to serve in that role, and I expect Pelosi's position as Speaker to, in part, lead to the use of more feminine process frames in coverage. I end with 2020 as this marked the end of the Trump administration, and because I started this data collection in 2021. Using news coverage through 2020 allows me to track over-time changes in response to women's representation.

My two predictions can occur at any level of office: local, state, or federal. In this chapter, I test my predictions using coverage of the US Congress at the federal level. I make this choice for several reasons. First, finding access to local news articles over time is difficult. Part of this difficulty is due to limited resources in existing news article databases. The decline of local news outlets compounds the problem of finding news articles to include in the dataset. Second, because the US Congress is a higher level of office more strongly associated with masculinity, it offers a tough case for finding feminizing effects. Third, if the effects of WDR lead to more feminine process news in national coverage of federal level institutions, then it is reasonable to expect trickle-down effects in coverage of state and local political processes—though this chapter does not go so far as to test these trickle-down effects.

I developed a set of keywords to identify articles that talked about Congress, the presidency, and policymaking to identify process news, such as debate over a key piece of legislation, votes on a bill, or key congressional hearings. I conducted this search for periods when Congress was actively in session, based on data from congress.gov.[9] With a set of keywords, I created a list of all the headlines that covered political process news. From this list, I then excluded op-eds, letters to the editor, obituaries, book reviews, and other non-routine news stories. I next selected a random sample of news articles from each congressional term included in the time frame. I culled approximately 80–100 stories each year in the dataset that I identified as being about political processes. The total dataset is N = 1499 articles.

I use news stories in the *New York Times* because the newspaper is largely considered the paper of record in the US, especially when it comes to political news coverage (Usher 2014; Winter and Eyal 1981), and the newspaper is a critical agenda-setter for other news outlets (Althaus and Tewksbury 2002; Dearing and Rogers 1996; Kiousis 2011; Shapiro and Hemphill 2016; Guo 2019; Su and Borah 2019). The *New York Times* is not only considered the "paper of record" in the US, but it is a paper with influence over both domestic and international news outlets (Archetti 2008; Segev and Blondheim 2013). The *NYT*, given its position in the media landscape, should be a leading

---

[9] See Chapter 6 Appendix for the full set of keywords.

indicator of broader trends in how the news media use gendered frames to report on politics (Shapiro and Hemphill 2016).

Coding Procedures

Every news article was read by two independent coders who were blind to the exact purpose of this research and who were provided with a codebook that defined different aspects of news coverage that can fit into feminine or masculine process frames. I include the full codebook procedures and protocols from the content analysis in Table 6.1.

Feminine process frames draw on themes of communality, compromise, collaboration, consensus-building, or bipartisanship. These are all behaviors that reflect broader stereotypes about women performing roles as caregivers (Prentice and Carranza 2002). Studies of women in leadership roles, such as business management, find that women leaders engage in and promote behaviors such as collaboration and consensus-building among groups (Eagly and Carli 2003a; Grant 1988; Hegelsen 1990; Fine 2009). These are also behaviors that women in legislative institutions perform more than men (Volden, Wiseman, and Wittmer 2013; Holman, Mahoney, and Hurler 2022; Holman and Mahoney 2019). An example of feminine process coverage is the following passage from an article on a Senate bill to consider whether prisoners can receive Pell Grants: "Mr. [Lamar] Alexander will find an *ally* in his committee's ranking Democrat, Senator Patty Murray of Washington, with *whom he has partnered* to broker deals, including reauthorizing the country's elementary and secondary education law and preserving insurance subsidies under the Affordable Care Act."[10] This passage reflects feminine processes because it highlights the collaboration between two Senators who are also of the opposing party.

Masculine process frames reinforce masculine behaviors and include game frames, the use of war or sports metaphors, and discussion of power-seeking behaviors. These elements of masculine process frames come from research in how men in leadership roles behave (Eagly and Karau 2002). An example of a masculine process frame is the following from an article about the government budget in 2015 and funding Planned Parenthood: "Democrats *accused* the Republicans of creating a *hostile* atmosphere that provided context—if not direct instigation—in Friday's *attack*. Five Republican-led congressional committees are investigating Planned Parenthood."[11] The article uses masculine

---

[10] March 18, 2018 New York Times, Senate Leaders Reconsider Ban on Pell Grants for Prisoners.
[11] December 1, 2015. *New York Times.* No Shutdown Expected on Planned Parenthood.

Table 6.1 Coding Procedures for Feminine and Masculine Process Frames

Coding Category	Description	Key Words
Masculine Process Frames		
Win Loss Frames	Does the language from the congressional process/outcomes in terms of winners and losers?	Lost Victory Victors Win Winners Losers Success Fail
War and Sports Metaphors	Does the story use language relating to war or sports? If the news story makes use of a language of sports and war, such as battle, competition, winning, or fight.	Attack Battle, Combat Fight Guarding Blew one of them up At war Trading blows, Curveball Blow up Trench warfare Pep rally Strike down Rally Bombshell Assault Scoring Umpire, Referee Score
Strategy and Tactics	Does the story refer to strategy or tactics? This includes discussions about potentially losing voters, calculating bases of support, etc.	Out on top Underdog Defense/offense Resistance Aim, assail
Power-Seeking/Agentic Motives	Does the story refer to power-seeking motives of elected leaders? This includes discussion of power-seeking motives; this is about individuals wanting to move onto a higher level of office, gain a leadership position, etc.	To benefit oneself Big win, Winning, Won, Lost, Losing Moving up, Advancing ahead
Feminine Process Frames		
Caregiving and/or Communal Motivations	Does this article talk about congressional leaders having the goal of helping people? Caregiving and communal goals refer to showing concerns for the community, and other groups.	Forgiving Humility Honesty Compassion, caring Kind Helpful Caring

Coding Category	Description	Key Words
Compromise and/or Collaboration	Does the article discuss behaviors such as compromise, consensus-building, working together? Includes discussion of Congress working together or discussion of Congress and presidency working together.	Trusting Consensus Compromise Collaborate Harmonious Patient Coalition
Congressional Bipartisanship	Does the article reference bipartisanship?	The two parties working together. Working together but not about the two parties is coded under the compromise category.

frames by setting up a conflict narrative between the political parties describing the relationship as "hostile." These themes in the news coverage could be used to talk about the behaviors of key political actors, either women or men, or these themes could be used to discuss the interactions between the two political parties or between Congress and the presidency. I used two researchers to separately read and code each article to allow me to assess for intercoder reliability. I include the tests on intercoder reliability in Chapter 6 Appendix Table A6.1.

Construction of Key Dependent Variables

Using the information from the content analysis, I created two dependent variables: a feminine process frame and a masculine process frame variable. Each of these variables is coded as 1 if one of the articles reflects at least one element of a feminine process or a masculine process frame, and 0 otherwise. Feminine frame use should increase as the number of women in Congress increases.

To test the gendered sourcing prediction, I recorded data on when the news media referred to women political leaders in Congress when discussing politics, and when stories included quotations from women. I make this distinction because choosing to directly quote a person's words can reflect the power, status, and prestige of that person's expertise. In other words, quoting a person gives more weight to that person. An example of a woman referenced in an article but not quoted comes from a 2008 article titled about the auto-bailout at the start of the Great Recession titled, "Deal to Rescue U.S. Automakers is Moving Ahead." The article paraphrases then Speaker of the House Nancy Pelosi stating: "The House speaker, Nancy Pelosi, said she hoped that Mr. Bush's appointee—or car czar, as the position has come to be known—would not need to be replaced by President-elect Barack Obama, raising the prospect that the outgoing and incoming administrations would cooperate in selecting someone." The article quotes Representative Barney Frank as a lead author on the bailout legislation. The decision to quote Frank but to paraphrase Pelosi, who was Speaker of the House at the time and would serve as a lead legislator on getting the bailout passed, is striking.[12]

For comparative purposes, the researchers also coded when the news media referenced men and quoted men in Congress. I use the data on men in sources to create an overall variable for the total number of political leaders referenced or quoted in a story. These data lead to two key outcome variables: the proportion of women leaders referenced in news articles and the proportion of women leaders directly quoted in news articles. I predict that a rise in WDR should lead to an increase in women being used as sources in political news coverage.

Construction of Key Independent Variables

The gendered discourse dataset includes covariates to account for other factors beyond WDR that might account for the use of gendered process frames and quoting women sources in stories. I created a series of variables to measure the proportion of women in the US House and the US Senate for each year. I combined these to make an overall woman in Congress variable that includes the House and Senate. I added a binary variable for when Nancy Pelosi served as Speaker of the House from 2007 through 2010, and from 2019 through 2020.[13] I recorded a binary variable to record the time frame when Hillary Clinton served as Secretary of State from 2009 through 2012. I carved out a separate variable documenting the proportion of women of color in Congress during this time period. These independent variables should have a positive and statistically significant effect on the use of feminine process frames and the use of women as sources.

With this database of political process news articles, I identified the number of authors listed in a story byline, the number of those authors who are women, and the number of women who are lead authors. I identified journalist gender using practices from past research (Bauer 2024b). I searched for each journalist's name to find a biography created by the journalist or from

---

[12] Of course, it may be that Speaker Pelosi decided not to publicly comment on the legislation.

[13] Pelosi's second tenure as Speaker ended at the end of 2022, but the data stop at 2020.

the journalist's news organization. From these biographies, I looked for the pronouns the journalists used to describe themselves. She/her pronouns led to the journalist being recorded as a woman and he/him pronouns I coded as a man. Just 28 percent of the articles included a woman author in the byline.

I collected data on the number of women serving in an editorial role at the *NYT*. I used the archives of the *NYT* to identify those listed in the paper's masthead. From year-to-year, the number of women editors ranged from 4 to 7, and the total proportion of women editors ranged from 0.23 to 0.54, with an $M = 0.372$ and an SD = 0.098. I also created a woman as executive editor variable coded as 1 for the period when Jill Abramson was the executive editor at the newspaper from 2011 to 2014; for the years Abramson was not editor, this variable was coded 0. These variables allow me to account for forces at the *NYT* that might lead journalists to use more feminine process frames regardless of WDR.

I created several other independent variables to account for factors that might affect the use of feminine process frames. I created a dummy variable to account for whether there was a presidential or midterm election that year. I recorded if there was unified party government for each year in the data. Unified government is when both houses of Congress and the presidency are controlled by the same political party. Divided government refers to when one or more houses of Congress is controlled by a political party that is not the president's political party. I record this as a dummy variable where 1 indicated unified government and 0 indicated divided government. Finally, I include the logged length in number of words for each article to include as a control. The average length of an article in number of words is 1192.98 words, with a standard deviation of 1212.89 words. The range for this variable is 41 to 21,759. Given this considerable range, I use the logged length of the article.

The Use of Gendered Process Frames

I start by examining descriptive patterns in the use of feminine and masculine process frames across the 13-year period of my dataset. A simple t-test comparison shows that, overall, there are more masculine frames, with an average of 28.30 percent, than feminine frames, with an average of 15.436 percent across the full dataset, $p < 0.001$. Figure 6.1 displays the trends showing a slow and steady increase in the use of feminine process frames. Several patterns stand out. First, there are always more masculine process frames than feminine process frames for each congressional term. This is not surprising given

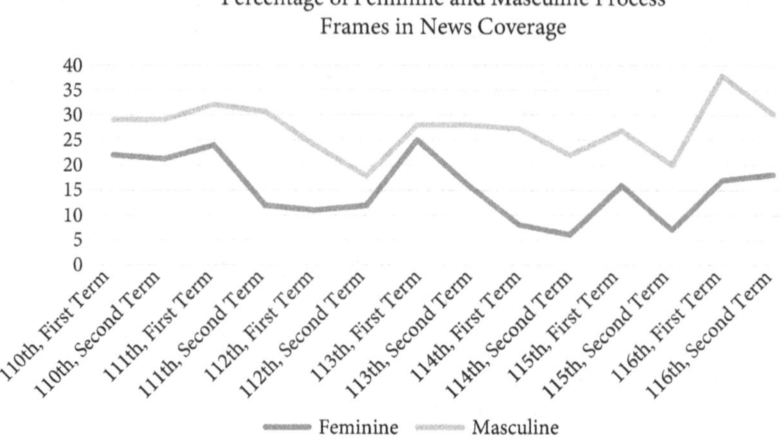

Figure 6.1 Gendered process frames in political news coverage, 2007–2020

that most news values favor masculinity. The congressional term with the highest percentage of masculine process frames at 42 percent was the second term of the 110th Congress which was in 2008. The use of masculine process frames may reflect the contentious debates in Congress over the economic crash that occurred that fall, and how best to address the impending fallout through legislation. Second, the trend line for the percentage of feminine process news coverage shows considerable variation across congressional terms. The first term of the 113th Congress, which was in 2013, has the highest use of feminine process frames at 25 percent, and the use of feminine process frames is almost equal to masculine process frames that year, which was 28 percent.

The gendered discourse prediction argues that as more women enter politics, journalists should shift from masculine to feminine process frames. To test how women's presence in politics affects the gendered language the media use, I estimated a series of logistic regression models to separately predict the use of a feminine frame or a masculine frame. The feminine process frame variable is coded as 1 if the article uses at least 1 element of a feminine frame, and 0 otherwise. The masculine process variable is coded the same way. Logistic regression allows me to model these dichotomous outcomes (Long 1997). All the models cluster the standard errors by congressional term. Table 6.2 includes the main results.

Starting with the feminine process frames, I find that the three key variables recording women's presence in politics, the Nancy Pelosi as Speaker variable, and the proportions of women in Congress are each insignificant. The results

Table 6.2 Gendered Process Frames

	Feminine Process Frames	Masculine Process Frames
Woman Speaker of the House	0.285	0.429***
	(0.329)	(0.110)
Proportion of women in Congress	−3.886	−0.460
	(4.055)	(1.553)
Proportion women authors	0.319	0.010
	(0.263)	(0.171)
Divided government	−0.102	−0.110
	(0.305)	(0.106)
Proportion of women editors at NYT	−0.151	0.636***
	(0.567)	(0.168)
Logged length (in words)	−0.211	−0.022
	(0.161)	(0.114)
Constant	0.537	−0.843
	(1.470)	(0.836)
Observations	1151	1151
Pseudo R^2	0.011	0.006

Note: Standard errors in parentheses; * $p<0.10$, ** $p<0.05$, *** $p<0.01$

suggest that WDR does not lead the news media to rely on more feminine process frames and indicate no support for the gendered discourse prediction.

The masculine process models show some curious patterns. The variable for Nancy Pelosi as Speaker of the House is statistically significant, $p < 0.001$, and positive. This effect is in the opposite direction of the gendered discourse prediction. The predicted probability of using a masculine process frame when Nancy Pelosi served as Speaker of the House is 0.382 (SE = 0.015), and when Nancy Pelosi was not speaker, the predicted probability falls to 0.287 (SE = 0.015), $p < 0.001$. This dynamic may simply capture the effects of divided government, or periods when a Democrat oversaw one branch of government and a Republican in charge of another branch of government. But the variable for divided government is not significant, $p = 0.298$. The first four years of the data are when Pelosi was Speaker and President Obama was president. This means that Pelosi was tasked with implementing Obama's legislative agenda, and their relationship in and of itself was not necessarily conflictual. However, there was considerable partisan conflict in Congress, especially over passage of the Affordable Care Act colloquially known as Obamacare, and this heightened level of partisan conflict could have led to the use of more masculine frames. Pelosi was a forceful presence, and, as a woman, she challenged the dominance of masculinity in political leadership given that she was the first woman Speaker of the House.

The other unexpected finding in the masculine process model is that the women editors variable is significant and positive, $p < 0.001$. In other words, when there are more women serving as editors at the *NYT*, journalists use more masculine process frames. When 50 percent of the editors at the paper are women, the predicted probability of using a masculine frame is 0.351 (SE = 0.010), or 35 percent, but when there are no women editors, the predicted probability of using a masculine frame drops to 0.283 (SE = 0.016), or 28.3 percent, $p < 0.001$. Women in media leadership roles can disrupt the usual gendered patterns of reporting by including women sources, for example (Mills 1997; Armstrong 2004; Katsuo et al. 2009), other research finds that women in media leadership can reify the norms and standards that already exist (de Bruin 2000). It may be that once women reach an editorial role at the paper of record in the US, they have been socialized to follow news norms that favor masculinity (Craft and Wanta 2004) and they may be unlikely to challenge such norms once they get into leadership roles.

The findings thus far do not indicate strong support for the gendered discourse prediction. I also tested if women of color in Congress affect the use of feminine and masculine process frames and do not find a significant effect. I include the full models in Chapter 6 Appendix Table A6.3. The findings suggest that women in political leadership can lead journalists to rely more heavily on masculinity. This may be a dynamic where the media rely on Speaker Pelosi's position to create a sense of gendered conflict between her, as a woman, and other political actors (who are mostly men) (Conroy 2015).

Women as Sources

The gendered sourcing prediction argues that women in Congress should lead to an increase in women referenced and quoted in the news. I start with Figure 6.2 which displays descriptive data on the use of women and men as sources in political news stories. The first key observation from the descriptive figure is that the number of women used as sources or directly quoted in news articles is never more than 15 percent. This means that 85 percent, or more, of the sources and people quoted in news articles are men. This relatively low rate of incorporating women's voices into political news stories does not mirror women's rates of representation in Congress. In the last two terms of the dataset, which encompass 2019 and 2020, women's representation was

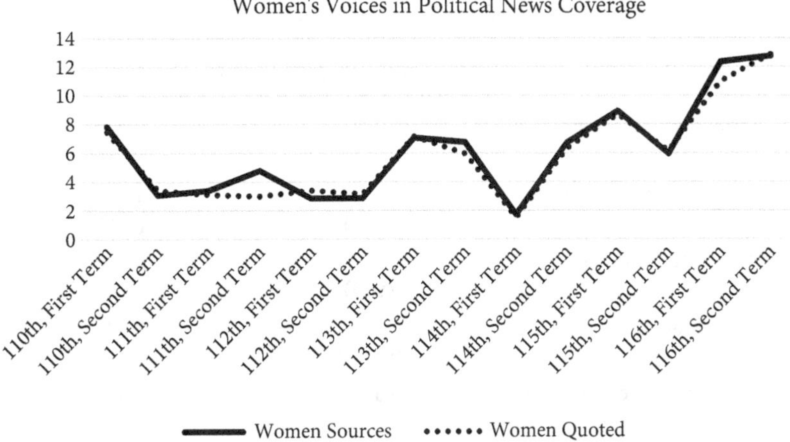

Figure 6.2 Percentage of women as sources in political news coverage

just over 25 percent in the US Congress, but women's use as sources is half that percentage. It is notable that 2019 saw a spike in women being used as sources in news coverage, and this is likely because of Nancy Pelosi as Speaker of the House frequently clashing with a Republican President. There is no comparable spike during Pelosi's first tenure as Speaker from 2007 to 2011. The coding for women being used as sources and being directly quoted did not just include women members of Congress but also women who lead non-profit or policy groups that have a stake in a particular piece of legislation. The general under-representation of women as sources in political process stories is quite striking.

My two outcome variables, women sources and women quoted, are proportions that capture the numbers of women and men in articles. Because of this variable construction, I use generalized linear models (GLMs) to estimate the effects of women's representation. GLM regression models recognize with the categorical nature of the outcome variable in the estimation procedures. I include the same set of controls from the previous models. The key independent variables are the variable for Pelosi as Speaker of the House and the proportion of women in Congress. Table 6.3 displays the full results.

For the women references model, I find a positive effect for the Pelosi variable and positive, significant effects for the proportions of women in Congress. The effect of Pelosi as speaker is such that the proportion of women referenced in political process coverage is 0.865 (SE = 0.009), or 8.65 percent, but when Pelosi is not speaker, that proportion falls to 0.053, or 5.5 percent, (SE = 0.010), $p = 0.033$. Having a woman in a high-profile political leadership

Table 6.3 Gendered Sources in Political Process News

	Women Referenced	Women Quoted
Woman Speaker of the House	0.033**	0.020
	(0.016)	(0.016)
Proportion of women in Congress	1.347***	1.312***
	(0.226)	(0.221)
Proportion women authors	0.034***	0.036**
	(0.013)	(0.015)
Divided government	0.017	0.023
	(0.015)	(0.015)
Proportion of women editors at *NYT*	0.016	−0.035
	(0.027)	(0.025)
Logged length (in words)	−0.003	0.001
	(0.008)	(0.007)
Constant	−0.202***	−0.206***
	(0.078)	(0.074)
Observations	1151	1151

Note: Standard errors in parentheses; * p<0.10, ** p<0.05, *** p<0.01

role leads to the inclusion of more women's voices in stories about political processes but not to women being directly quoted more in political process coverage. The women quoted model shows an insignificant effect for Pelosi as Speaker of the House. Important to remember is that these data do not just record when Pelosi is referenced or quoted in coverage, but when the media reference women more generally in stories about the legislative process, how policies might affect everyday people, and the types of experts used to fill out a story.

Figure 6.3 displays the predicted proportions of women either referenced or quoted in political process news based on when women's representation is at a low, moderate, or a high level. The figure shows a striking increase in the number of women sources quoted or referenced in news coverage moving from a low level of WDR where references to women make up 0.0317, or 3.17 percent (SE = 0.101) of sources in news coverage, to 0.1125, or 11.25 percent (SE = 0.007) of references to experts. This 8 percent increase is statistically significant, $p < 0.001$, but it is also important to note that women still made up a very small share of the experts referenced or quoted in news coverage. At the height of women's representation, women comprise 11 percent of sources referenced in news articles. This means that just under 90 percent of the sources cited in political process news articles are men.

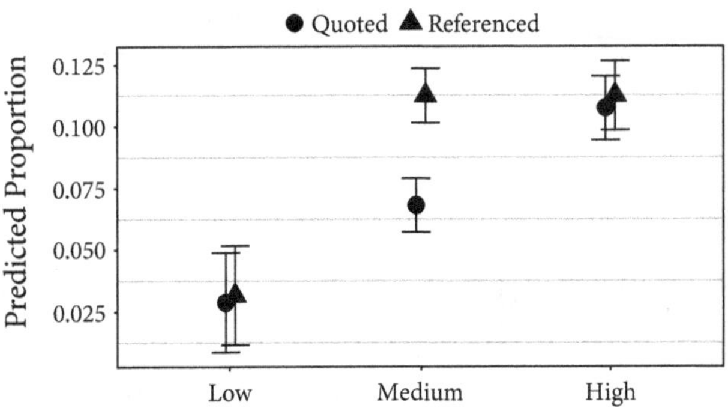

Figure 6.3 Women experts in political process news
Note: 95 percent confidence intervals included.

Together, the results of these two models show that when a woman serves in a high-profile political leadership role, the news media will reference women as sources or experts in political process coverage more frequently, but the news media do not take the extra step of quoting those women's voices. It may be that women are less likely to agree to be quoted in news stories relative to men, and there is just no way to know if this effect of women taking themselves out of the story occurs. I also estimated models using the men as references and men quoted variables which I include in the appendices, Table A6.2. The models for the men in news stories confirm this null effect as none of the women's representation variables are significant.

Women of Color's Descriptive Representation and Gendered Sourcing

I tested whether women of color's presence in Congress, more specifically, affects the gendered sourcing patterns of political process news stories. Based on the results from Chapter 4, I expect that women of color might have a uniquely different effect than just women's overall representation. I estimated generalized linear models estimating the proportion of women experts cited or quoted in political process news coverage. I include these full models in Table A6.4, and I graphed the effects of women of color in Congress on gendered sourcing patterns in Figure 6.4. The effects of women of color in Congress are significant and positive for models predicting the women experts referenced and quoted in political process news. When women of color are in Congress at a low rate, about 4 percent, the predicted proportion

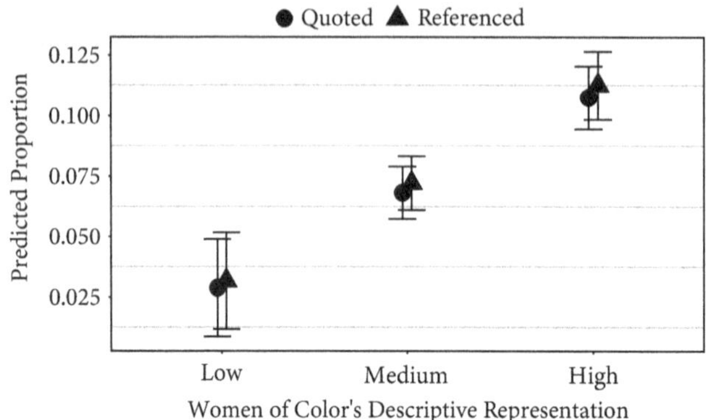

Figure 6.4 Women experts in political process news based on women of color's descriptive representation
Note: 95 percent confidence intervals included.

of women references is 0.044 (SE = 0.009), or 4.4 percent. The proportion of women referenced in news articles increases to 0.105 (SE = 0.007) when women of color reached their highest rate of representation at 10.5 percent. The effect is similar for women quoted in news articles. More women of color in Congress lead to more women being referenced or directly quoted in news coverage. As with the initial analyses of gendered sourcing patterns, I also estimated the effect of women of color in Congress on the inclusion of men as sources, and I find insignificant effects, which is what I would expect.

The strong and positive effects for both women's descriptive representation and women of color's descriptive representation on the gendered sourcing patterns in the news media are important findings. I separated the use of women as sources from the overall use of feminine process frames, but the sourcing analyses find that high levels of WDR can increase the presence of women in the news in important ways that enhance women's representation in public discourse.

Results Summary

This chapter presented two sets of analyses. First, I examined how WDR affected the use of feminine and masculine process frames. I found that masculine process frames dominate routine political news coverage. This does not strongly support the gendered discourse prediction. Second, I examined how WDR affected the use of women as sources in political process news. I found that women's, and women of color's, descriptive representation, increases the use of women as sources and the use of direct quotations in articles from women. These findings support the gendered sourcing prediction.

Conclusion

This chapter addressed one potential mechanism by which the information learns about WDR and information about institutional stereotype change are transmitted to the public. The results suggest that higher rates of WDR can change the gendered patterns of public discourse in the news media, but masculinity never quite disappears. Higher rates of WDR leads to more feminine language used in political process news but there are always higher rates of masculine language. Indeed, these results, while not quite perfectly matching up to my predictions, do mirror the shifts seen in the experiments from Chapter 3. Higher rates of WDR do, more promisingly, lead to more women's voices included in political process news coverage.

Where the previous empirical chapters highlighted how WDR affects voters and the stereotypes held of political institutions, I track the effects of WDR on the types of information available to voters about politics. While there is a robust body of scholarship on the role of campaign news coverage on candidates (van der Pas and Aaldering 2020; Bauer and Taylor 2023; Bauer 2024b) and how such coverage affects voters (Rohrbach, Aaldering, and Van Der Pas 2023), there is less scholarship on routine news coverage. An exception is Aaldering and van der Pas (2020) who found substantial differences in the coverage of women political leaders across routine times and campaign times. The findings in this chapter show that masculine process frames are the dominant frame that appears in news coverage about politics. It is striking that masculine frames are so dominant in news media coverage even when women serve in prominent political leadership roles. News outlets not only play a "watchdog" role over political institutions, but they also face market-based pressures that may lead to an over-reliance on masculine tropes when characterizing political events and activities. Reading about conflict is more attractive than reading about people happily getting along. Until these market-based pressures alleviate, it may be difficult to eradicate the dominant masculine frames in political news coverage.

On a more promising note, the results surrounding the gendered sourcing prediction show that when there are more women in office, there are more women included in news stories. Part of this effect is likely due to women's presence in top leadership roles, and it is natural to quote these women when covering a contentious political fight. However, more women's voices are included in news coverage as experts or stakeholders who are separate from government. The dominance of men as "experts" in the news media is a well-documented phenomenon (see, e.g., Searles et al. (2023)). Multiple public initiatives have worked to make it easier for journalists to find a more diverse range of sources for their news stories. Efforts like Women Also Know Stuff in political science, which spawned several spinoffs for other disciplines, aim to make the work of finding an expert easier for reports. Many of these efforts to promote women experts emerged at the tail-end of my dataset, and the effects of such efforts may not be fully captured in this chapter. This chapter offers mixed support for the extent to which the news media transmit information about WDR that can lead to the feminizing effects documented in my experiments. Future work should do more to identify how WDR disrupts masculine news norms. I spend more time in the concluding chapter outlining possibilities for future research on this front.

7

Does Women's Descriptive Representation Matter?

The Kanab County all-women city council, elected in 1912, was certainly noteworthy for the council's representation of women. More than 100 years later, all-women city councils or even just majority-women city councils are still rare enough to garner headlines and news attention. Gains for women's representation can be slow in coming. Turning to recent elections, Vermont, in 2022, became the very last state to elect a woman to the US Congress with the election of Becca Balint to the state's House seat. It is remarkable that Vermont held off sending a woman to Congress until 2022 considering that Vermont became a state in 1791. This means that Vermont, for nearly 230 years, had an all-men delegation they sent to Congress. New Hampshire, just right next door, represents quite a contrast as the state regularly has periods where their congressional delegation is all-women and has had multiple women governors. Katie Britt, a Republican and the former chief of staff for Alabama Senator Richard Shelby, won election to the seat vacated by her former boss becoming the first woman senator from Alabama. The 2022 elections also saw some gains for women governors as New York elected Kathy Hochul to the gubernatorial office she took over upon her predecessor's resignation, bringing the total number of women governors currently serving to twelve, a record high. Despite these recent gains, there are still disparities in women's representation. As of 2025, seventeen states have yet to elect a woman to the US Senate, eighteen states have yet to elect a woman governor, and five states have never elected a woman governor or senator.[1] Of course, very few women of color currently serve as governor, and no Black women have ever won election to a gubernatorial office in the US. Clearly, there is room for WDR to grow.

The gains made in WDR in recent elections were certainly precarious as the US entered the 2024 election cycle. The 2024 election featured a presidential contest, and appeared at the onset to be a repeat of the 2020 race. Trump's

---

[1] https://www.pewresearch.org/short-reads/2024/11/01/17-states-havent-had-a-female-us-senator-and-18-havent-had-a-woman-governor/.

Feminizing Political Institutions. Nichole M. Bauer, Oxford University Press. © Nichole M. Bauer (2026).
DOI: 10.1093/9780197841556.003.0007

bid for another term in the White House did not go unchallenged among Republicans as he faced several contenders. Only one woman, former South Carolina Governor and United Nations Ambassador Nikki Haley, a woman of South Asian descent, was among the potential contenders in 2024. The dearth of women running for political office in the Republican Party reflects broader trends where most of the women who run for political office do so as Democrats (Crowder-Meyer and Lauderdale 2014; Crowder-Meyer 2013). With only nominal competition, Trump successfully secured the Republican nomination.

After weeks of speculation about incumbent President Joe Biden's health and fitness to successfully run a presidential campaign against Donald Trump, and hypothetically serve another four-year term, the incumbent president stepped aside. Joe Biden's decision to bow out of the 2024 presidential contest less than four months before the general election opened the way for Kamala Harris's candidacy. For the first time, a Black, South Asian woman became the party's nominee. And, for the second time, a woman ran against Donald Trump for the presidency. The short presidential campaign of Harris, just about 100 days, appeared to set the stage for a close match between Harris and Trump. The very short campaign Harris had to put together at the last minute certainly gave her a steep uphill battle in the campaign. Her selection as the nominee, without a formal nominating contest, may reflect the "glass-cliff" phenomenon where businesses select women as CEOs when companies are in financial trouble (Ryan et al. 2016; Ryan, Haslam, and Kulich 2010; Ryan and Haslam 2007). Appointing women CEO when a business is already failing sets up the woman CEO to fail. In the end, it was not that close of a contest. Trump handily won the presidency. For four more years, the presidency in the United States will remain an institution without women's descriptive representation.

At the congressional level, the number of women serving held steady in 2024. Since 1992, women increased their numbers in Congress every election cycle except for 2010 where women lost seats. Women face steep challenges in keeping their gains in descriptive representation as women incumbents are far more likely to face high-quality challengers relative to men (Branton et al. 2018). From 2022 to the 2024 election, women gained about five more seats across the House and the Senate moving their level of representation to 28.2 percent, up about a half of a percent from 2022. Black women made notable gains in the Senate with Angela Alsobrooks of Maryland and Lisa Blunt Rochester of Delaware, both Democrats, winning their elections to become the first Black women to represent their respective states. Prior to the start of the 2025 congressional term, the Senate only had two Black women who had ever won election to that body, Carol Mosley Braun, who served from 1993–1998, and Kamala Harris, who served from 2017 until the end of 2020.[2] Women still have a long way to achieve gender parity.

This book tracked the effects of WDR arguing that more women in elected political office can lead people to see institutions as more feminine and inclusive. I addressed several core questions: (1) *Do individuals stereotype political institutions that are more diverse along racial and gender lines as less masculine and less white compared to institutions that under-represent women and people of color?* (2) *Are the feminizing effects of more diverse institutions more likely to be felt at different types of political office?* (3) *How does changing the stereotypic perceptions the public holds of political institutions change the way women and men engage in political participation and evaluate political institutions?* and (4) *How do the news media communicate the feminizing effects of WDR?*

The research in this book shows that WDR affects how the public view and interact with institutions. Changes in WDR lead people to see institutions as more feminine, and these feminine perceptions can enhance political engagement and feelings of trust in government. The masculine stereotypes that people have of political institutions contribute to the overall negative perceptions that people have about politics. The link between masculinity and politics is not immutable. In this concluding chapter, I review the main findings from each previous chapter. I also chart out directions for future research that can build upon the work started in this book. Finally, I conclude by identifying the broader implications that emerge from the findings laid out in this book.

Summaries of Main Chapters

The first chapter identified one of the central puzzle motivating this book: theories of descriptive representation suggest that having more women in political office should change how individuals view political institutions and how people engage with political institutions. The past work in this area presents a mix of findings regarding whether WDR matters for individual levels of political engagement with some work showing that more women in politics lead to more participation (Hinojosa and Kittilson 2020) and other works suggesting that more women does not, in fact, lead to more

---

[2] Laphonza Butler was appointed to the Senate to fill Senator Dianne Feinstein's seat after the Senator's death. Butler, a Black woman, did not run for the seat in 2024, and the seat was won by a white man. The start of the 2025 congressional term marks the first time in over 30 years that California sent an all-male senate delegation to Congress.

participation (Dolan 2006). In Chapter 1, I outlined how past scholarship overlooks the connection between descriptive representation and the raced-gendered impressions individuals have of political institutions (see, e.g., Atkeson (2003); Dolan (2006)). I argue that a missing link in this literature is whether having more women in political office changes the white-masculine stereotypes that people hold of political institutions. If WDR increases political participation, then, I argue, WDR should change the stereotypes associated with political institutions. This perceptual shift is pivotal. Showing these connections, that the demographic characteristics of political institutions affect the racial and gender stereotypes of institutions held by people, is critical to understanding when and how people will engage with politics.

Chapter 2 explained what it means to have white-masculine institutions, and how political institutions came to have this association. I drew on multiple strands of research to identify how and why individuals apply gender stereotypic qualities to objects and institutions in ways that are not dissimilar from how people apply stereotypes to individual women and men. This chapter elaborated my main theory of institutional stereotype change which argues that as the visible demographic characteristics of a political institution change so that one group moves from being a minority in the institution to being more visible, the gendered and racialized stereotypes of the institution will also change. Within this broad theoretical framework, I outlined each of the predictions I test in the empirical chapters, Chapters 3–6. Table 7.1 revisits these predictions with updates identifying those that were upheld and those that were not. These predictions not only test my central theory of institutional stereotype change but also test how WDR can improve political engagement and institutional trust. Beyond constructing my theory of stereotype change, this chapter also offers a test showing that people see nearly all types of political institutions, from city councils to the presidency, as masculine bodies.

Chapter 3 started to address the first major research question of this book: *Do individuals stereotype political institutions that are more diverse along racial and gender lines as less white and less masculine compared to institutions that under-represent women and people of color?* I test the feminizing effects of WDR with a survey experiment using a national sample of adults in the US. The experiment presented vignettes that told individuals that a recent election ushered in majority-women or majority-men institutions varying whether the institution is a city council chamber, state legislature, mayor, or governor. I then measured the gendered traits associated with each political institution to track differences in majority-women and majority-men institutions within each type of office and across types of offices. The experiments show

Table 7.1 Key Predictions and Results

Predictions	Empirical Test	Chapter	Results
Gendered Shifts Prediction: Higher rates of women's descriptive representation will lead people to associate political institutions with more feminine and fewer masculine stereotypic qualities.	Experiments	Chapter 3	Upheld, People evaluate majority-women city councils, state legislatures, mayors, and governors as having more feminine traits than majority-men institutions, but people see majority-women institutions as having feminine and masculine traits
Institutional Type Prediction: The feminizing effects of women's descriptive representation are more likely to occur in a legislative (local) relative to an executive (state-level) political institution.	Experiments	Chapter 3	Not upheld. The shifts occur across both types of institutions.
Partisan Differences Prediction: The feminizing effects of WDR will be stronger among Democrats relative to Republicans or Independents.	Experiments	Chapter 3 and Chapter 4	Upheld. Feminizing effects are stronger for Democratic participants relative to Republican participants.
Raced-Gendered Prediction: Women of color's descriptive representation will weaken the white-masculine stereotypes associated with political institutions more so than the descriptive representation of white women and people of color more generally.	Experiments	Chapter 4	Upheld. Women of color's descriptive representation increases feminine stereotypes of institutions over masculine stereotypes.
Linked Fate Prediction: Voters of color will be more likely to see institutions that descriptively represent women of color as more feminine and inclusive relative to white voters.	Experiments	Chapter 4	Upheld. Voters of color relative to white voters see majority-women of color institutions as more feminine than masculine.

continued

Table 7.1 *continued*

Predictions	Empirical Test	Chapter	Results
Political Engagement Prediction: Individuals, both women and men, will express more willingness to participate in politics when stereotyping institutions as more feminine relative to more masculine institutions.	Experiments	Chapter 5	Partially Upheld. People report higher levels of engagement for only majority-women city council councils.
Institutional Evaluation Prediction: Individuals will rate more feminine institutions more positively than masculine institutions.	Experiments	Chapter 5	Partially Upheld. People are more trusting of majority-women city councils, state legislatures, and mayors; but people do not see more feminine institutions as more productive.
Gendered Engagement Prediction: More feminine political institutions will lead to higher levels of engagement and more positive institutional evaluations among those who have more feminine traits over masculine traits.	Experiments	Chapter 5	Partially Upheld. People with feminine PAQ traits are more willing to contact an elected official when institutions are majority-women relative to majority-men.
Gendered Discourse Prediction: As the number of women in Congress increases, news coverage of political processes will reflect more feminine process frames compared to when there are lower levels of women in Congress.	Longitudinal Content Analysis of New Coverage	Chapter 6	Not Upheld. More women in Congress do not lead to more feminine process frames. And the media used masculine process frames more frequently during Nancy Pelosi's time as Speaker of the House.
Gendered Source Prediction: Women's increased representation should lead the news media to rely on women political leaders as sources in news coverage.	Longitudinal Content Analysis of New Coverage	Chapter 6	Upheld. WDR leads to more women used as sources in the news.

that across all levels of office, people associate majority-women institutions with feminine and masculine traits, but people see majority-men institutions through the lens of just masculinity. This first pivotal test of my theory of institutional stereotype change confirms that the demographic characteristics of institutions do, in fact, shift the gendered lens through which people view these institutions.

Chapter 4 focused more specifically on the distinct impact of women of color's descriptive representation in political institutions. Women's representation, as Chapter 3 showed, has the power to feminize institutions, but it is women of color who are uniquely positioned, due to their intersectional identities, to undo both the raced and gendered perceptions of political institutions. I extended my theory of institutional stereotype change to consider how women of color can uniquely undo the raced-gendered perceptions of political institutions. I conducted a series of experiments to track how women of color's descriptive representation affects the stereotypes people associate with political institutions. These results show that people rate institutions that are majority-women of color as more feminine compared to institutions that do not have strong representation for women of color. This finding confirms that the gender stereotypes of political institutions change with women of color's descriptive representation. People also think that majority-women of color institutions will represent a broader range of minoritized groups—these findings show how the raced perceptions of institutions shift under majority-women of color institutions leading people to see political institutions as more inclusive. The studies in this chapter also illustrate the unique feminizing and diversifying effects of women of color's descriptive representation relative to not just women as a general group but also men of color's descriptive representation. These raced-gendered effects I document are especially strong among voters who belong to a minoritized ethnorace group.

Chapter 5 centers on the question: *How does changing the stereotypic perceptions the public holds of political institutions change the way women and men engage in political participation and evaluate political institutions?* I find that more women in city councils increase political engagement, but this is the only level of office where I find effects. I also find that people rate majority-women institutions as more trustworthy than majority-men institutions but not as more productive. The null effects on productivity are curious given that women in elected office are very, very productive legislators (Volden, Wiseman, and Wittmer 2013; Anzia and Berry 2011). The tests of the gendered engagement hypothesis find that people who see themselves as more feminine than masculine are more likely to participate in politics and think more favorably of majority-women rather than majority-men institutions. I tested these hypotheses with experimental data on women of color's descriptive representation and found no differences in downstream effects based on majority-women relative to majority-women of color institutions.

Chapter 6 turned to identifying whether and how the news media play a role in feminizing institutions. Indeed, the news media are a critical mechanism by which the public learn about political institutions. I proposed a framework of feminine and masculine political process news coverage to explain when and how the news media will shift the gendered frames used to talk about the process by which Congress, and other key political actors, considers, negotiates, and passes legislation. Past work shows quite clearly that the news media rely on frames of conflict and gridlock (Cappella and Jamieson 1996), all stereotypically masculine behaviors, to cover political processes—and these frames turn individuals off politics (Groenendyk and Krupnikov 2021). I argue that breaking down the white-masculine stereotypes of political institutions will shift how the news media talk about political processes to rely on feminine over masculine frames. Feminine political process frames, a new concept I introduce in this book, highlight compromise and consensus-building over fighting and obstructionism. I analyzed that the use of feminine process frames emerges by tracking news coverage of Congress and its passage of key legislation from 2007 through to the present. I match these time frames with data on women's representation in Congress which includes periods with Nancy Pelosi as Speaker of the House and the leader of the Democratic Party. I show some small shifts from masculine political process frames to feminine political process frames, but, overwhelmingly, masculinity persists. Lawmakers, especially in eras of divided government, generally must forge some kinds of consensus across disparate interests, but the public rarely hears about this process. Interestingly, these analyses showed that during Nancy Pelosi's time as Speaker of the House, the use of masculine political process frames increased. While masculinity persists in the news media's political discourse, I find that increased levels of WDR lead to more women cited and quoted in news articles demonstrating that women's descriptive representation can shift, in part, who the news media talk to about politics.

Critical Questions for Future Scholarship

A lingering question from this book is how many women is enough to achieve the feminizing effects of WDR. Past scholarship long argued for, and then against, a critical mass level of 15 percent (Childs and Krook 2009, 2008;

Grey 2006; Tremblay 2006; Kanter 1977b). Chapter 3 presented data from a pre-test I conducted varying whether a city council was majority-women or all-women, and I found no difference between the majority-women and the all-women conditions—though this experimental study does not exactly answer the question of how many women are enough. Hinojosa and Kittilson (2020) argue that women's *visibility* is what leads to higher levels of political efficacy and a higher level of political connectedness among the public. As I have already recounted throughout this book, women's levels of descriptive representation are still well below gender parity except for a handful of state legislatures. Nevertheless, the feminizing effects of WDR can still occur if there is a substantial and visible number of women in elected political office even if those women do not comprise more than 50 percent of an institution.

My tests of institutional stereotype change rely largely on an experimental approach. I chose to use experiments because this method allows me to control the information people have about the gender composition of political institutions. While the experiments show the stereotype changes that occur in response to increased WDR, I cannot say for certain how sustainable or durable these effects are. Sometimes, effects induced in an experiment can be relatively short-lasting. For example, seminal work on the priming effects of the news media found that the effects dissipated after just a few days (Iyengar and Kinder 1987). The extent to which people receive direct information about the numbers of women in political office outside of an electoral context is not very clear. An emerging question is when and how the news media report on WDR in local, state, and federal institutions. The effects of WDR may depend on how much people follow the news, and how much state and local news outlets report on political processes. As local news outlets continue to struggle, it may be harder for citizens to learn about who holds political power in their town, city, or state, and this means that the stereotype change effects may not be durable over time.

Future research should examine how the partisan make-up of WDR matters. Early research on the behaviors of women in elected office suggests strong levels of convergence in the policy agendas and priorities of Democratic and Republican women (Swers 2002). As polarization between the political parties increased, the shared set of policy issues that might give rise to bipartisanship among women has shrunk. Republican women, for example, often lead the charge in favor of legislation that restricts or completely bans access to abortion across state legislatures (Reingold et al. 2021). Abortion was once an issue where Democratic and Republican women favored allowing some level of access for people who might become pregnant but partisan divisions are more pronounced with this issue such that the partisan leanings of a state strongly correlate with whether a state protects or bans abortion

(Kim et al. 2023). If women in political office behave primarily as partisans, then the stereotypic shifts identified in this book may be weaker or may not occur at all.

Women's behavior in elected office, beyond their support or lack of support for legislation to improve women's lives, can affect the stereotypic lens through which others view political institutions. Recent research shows that women who spend long periods of time in institutions dominated by men will adopt the behavioral norms of men (Jones 2016; Silva and Pullan 2025). Women in elected office who work against bipartisanship or other forms of compromise can face a backlash for failing to behave in ways that uphold feminine norms (Bauer, Yong Harbridge, and Krupnikov 2017). These types of behaviors can also weaken the institutional stereotype change patterns identified in this manuscript. Women who engage in behaviors that are more in line with masculine stereotypes and not feminine stereotypes can stop people from seeing majority-women political institutions as more feminine and less masculine. Identifying the extent to which women in elected office uphold feminine norms of behavior or masculine norms can shed light on the potential for stereotype shifts in American political institutions. Moreover, conducting experiments that vary the behaviors of women, and men, in elected political office can clarify the limits of institutional stereotype change.

The model of institutional stereotype change proposed here focuses on the stereotypes associated with women, but feminine traits and behaviors can be displayed by anyone regardless of their gender. A next step in this line of inquiry is to examine whether men's behaviors in political institutions can erode the masculinity of these institutions. Indeed, men in political institutions often adopt and model the feminine behaviors of women in those bodies (Bauer and Cargile 2023; Nugent 2019; Homola 2022). For example, Dietrich, Hayes, and O'Brien (2019) find that when women deliver emotionally charged speeches about women and children on the floor of Congress, men display similar levels of emotions in their floor speeches on the same topics. In this way, when men adopt feminine traits and behaviors, they may be able to weaken the masculinity associated with political institutions. This means that the burden of improving how the public views our political institutions may not be entirely contingent on women's behaviors.

The experiments in Chapter 4 varied the race and gender of descriptive representation to track changes in racialized and gendered stereotypes. My experiments considered institutions with majority-women of color but did not specify the race or ethnicity of those women. Future work should do more to parse out how Black women, Latinas, Asian American women, and women of other minoritized backgrounds can shift the racialized and gendered perceptions of institutions as women of color are not a monolith (Greene, Matos, and Sanbonmatsu 2021). Research offers mixed conclusions on the extent to which people associate women of different minoritized ethnoracial backgrounds with separate stereotype constructs (Gonzalez and Bauer 2022). Future work can do more to investigate the content of these stereotype constructs and how women's representation shifts institutional stereotypes in different ways based on a woman's ethnorace. Asian American women, often bound by the model minority stereotype (Qi, Kim, and Bauer 2023), may lead people to associate political institutions with *different* sets of stereotypes relative to Black women or Latinas. Beyond considering race and gender, there are a multitude of other identities that have the potential to weaken the entrenched masculine stereotypes of political institutions. Having leaders with non-gender conforming identities, trans women and trans men, people from working class backgrounds all have the potential to shift stereotypic perceptions because of the unique stereotypes associated with each of these groups (Jones 2022; Golebiowska 2003; Carnes and Lupu 2016; Flores, Strode, and Haider-Markel 2025; Barnes, Beall, and Holman 2020).

I based much of my theory on work in behavioral economics tracking how the gender composition of occupations has changed over time (Levanon, England, and Allison 2009). This work finds that more feminine occupations come with less prestige, power, and status compared to masculine institutions. I did not address whether the prestige of institutions affects the extent to which feminizing effects occur (see, e.g., Crowder-Meyer, Gadarian, and Trounstine 2015). A natural extension of this research is to examine the question: Do people see majority-women political institutions as less important, prestigious, and powerful? Some of the strongest feminizing effects I found were in local institutions, and these are generally considered less prestigious institutions. Tracking changes in perceived prestige of institutions based on levels of WDR is a question I hope to tackle in my future research agenda.

A fundamental question for future scholarship is the extent to which there are spillover effects from WDR to other political institutions. It is not unreasonable to hypothesize that in places with a high level of WDR, such as Nevada or New Mexico, people might think of other political institutions as more feminine. These spillover effects might be constrained to state and local offices where people's impressions of these political institutions might be more malleable relative to national-level political institutions. For example, Moyer (2025) finds that people have more confidence in courts that descriptively represent women, but these effects are constrained to lower courts. It may be that places with high WDR on local courts will also have more confidence in city councils and other local governments. If these spillover effects occur, it means that the engagement effects and improved levels of institutional trust may be broader than the results I presented in Chapter 5 find.

How to Get More Women in Political Office

A key takeaway from this book is that important benefits accrue from having more women in political office. Indeed, there already exists a substantial body of scholarship highlighting how women's representative matters for political efficacy (Stauffer 2021), engagement (Atkeson 2003), and democratic legitimacy (Clayton, O'Brien, and Piscopo 2019), among other important outcomes. Despite these tremendous benefits, Congress is far from being a majority-women institution. This begs the question: How do we achieve gender parity in representation? A vast literature documents barrier facing women in political office including childhood socialization patterns (Bos et al. 2022), fostering nascent ambition (Crowder-Meyer 2020), entering the political pipeline (Maestas et al. 2006), running for office (Dittmar 2015), and then winning election (Pearson and McGhee 2013). In this section, I briefly review this literature on the barriers to women's representation with an eye toward considering how these barriers can be overcome to increase women's descriptive representation.

From a young age, boys and girls are socialized into gendered roles. Young girls are socialized to be modest, not speak out of turn, and to be helpful to others while young boys are socialized to tout their achievements, speak up, and show strength and authority (Liben, Bigler, and Krogh 2001; Bigler et al. 2008; Hilliard and Liben 2019, 2010). In short, boys are socialized to be leaders and girls are not. These socialization patterns become more ingrained in boys and girls as they enter adolescence and young adulthood. Studies show that exposing children to women leaders in grade school curricula can blunt the patterns of gendered socialization (Clayton, O'Brien, and Piscopo 2024; Oxley et al. 2020; Lay et al. 2021). Of course, having more women serving in political leadership roles can also shift socialization patterns. But this type of solution leads to a circular problem: More women in political leadership can lead girls to think about themselves as leaders but there need to be more women in political leadership for this to happen. Certainly, more women running for high-level political offices expose girls to the idea that women can be leaders. For example, during Elizabeth Warren's 2020 primary campaign, she often spoke to young girls whose parents brought them to campaign events, would make a pinkie promise with them so that they would remember that girls run for president, and she even wrote a children's book called *Pinkie Promises*.[3] Exposing girls and boys to the idea that girls and women can be leaders, especially through elementary school curricula, has the potential to increase women's political ambition in the long term (Lay et al. 2021). Not every parent can take their child to meet a presidential candidate. One of the important findings from this book is that the effects of WDR are the strongest at the local level. Engaging with local women leaders at school board or city council meetings can start to erode the idea that politics is for men.

Over the last decade, more women are choosing to run for political office, though not all these women are successful (Shah, Scott, and Juenke 2019). Slowly, the long-standing partisan gap in women's representation is starting to close (Crowder-Meyer and Lauderdale 2014; Crowder-Meyer 2013). Since 2020, Republican women steadily increased their ranks at the federal level. Nevertheless, entering the political pipeline can be a daunting task. A potential candidate needs to be able to tap into local political networks to have a viable candidacy (Carroll and Sanbonmatsu 2013). Candidate-training organizations geared at recruiting women candidates can demystify the process (Schneider, Sweet-Cushman, and Gordon 2023; Kreitzer and Osborn 2019)—though there are still important gaps in these types of programs (Piscopo 2019). For example, these programs do not often address the raced-gendered barriers that Black women or Latinas face in running for office (Brown and Lemi 2021; Cargile 2023), and few organizations focused on recruiting and training women of color exist (Bejarano and Smooth 2022; Sanbonmatsu 2015).

Recruiting more women to run for political office especially at the local level may be the best effective way for the feminizing effects of institutions to be realized. The largest effects in the stereotypic shifts of political institutions coupled with downstream effects were in local political offices. Local offices are also especially important to how women build their political careers (Sweet-Cushman 2020). Women, more so than men, are more likely to start their careers in local offices, and to strategically work their way through the political pipeline to higher levels of office (Carroll and Sanbonmatsu 2013). Recruiting and providing support for women pursuing office at the local level can not only lead people to see institutions as more feminine but can also help to create a pool of qualified women candidates who can run for higher offices in the future.

---

[3] https://www.npr.org/2021/10/30/1050438969/you-can-do-it-elizabeth-warren-makes-a-pinkie-promise-to-girls.

Ample studies show that when women run for political office, they win (Pearson and McGhee 2013; Dolan 2014; Lawless and Fox 2005). Of course, this finding comes with an asterisk as the women who win tend to be more qualified than the men who win (Fulton and Dhima 2021; Fulton 2012; Bauer 2020c, a), and women have to make different types of strategic considerations in their campaign strategies compared to men (Dittmar 2015; Bauer and Santia 2023, 2021). Voters tend to pick candidates, both women and men, who fit into the long-held masculine traits and behaviors associated with political leadership (Bauer 2020a, c). The use of masculine stereotypes in voter decision-making could be a problem of demand, where voters prefer to see candidates who adhere to masculine rather than feminine stereotypes (Bauer 2017; Karpowitz et al. 2024). The problem could also be one of supply where voters are most often exposed to candidates who reinforce masculinity (Bauer and Santia 2023). A larger question underlying this book is how to get voters to see feminine traits and behaviors as valuable qualities for political leaders.

WDR provides normative benefits from the perspective of democratic inclusion. Political systems in the US do not always make overt efforts to increase women's inclusion. Research in comparative politics points to numerous institutional mechanisms that can limit the opportunity for voter biases to negatively affect women's inclusion in politics (Clayton, O'Brien, and Piscopo 2023a). For example, mandatory quotas on party lists in parliamentary systems increase women's representation in elected office (Springer, Klein, and Ludecke 2024; Bush 2011). The extent to which such mechanisms can be used in the American political system is not entirely clear. Some states have undertaken initiatives to change the processes by which voters select candidates at the ballot, and some of these measures increase women's representation. For example, Maine and Alaska recently made switches to ranked choice voting in congressional elections. In Alaska's August 2022 special election to fill the vacancy left by the death of long-time Representative Don Young, Alaska selected a woman to represent the state in the House. Democrat Mary Peltola's election was particularly noteworthy as she became the first woman to represent Alaska in the US House since becoming a state in 1959,[4] and she became the first Native Alaskan to win election to the US Congress, House and Senate combined. Indeed, since achieving statehood, Alaska had yet to elect a native Alaskan to the state's congressional delegation. The use of ranked choice voting contributed to Peltola's victory as Democratic voters coalesced behind her candidacy, and Republicans were

---

[4] Alaska, as of 2025, has only had six US House members since statehood.

split between the choice of Sarah Palin and Nick Begich Jr. Many Republicans who put either Palin or Begich first in the ranked choice voting put Peltola second thereby creating a pathway for her victory.[5] Electoral institutions such as ranked-choice voting can create opportunities for candidates from marginalized groups to find a path to winning elected political office. After Peltola's victory in the special election, she again ran in the 2022 general election, which again used ranked choice voting, and Peltola won a full term in the House.[6]

The barriers to women's descriptive representation do not end when women win elections. Women incumbents tend to have higher-quality challengers (Milyo and Schlosberg 2000; Barnes, Branton, and Cassese 2017; Anzia and Berry 2011). Recent studies suggest that voters demonstrate a lot of gender parity in how they rate the legislative accomplishments of women and men incumbents (Bauer et al. 2025; Hamel and Bauer 2024; Bauer 2024a; McLaughlin 2023). Indeed, research suggests that voters tend to care more about policy alignment rather than the gender of their legislator (Kaslovsky and Rogoswki 2022). Women in elected political office still need to develop a strong profile of accomplishments to prevent re-election challengers and to stay in political office.

Why Does Women's Descriptive Representation Outside Politics Matter?

In this section, I discuss the underlying implications for this research as it relates to women's inclusion in public life more broadly. One way to address this question about why WDR matters is from a theoretical perspective about the normative ideals for a healthy and functioning democracy. Descriptive representation occurs when elected legislative bodies mirror the characteristics of the population represented (Pitkin 1967). Pitkin (1967) argues that descriptive representation matters for other types of representation such as substantive representation and symbolic representation. Electing more women to political institutions accomplishes many of the goals of substantive representation (Swers 2013, 1998). Women in elected political office are more likely to advocate for women, children, families, and other under-represented groups (Dietrich, Hayes, and O'Brien 2019). The extent to which women's

---

[5] When Peltola ran for re-election in 2024, she was defeated.

[6] Alaska appears to have some buyer's remorse over ranked choice voting but narrowly voted to keep the voting scheme in the 2024 election: https://alaskabeacon.com/2024/11/20/alaska-chooses-to-keep-ranked-choice-voting-begich-defeats-peltola-unofficial-results-show/.

descriptive representation can change perceptions of political institutions extends to informal as well as formal institutions. For example, people are less likely to endorse the repression of protestors when the protestors are women (Naunov 2025).

Politics is certainly not the only public institution in the US dominated by men. Indeed, many of the professions considered the most prestigious and the highest paying are dominated by men and associated with masculine stereotypes (Levanon, England, and Allison 2009; Glick, Wilk, and Perreault 1995). People still see professions such as being a lawyer or a medical doctor through the lens of masculinity, even though in some of these fields, women have increased their ranks considerably (ABA 2017). In fact, in higher education, women are approximately 60 percent of all college students.[7] Despite these gains, disparities in women's representation in academia, especially at the ranks of tenured associate and full professors, persist. Gendered dynamics affect women's inclusion into collegiate sports, a stereotypically masculine institution (Druckman and Sharrow 2023).

A long-standing "fun fact," that is not all that fun, is that there are more CEOs of Fortune 500 companies named John than there are women CEOs. Business, especially business management, is an arena long dominated by men and where masculine behaviors are preferred and encouraged from business leaders (Heilman 2012; Heilman and Okimoto 2007; Heilman et al. 2004). Other institutions, such as the US military, have enacted policies to increase women's inclusion, such as lifting the ban on women filling combat roles which then opened opportunities for women to compete for spots on elite special forces teams such as the Navy Seals, but progress toward gender equity is slow. However, many of these initiatives are being rolled back in the second Trump administration in sometimes dramatic ways. One of Trump's first tasks in 2025 was to remove or have his controversial Secretary of Defense Pete Hegseth, remove any woman or person of color in a top leadership role in any branch of the armed forces. Secretary Hegseth has recently, as of June 2025, gone so far as to remove the names of women, people of color, and LGBTQ individuals from military bases and battleships. Stripping a naval ship of Harvey Milk's name, a navy veteran and the first out gay elected official in the US who was assassinated in 1978, send a powerful signal about what the military represents.

The extent to which demographic shifts in majority-men institutions outside of politics can lead to changes in the stereotypes associated with these

---

[7] https://feed.georgetown.edu/access-affordability/women-increasingly-outnumber-men-at-u-s-colleges-but-why/.

institutions is not entirely clear. Work in behavioral economics suggests that these types of shifts do occur as the demographics of an industry change, but these shifts can be very slow and gradual shifts (Levanon, England, and Allison 2009). But as an earlier section of this chapter noted, feminizing effects come with a decline in pay and prestige for women's jobs. Policies that open more opportunities for women to enter and succeed in traditionally masculine institutions can certainly help to speed up the demographic change needed for stereotype change to occur. However, efforts at inclusion are not always met with a positive reception by those currently in the institutions and they do not always achieve more inclusion. Moreover, many policies or practices that restrict, formally or informally, people's entries into masculine institutions and reinforce norms and standards of masculinity are thought to be "gender neutral."

I completed my first draft of this book in December 2023. In the time since completing the first draft of the manuscript and my revisions taking place in the summer of 2025, there has been a remarkable and strong push-back among the public and among elected leaders against efforts around increasing the diversity of people in public institutions. Programs designed to provide opportunities to under-represented and often marginalized groups, often termed DEI Initiatives for Diversity, Equity, and Inclusion, are often characterized as providing special benefits for a group of people at the cost of merit-based selections for jobs, promotions, contracts, and admission into institutions dominated by white-masculinity. In the early days of the second Trump term, Facebook founder and CEO Mark Zuckerberg publicly talked about the need for more "masculine energy"[8] in the tech industry. About 75 percent of those working in the tech industry are men, and the vast majority of these are white men. Indeed, there seems to already be a lot of "masculin energy" in the tech sector. Emerging scholarship finds that ideas about masculinity serve as a legitimizing force for the bad behaviors of men in masculine institutions (Huber, Pruett, and Karim 2022). Even just a small increase in the presence of women in a conventionally masculine institution can produce a backlash effect. This backlash effect to inclusion can limit the presence of not just women in public institutions but the presence of ethnoracial minority groups, individuals from low-income backgrounds, those with disabilities, veterans, or other groups of individuals who do not fit into strict notions of white-masculinity.

---

[8] https://www.forbes.com/sites/gemmaallen/2025/01/19/mark-zuckerbergs-masculine-energy-is-techs-power-play-laid-bare/.

Conclusion

The theory developed and research presented in this manuscript show the subtle ways that women's representation can shift how the public views political institutions. These findings have broad ramifications for how and why women's inclusion in masculine institutions matters. A premise underlying this book is that more women in political office are a public good. Of course, it is important to caution that the goal of increasing WDR in politics is never to purposefully exclude men from political institutions. The goal of WDR is to create more opportunities for historically minoritized groups to have descriptive, symbolic, and substantive representation. Women's descriptive representation can lead the public to see political institutions as more inclusive. The positive benefits of WDR can only come by electing a diverse set of women, and men, to political office.

Chapter 2 Appendix

Table A2.1 Cities and Counties Included in Data

City/County	State	County Board	City/County	State	County Board
Akron	OH	0	Colorado Springs	CO	0
Alameda County, Oakland	CA	1	Columbia	SC	0
Albany	NY	0	Columbus	OH	0
Albany County	NY	1	Concord	NH	0
Albuquerque	NM	0	Concord	CA	0
Allentown	PA	0	Contra Costa County, Concord	CA	1
Anchorage	AK	0	Dallas	TX	0
Atlanta	GA	0	Dane County	WI	1
Augusta	GA	0	Dayton	OH	0
Augusta	ME	0	Denver	CO	0
Austin	TX	0	Des Moines	IA	0
Bakersfield	CA	0	Detroit	MI	0
Baltimore	MD	0	Dover	DE	0
Baton Rouge	LA	0	Dutchess County, Poughkeepsie	NY	1
Billings	MT	0	El Paso	TX	0
Birmingham	AL	0	Erie County	NY	1
Bismarck	ND	0	Fargo	ND	0
Boise	ID	0	Fresno	CA	0
Boston	MA	0	Fresno County	CA	1
Bridgeport	CT	0	Grand Rapids	MI	0
Buffalo	NY	0	Greenville	SC	0
Burlington	VT	0	Harrisburg	PA	0
Cape Coral	FL	0	Hartford	CT	0
Charleston	SC	0	Helena	MT	0
Charleston	WV	0	Henrico County, Richmond	VA	1
Charlotte	NC	0	Honolulu	HI	0
Cheyenne	WY	0	Houston	TX	0
Chicago	IL	0	Indianapolis	IN	0
Cincinnati	OH	0	Jackson	MS	0
Cleveland	OH	0	Jacksonville	FL	0
Juneau	AK	0	Phoenix	AZ	0
Kansas City	MO	0	Pierre	SD	0
Lancaster	PA	0	Pima County, Tucson	AZ	1

continued

Table A2.1 *continued*

City/County	State	County Board	City/County	State	County Board
Las Vegas	NV	0	Pittsburgh	PA	0
Layton	UT	0	Polk County	IA	1
Little Rock	AR	0	Portland	OR	0
Los Angeles	CA	0	Portland	ME	0
Louisville	KY	0	Poughkeepsie	NY	0
Madison	WI	0	Providence	RI	0
Manchester	NH	0	Provo	UT	0
Maricopa County, Phoenix	AZ	1	Raleigh	NC	0
McAllen	TX	0	Reno	NV	0
Memphis	TN	0	Richmond	VA	0
Miami	FL	0	Riverside	CA	0
Milwaukee	WI	0	Riverside County	CA	1
Milwaukee County	WI	1	Riverside County	CA	1
Minneapolis	MN	0	Rochester	NY	0
Mission Viejo	CA	0	Sacramento	CA	0
Monroe County	NY	1	Sacramento County	CA	1
Montpelier	VT	0	Salt Lake City	UT	0
Murrieta	CA	0	San Antonio	TX	0
Nashville	TN	0	San Bernadino	CA	0
New Haven	CT	0	San Bernadino County	CA	1
New Orleans	LA	0	San Diego	CA	0
New York	NY	0	San Diego County	CA	1
Newark	NJ	0	San Francisco	CA	0
Oakland	CA	0	San Francisco County	CA	1
Ogden	UT	0	San Jose	CA	0
Oklahoma City	OK	0	San Juan	PR	0
Omaha	NE	0	Santa Clara County	CA	1
Onondaga County, Syracuse	NY	1	Sarasota	FL	0
Orange County	CA	1	Seattle	WA	0
Orlando	FL	0	Sioux Falls	SD	0
Palm Bay	FL	0	Spokane	WA	0
Philadelphia	PA	0	Springfield	MA	0
St. Louis	MO	0			
St. Paul	MN	0			
Stamford	CT	0			
Suffolk County	NY	1			
Syracuse	NY	0			
Tampa	FL	0			
Toledo	OH	0			
Tucson	AZ	0			
Tulsa	OK	0			
Virginia Beach	VA	0			
Virginia Beach County	VA	1			
Washington	DC	0			

City/County	State	County Board	City/County	State	County Board
Wichita	KS	0			
Wilmington	DE	0			
Winston-Salem	NC	0			
Worcester	MA	0			
Youngstown	OH	0			

Table A2.2 Sample Characteristics, 2018 CCES Stereotype Test

	Empirical Test 1 Masculine Stereotype Test
Sample	CCES, 2018
% Female	56%
Age (Mean)	48 years old
% White	76%
College Degree	47.6%
Live in South	39%
% Liberal	29%

Table A2.3 Feminine and Masculine Levels of Office, by Political Party

Democratic Participants			
Political Institution	% Very or Somewhat Feminine	% Very or Somewhat Masculine	p-value
City Council	38.83%	61.16%	0.001
State Legislature	30.93%	69.07%	0.001
Senate	30.03%	69.97%	0.001
Governor	25.00%	75.00%	0.001
President	22.87%	77.13%	0.001

Republican Participants			
Political Institution	% Very or Somewhat Feminine	% Very or Somewhat Masculine	p-value
City Council	34.12%	65.88%	0.001
State Legislature	19.52%	80.48%	0.001
Senate	11.00%	88.99%	0.001
Governor	10.95%	89.04%	0.001
President	2.40%	97.63%	0.001

continued

Table A2.3 *continued*

Democratic Participants			
Political Institution	**% Very or Somewhat Feminine**	**% Very or Somewhat Masculine**	**p-value**
% Very or Somewhat Masculine across Political Party			
	Democrats	**Republicans**	**p-value**
City Council	61.16%	65.88%	0.2813
State Legislature	69.07	80.48%	0.041
Senate	69.97%	88.99%	0.001
Governor	75.00%	89.04%	0.001
President	77.13%	97.63%	0.001

Note: All p-values rely on two-tailed t-tests.

Table A2.4 Feminine and Masculine Levels of Office, by Participant Gender

Female Participants			
Political Institution	**% Very or Somewhat Feminine**	**% Very or Somewhat Masculine**	**p-value**
City Council	32.22%	67.78%	0.001
State Legislature	24.33%	75.67%	0.001
Senate	22.27%	77.72%	0.001
Governor	17.72%	82.77%	0.001
President	13.05%	86.95%	0.001

Male Participants			
Political Institution	**% Very or Somewhat Feminine**	**% Very or Somewhat Masculine**	**p-value**
City Council	42.20%	57.80%	0.0036
State Legislature	26.30%	73.69%	0.001
Senate	22.48%	77.52%	0.001
Governor	19.60%	80.40%	0.001
President	13.20%	86.78%	0.001

% Very or Somewhat Masculine across Participant Gender			
	Women	**Men**	**p-value**
City Council	67.78%	57.80%	0.0037
State Legislature	75.67%	73.69%	0.5266

	Female Participants		
Political Institution	**% Very or Somewhat Feminine**	**% Very or Somewhat Masculine**	**p-value**
Senate	77.72%	77.52%	0.9448
Governor	82.77%	80.40%	0.3918
President	86.95%	86.78%	0.9454

Note: All p-values rely on two-tailed t-tests.

Table A2.5 % Rating Each Office as Masculine, Moving up the Political Ladder

Office	% Masculine	p-value
City Council	63.34%	0.001
State Legislature	74.47%	
State Legislature	74.47%	0.0359
Senate	77.75%	
Senate	77.75%	0.0026
Governor	81.79%	
Governor	81.79%	0.001
President	86.78%	

Chapter 3 Appendix

Table A3.1 Sample Characteristics

Sample	CCES, 2021
% Female	57%
Age (Mean)	51 years old
% White	67%
College Degree	45.8%
Live in South	38%
% Liberal	32%

Table A3.2 Balance Checks

	Assignment to Conditions
Majority-Women State Legislature	
Nonbinary Gender Identity	0.846
	(1.250)
Household Income	0.264
	(0.182)
Marital Status	0.032
	(0.070)
Participant Racial/Ethnic Minority	0.679**
	(0.281)
Participant Education Level	−0.187
	(0.195)
Employed	−0.312
	(0.259)
Personality Attributes Questionnaire	0.189
	(0.601)
Women Participants	0.034
	(0.272)
Democratic Participant	−0.067
	(0.297)
Republican Participant	0.426
	(0.335)

	Assignment to Conditions
Constant	−0.578
	(0.677)
Majority-Men State Legislatures	
Nonbinary Gender Identity	−0.555
	(1.471)
Household Income	−0.866***
	(0.175)
Marital Status	0.134*
	(0.071)
Participant Racial/Ethnic Minority	0.722**
	(0.290)
Participant Education Level	−0.482***
	(0.186)
Employed	−0.076
	(0.263)
Personality Attributes Questionnaire	0.223
	(0.611)
Women Participants	0.242
	(0.274)
Democratic Participant	0.365
	(0.296)
Republican Participant	−0.167
	(0.363)
Constant	2.828***
	(0.611)
Majority-Women City Council (base conditions)	
Majority-Men City Council	
Nonbinary Gender Identity	0.719
	(1.193)
Household Income	−0.816***
	(0.175)
Marital Status	0.120*
	(0.072)
Participant Racial/Ethnic Minority	0.343
	(0.299)
Participant Education Level	−0.580***
	(0.185)
Employed	−0.071
	(0.264)

continued

Table A3.2 *continued*

	Assignment to Conditions
Personality Attributes Questionnaire	0.029
	(0.607)
Women Participants	−0.137
	(0.279)
Democratic Participant	0.206
	(0.302)
Republican Participant	0.129
	(0.346)
Constant	3.256***
	(0.609)
Woman Governor	
Nonbinary Gender Identity	1.070
	(1.161)
Household Income	−0.257
	(0.177)
Marital Status	0.033
	(0.071)
Participant Racial/Ethnic Minority	0.823***
	(0.283)
Participant Education Level	−0.317*
	(0.192)
Employed	−0.598**
	(0.265)
Personality Attributes Questionnaire	0.871
	(0.613)
Women Participants	0.034
	(0.275)
Democratic Participant	0.125
	(0.289)
Republican Participant	−0.349
	(0.368)
Constant	1.529**
	(0.634)
Man Governor	
Nonbinary Gender Identity	−0.488
	(1.474)
Household Income	−0.544***
	(0.174)
Marital Status	0.111
	(0.071)

	Assignment to Conditions
Participant Racial/Ethnic Minority	0.197
	(0.298)
Participant Education Level	−0.576***
	(0.186)
Employed	0.146
	(0.261)
Personality Attributes Questionnaire	−1.143*
	(0.597)
Women Participants	0.152
	(0.273)
Democratic Participant	0.069
	(0.296)
Republican Participant	−0.099
	(0.348)
Constant	2.444***
	(0.614)
Woman Mayor	
Nonbinary Gender Identity	−0.233
	(1.438)
Household Income	−0.117
	(0.174)
Marital Status	0.149**
	(0.068)
Participant Racial/Ethnic Minority	0.222
	(0.284)
Participant Education Level	−0.294
	(0.190)
Employed	−0.089
	(0.254)
Personality Attributes Questionnaire	0.391
	(0.593)
Women Participants	0.161
	(0.265)
Democratic Participant	0.156
	(0.286)
Republican Participant	−0.043
	(0.345)
Constant	0.654
	(0.636)

continued

Table A3.2 *continued*

	Assignment to Conditions
Man Mayor	
Nonbinary Gender Identity	−12.669
	(507.756)
Household Income	−0.488***
	(0.172)
Marital Status	0.096
	(0.070)
Participant Racial/Ethnic Minority	0.302
	(0.296)
Participant Education Level	−0.526***
	(0.185)
Employed	0.056
	(0.260)
Personality Attributes Questionnaire	−0.247
	(0.603)
Women Participants	0.323
	(0.270)
Democratic Participant	0.149
	(0.302)
Republican Participant	0.300
	(0.335)
Constant	2.142***
	(0.617)
Observations	985
Pseudo R^2	0.056

Standard errors in parentheses
* $p<0.10$, ** $p<0.05$, *** $p<0.01$

Trait Measures: Next, think about the characteristics associated with the newly elected [state legislature/city councilor/governor/mayor] you read about earlier. To what extent does each of the traits below describe the [state legislature/city councilor/governor/mayor]?

> Traits: assertive, tough, aggressive, warm, empathetic, caring
> Response options: Very well, somewhat well, somewhat unwell, very unwell

Issue Measures: Based on the information you read, which issues do you think the new [state legislature/city councilor/governor/mayor] will prioritize.

> Issues: infrastructure, economic development, education, crime, healthcare, race relations, income inequality, social welfare issues
> Response Options: very high priority, somewhat high priority, somewhat low priority, very low priority

Table A3.3 Full Means and Standard Deviations, Feminine and Masculine Stereotypes, Mean (SD)

City Councils			
	Majority Women	**Majority Men**	**p-value**
Feminine Stereotypes	0.5923 (0.2241)	0.4151 (0.2285)	0.0001
Masculine Stereotypes	0.5776 (0.1822)	0.5717 (0.2027)	0.8083
p-value	0.3809	0.0001	

State Legislature			
	Majority Women	**Majority Men**	**p-value**
Feminine Stereotypes	0.5692 (0.2538)	0.3857 (0.2104)	0.0001
Masculine Stereotypes	0.5803 (0.2178)	0.5781 (0.2002)	0.9343
p-value	0.5390	0.0001	

Mayors			
	Woman	**Man**	**p-value**
Feminine Stereotypes	0.5802469 (0.2347108)	0.4872495 (0.2723329)	0.0043
Masculine Stereotypes	0.5582011 (0.2276945)	0.4817851 (0.2569752)	0.0138
p-value	0.2374	0.7572	

Governors			
	Woman	**Man**	**p-value**
Feminine Stereotypes	0.5630 (0.2592)	0.4981 (0.2389)	0.0451
Masculine Stereotypes	0.5130 (0.2516)	0.4991 (0.1975)	0.6348
p-value	0.0035	1.0000	

Note: All t-tests are two-tailed.

Table A3.4 Additional Comparisons for Traits across Institutional Types, Mean (SD)

Comparisons between Legislative Institutions				
Stereotypes	Gender Composition	City Council	State Legislature	p-value
Feminine	Majority-Women	0.5692 (0.2538)	0.5923 (.2241)	0.4440
Feminine	Majority-Men	0.4150 (0.2285)	0.3857 (0.2104)	0.2991
Masculine	Majority-Women	0.5803 (0.2178)	0.5776 (0.1822)	0.9143
Masculine	Majority-Men	0.5717 (0.2027)	0.5781 (0.2002)	0.8014

Comparisons between Executive Institutions				
		Mayor	Governor	p-value
Feminine	Majority-Women	0.5802 (0.2347)	0.5630 (0.2592)	0.5837
Feminine	Majority-Men	0.4872 (0.2723)	0.4981 (0.2389)	0.7411
Masculine	Majority-Women	0.5582 (0.2277)	0.5130 (0.2516)	0.1402
Masculine	Majority-Men	0.4818 (0.2570)	0.4991 (0.1975)	0.5583

Comparisons between Legislative and Executive Institutions				
Stereotypes	Gender Composition	Legislative	Executive	p-value
Feminine	Majority-Women	0.5811 (0.2387)	0.5718 (0.2466)	0.6687
Feminine	Majority-Men	0.4004 (0.2200)	0.4927 (0.2558)	0.0001
Masculine	Majority-Women	0.5789 (0.2000)	0.5361 (0.2403)	0.0320
Masculine	Majority-Men	0.5749 (0.2011)	0.4904 (0.2291)	0.0001

Comparisons between Local and State Institutions				
Stereotypes	Gender Composition	Local	State	p-value
Feminine	Majority-Women	0.5864 (0.2290)	0.5661 (0.2559)	0.3519
Feminine	Majority-Men	0.4513 (0.2535)	0.4417 (0.2315)	0.6630

Masculine	Majority-Women	0.5679 (0.2060)	0.5468 (0.2371)	0.2914
Masculine	Majority-Men	0.5390947 (0.2023566)	0.5271003 (0.2350992)	0.5459

Table A3.5 Differences in Feminine Stereotyping across Participant Gender

Level of Office	Gender Composition	Women	Men	p-value
City Council	Majority-Women	0.6213 (0.2171)	0.5514 (0.2294)	0.0796
City Council	Majority-Men	0.4021909 (0.2393157)	0.4333 (0.2132)	0.4627
State Legislature	Majority-Women	0.5997 (0.2578)	0.5238 (0.2432)	0.1057
State Legislature	Majority-Men	0.3616 (0.1945)	0.4119 (0.2251)	0.1898
Mayor	Majority-Women	0.5926 (0.2230)	0.5653 (0.2415)	0.5181
Mayor	Majority-Men	0.4870 (0.2850)	0.4875 (0.2618)	0.9933
Governor	Majority-Women	0.5990 (0.2174)	0.5142 (0.3022)	0.0761
Governor	Majority-Men	0.4876 (0.2384)	0.5115 (0.2410)	0.5873

Table A3.6 Gender Differences in Masculine Stereotyping across Participant Gender

Level of Office	Gender Composition	Women	Men	p-value
City Council	Majority-Women	0.5871 (0.1898)	0.5641 (0.1716)	0.4879
City Council	Majority-Men	0.5991 (0.2079)	0.5311 (0.1895)	0.0667
State Legislature	Majority-Women	0.619482 (0.2167)	0.5208 (0.2078)	0.0142
State Legislature	Majority-Men	0.5897 (0.1914)	0.5651 (0.2105)	0.4983
Mayor	Majority-Women	0.5813 (0.2157)	0.5302 (0.2403)	0.2112

continued

Table A3.6 *continued*

Level of Office	Gender Composition	Women	Men	p-value
Mayor	Majority-Men	0.4667 (0.2796)	0. 4964 (0.2344)	0.5249
Governor	Majority-Women	0.531401 (0.2261656)	0.4880 (0.2829)	0.3527
Governor	Majority-Men	0.5041 (0.2004)	0.4927 (0.1955)	0.7532

Table A3.7 Gender Differences in Feminine Stereotyping across Participant Party

Level of Office	Gender Composition	Democrats	Republicans and Independents	p-value
City Council	Majority-Women	0.6667 (0.2152)	0.5473 (0.2186)	0.0029
City Council	Majority-Men	0.3901 (0.2304)	0.4298 (0.2276)	0.3578
State Legislature	Majority-Women	0.6589 (0.2280)	0.5204 (0.2551)	0.0036
State Legislature	Majority-Men	0.3816 (0.2003)	0.3889 (0.2193)	0.8500
Mayor	Majority-Women	0.6239 (0.2202)	0.5495 (0.2411)	0.0798
Mayor	Majority-Men	0.5685 (0.2614)	0.4430 (0.2695)	0.0145
Governor	Majority-Women	0.6440 (0.2313)	0.5070 (0.2641)	0.0040
Governor	Majority-Men	0.4765 (0.2435)	0.5111 (0.2368)	0.4451

Table A3.8 Gender Differences in Masculine Stereotyping across Participant Party

Level of Office	Gender Composition	Democrats	Republicans and Independents	p-value
City Council	Majority-Women	0.6009 (0.1602)	0.5628 (0.1944)	0.2536
City Council	Majority-Men	0.5725 (0.1844)	0.5712 (0.2139)	0.9739
State Legislature	Majority-Women	0.6376 (0.1610)	0.5499 (0.2380)	0.0345

Level of Office	Gender Composition	Democrats	Republicans and Independents	p-value
State Legislature	Majority-Men	0.5843 (0.1646)	0.5733 (0.2252)	0.7617
Mayor	Majority-Women	0.5422 (0.1978)	0.4921 (0.2835)	0.2836
Mayor	Majority-Men	0.5051 (0.2082)	0.4956 (0.1924)	0.8021
Governor	Majority-Women	0.5769 (0.2134)	0.5450 (0.2378)	0.4413
Governor	Majority-Men	0.5297 (0.2610)	0.4557 (0.2526)	0.1291

Table A3.9 Full Means and Standard Deviations, Feminine and Masculine Issues

City Councils			
	Majority-Women	**Majority-Men**	**p-value**
Feminine Issues	0.7757 (0.1718)	0.5873 (0.2033)	0.0001
Masculine Issues	0.7294 (0.1720)	0.7183 (0.1567)	0.5835
p-value	0.0019	0.0001	

State Legislature			
	Majority-Women	**Majority-Men**	**p-value**
Feminine Issues	0.7843 (0.1447)	0.6 (0.1923)	0.0001
Masculine Issues	0.7295 (0.1752)	0.7033 (0.1620)	0.2238
p-value	0.0003	0.0001	

Mayors			
	Majority-Women	**Majority-Men**	**p-value**
Feminine Issues	0.7431 (0.1729)	0.6382 (0.1786)	0.0001
Masculine Issues	0.7290 (0.1738)	0.6714 (0.1837)	0.0115
p-value	0.1412	0.0107	

continued

Table A3.9 *continued*

Governors		
	Woman	**Man**	**p-value**
Feminine Issues	0.7167 (0.2066)	0.6343 (0.1859)	0.0012
Masculine Issues	0.6981 (0.2160)	0.6563 (0.1696)	0.0952
p-value	0.1646	0.0807	

Table A3.10 Additional Issue Comparisons across Institutional Types, Mean (SD)

Comparisons between Legislative Institutions

Issues	Gender Composition	City Council	State Legislature	p-value
Feminine	Majority-Women	0.7757 (0.1718)	0.7843 (0.1447)	0.6642
Feminine	Majority-Men	0.5873 (0.2033)	0.6000 (0.1923)	0.6117
Masculine	Majority-Women	0.7295 (0.1720)	0.7295 (0.1752)	0.9989
Masculine	Majority-Men	0.7183 (0.1567)	0.7033 (0.1620)	0.4590

Comparisons between Executive Institutions

Issues	Gender Composition	Mayor	Governor	p-value
Feminine	Majority-Women	0.74311 (0.1729)	0.7167 (0.2066)	0.2744
Feminine	Majority-Men	0.6382 (0.1786)	0.6343 (0.1859)	0.8669
Masculine	Majority-Women	0.7290 (0.1738)	0.6981 (0.2160)	0.2136
Masculine	Majority-Men	0.6714 (0.1836)	0.6563 (0.1696)	0.5062

Comparisons between Legislative and Executive Institutions

Gender Composition	Gender Composition	Legislative	Executive	p-value
Feminine	Majority-Women	0.7798 (0.1592)	0.7302 (0.1902)	0.0016
Feminine	Majority-Men	0.5936 (0.1976)	0.6363 (0.1819)	0.0129

| Masculine | Majority-Women | 0.7294
(0.1732) | 0.7139
(0.1958) | 0.3420 |
| Masculine | Majority-Men | 0.7108
(0.1592) | 0.6639
(0.1766) | 0.0020 |

Comparisons between Local and State Institutions				
Gender Composition	**Gender Composition**	**Local**	**State**	**p-value**
Feminine	Majority-Women	0.7598 (0.1728)	0.7505 (0.1812)	0.5549
Feminine	Majority-Men	0.6124 (0.1928)	0.6169 (0.1896)	0.7972
Masculine	Majority-Women	0.7292 (0.1726)	0.7138 (0.1969)	0.3480
Masculine	Majority-Men	0.6951 (0.1718)	0.6802 (0.1671)	0.3287

Table A3.11 Full Means and Standard Deviations, Feminine and Masculine Issues, by Participant Party

City Councils, Feminine Issues			
	Majority Women	**Majority Men**	**p-value**
Democratic Participant	0.8395 (0.0215)	0.5824 (0.2306)	0.0001
Republican Participant	0.7364 (0.1713)	0.5902 (0.1866	0.0001
p-value	0.0006	0.8371	

State Legislature, Feminine Issues			
	Majority-Women	**Majority-Men**	**p-value**
Democratic Participant	0.8619 (0.119)	0.6011 (0.205)	0.001
Republican Participant	0.742 (0.140)	0.599 (0.022)	0.001
p-value	0.001	0.9536	

Mayors, Feminine Issues			
	Woman	**Man**	**p-value**
Democratic Participant	0.7133 (0.1713)	0.6948 (0.1693)	0.0100

continued

Table A3.11 *continued*

Republican Participant	0.7861 (0.1676)	0.6078 (0.1770)	0.002
p-value	0.0192	0.0095	

Governors, Feminine Issues			
	Woman	**Man**	**p-value**
Democratic Participant	0.7825 (0.1750)	0.6208 (0.1956)	0.0001
Republican Participant	0.6710 (0.2155)	0.6423 (0.1807)	0.3799
p-value	0.0030	0.5420	

City Councils, Masculine Issues			
	Majority-Women	**Majority-Men**	**p-value**
Democratic Participant	0.7925 (0.1206)	0.7287 (0.1438)	0.0190
Republican Participant	0.6908 (0.1875)	0.7120 (0.1644)	0.4449
p-value	0.0007	0.5649	

State Legislature, Masculine Issues			
	Majority-Women	**Majority-Men**	**p-value**
Democratic Participant	0.7965 (0.1303)	0.7242 (0.1562)	0.0165
Republican Participant	0.6930 (0.1861)	0.6869 (0.1657)	0.8330
p-value	0.0016	0.2022	

Mayors, Masculine Issues			
	Woman	**Man**	**p-value**
Democratic Participant	0.7725 (0.1694)	0.7306 (0.1442)	0.2087
Republican Participant	0.6989 (0.1693)	0.6396 (0.1952)	0.0457
p-value	0.0184	0.0082	

Governors, Masculine Issues			
	Woman	**Man**	**p-value**
Democratic Participant	0.78 (0.1522)	0.6611 (0.1623)	0.004
Republican Participant	0.6412 (0.1522)	0.6535 (0.1748)	0.7178
p-value	0.0004	0.8128	

Table A3.12 Full Means and Standard Deviations, Feminine and Masculine Issues, by Participant Gender

City Councils, Feminine Issues			
	Majority-Women	**Majority-Men**	**p-value**
Woman Participant	0.7986 (0.1656)	0.6037 (0.1876)	0.0001
Man Participant	0.7466 (0.1778)	0.5775 (0.2123)	0.0001
p-value	0.1024	0.4865	

State Legislature, Feminine Issues			
	Majority-Women	**Majority-Men**	**p-value**
Woman Participant	0.7793 (0.1289)	0.5954 (0.1658)	0.0001
Man Participant	0.7875 (0.1545)	0.6039 (0.2131)	0.0001
p-value	0.7607	0.8075	

Mayors, Feminine Issues			
	Woman	**Man**	**p-value**
Woman Participant	0.7288 (0.1587)	0.6280 (0.1844)	0.0020
Man Participant	0.7544 (0.1837)	0.6486 (0.1734)	0.0009
p-value	0.4095	0.5259	

Governors, Feminine Issues			
	Woman	**Man**	**p-value**
Woman Participant	0.6676 (0.2463)	0.6406 (0.1949)	0.5458
Man Participant	0.7475 (0.1721)	0.6295 (0.1801)	0.0001
p-value	0.0370	0.7466	

City Councils, Masculine Issues			
	Majority-Women	**Majority-Men**	**p-value**
Woman Participant	0.6697 (0.1674)	0.7376 (0.1474)	0.0335
Man Participant	0.7711 (0.1637)	0.7068 (0.1617)	0.0140
p-value	0.0006	0.2870	

continued

Table A3.12 *continued*

State Legislature, Masculine Issues			
	Majority-Women	**Majority-Men**	**p-value**
Woman Participant	0.7145 (0.1820)	0.7076 (0.1444)	0.8289
Man Participant	0.7389 (0.1713)	0.6998 (0.1764)	0.1808
p-value	0.4572	0.7886	

Mayors, Masculine Issues			
	Woman	**Man**	**p-value**
Woman Participant	0.7307 (0.1798)	0.6667 (0.1854)	0.0600
Man Participant	0.7277 (0.1702)	0.6762 (0.1833)	0.0969
p-value	0.9246	0.7741	

Governors, Masculine Issues			
	Woman	**Man**	**p-value**
Woman Participant	0.7433 (0.1643)	0.6554 (0.1723)	0.5090
Man Participant	0.6259 (0.2657)	0.6570 (0.1688)	0.0023
p-value	0.0031	0.9604	

Experimental Test for Proportion of Women/Men in City Councils

The city council pre-test experiment includes four conditions: an all-women city council, an all-men city council, a female-majority city council, and a male-majority city council (see Table A3.13). Participants received a newspaper vignette that described the results of recent elections. Table A3.13 includes the text for each condition. I include conditions where one gender completely dominates the city council and where one gender just has a majority to test whether the numbers of women, or men, on city councils matter for shifting the stereotypes associated with that chamber. This aspect of the experiment allows me to test whether the ratio of women's representation matters in shifting gendered impressions.

The City Council Experiment sample comes from Amazon's Mechanical Turk. MTurk is an online recruitment platform where participants complete small tasks for a nominal fee.

The results produced by MTurk samples frequently mirror those conducted with nationally representative samples (Berinsky, Huber, and Lenz 2012; Mullinix et al. 2015). MTurk samples are also particularly useful for research on perceptions of gender and politics (Hannagan, Schneider, and Greenlee 2012) because these samples are less likely to misreport preferences for female candidates due to social desirability pressures (Krupnikov, Piston, and Bauer 2016).

I measure the stereotypic associations individuals have of political institutions using an expanded version of the stereotype measure from the main tests in Chapter 3. The feminine and masculine measures come from existing research on the extent to which gender stereotypes affect evaluations of female and male candidates (Huddy and Terkildsen 1993b; Bauer 2017). I use feminine and masculine traits to test the way individuals stereotype institutions because the traits associated with organizations and occupations are, according to social psychology research, one of the key ways that stereotypic impressions are formed (Shinar 1975; Glick, Wilk, and Perreault 1995). The feminine traits included: gentle, sensitive, feminine, emotional, talkative, and cautious; the masculine traits included: assertive, coarse, tough, aggressive, stern, masculine, active, rational, and self-confident. The final feminine and masculine measures average the trait attributions, and I recoded it to range from 0–1 and higher values indicate a stronger association with a specific stereotype.

The results in Table A3.15 show that there are no differences in the stereotyping patterns between the majority-women and the all-women conditions and the majority-men and all-men conditions. The main findings replicate the results from the study in Chapter 3. Majority-women institutions are rated higher on feminine stereotypes relative to majority-men institutions but majority-women institutions do not lose on masculine traits.

Table A3.13 Experimental Conditions, N = 394

Condition	N	Treatment
All-women	101	When the new city council takes over next year, the majority of its members will be women. Indeed, women will hold 12 out of 12 city council seats. Residents are looking forward to seeing what new policies the majority-female city council puts into place next year.
All-men	99	When the new city council takes over next year, none of its members will be women. Indeed, women will hold 0 out of 12 city council seats. Residents are looking forward to seeing what new policies the majority-male city council puts into place next year.
Majority-women	101	When the new city council takes over next year, the majority of its members will be women. Indeed, women will hold 8 out of 12 city council seats. Residents are looking forward to seeing what new policies the majority-female city council puts into place next year.
Majority-men	93	When the new city council takes over next year, the majority of its members will be men. Indeed, men will hold 8 out of 12 city council seats. Residents are looking forward to seeing what new policies the majority-male city council puts into place next year.

Table A3.14 City Council Pre-test, Balance Checks

	Assignment to Conditions
All-Women City Council (Base Condition)	
All-Men City Council	
Political Interest	0.183
	(0.125)
Age	0.003
	(0.011)
Respondent Gender	−0.010
	(0.291)
Region	0.044
	(0.139)
Race/Ethnicity	−0.094
	(0.115)
Education	0.094
	(0.119)
Partisanship	−0.021
	(0.106)
Ideology	0.035
	(0.158)
Constant	−0.910
	(1.292)
Majority-Women City Council	
Political Interest	−0.045
	(0.129)
Age	−0.001
	(0.011)
Respondent Gender	−0.031
	(0.288)
Region	0.063
	(0.138)
Race/Ethnicity	−0.064
	(0.112)
Education	0.058
	(0.120)
Partisanship	0.114
	(0.106)
Ideology	0.118
	(0.158)

	Assignment to Conditions
Constant	−1.006 (1.313)
Majority-Men City Council	
Political Interest	−0.089 (0.135)
Age	0.015 (0.011)
Respondent Gender	−0.392 (0.300)
Region	0.107 (0.144)
Race/Ethnicity	0.005 (0.117)
Education	0.006 (0.124)
Partisanship	0.004 (0.105)
Ideology	−0.138 (0.160)
Constant	0.189 (1.316)
Observations	387
Pseudo R^2	0.015

Table A3.15 Full Means and Standard Deviations, Feminine and Masculine Stereotypes, City Council Experiment, Pre-Test

Political Institution	Feminine	Masculine	p-value
Majority-Female	0.644 (0.195)	0.545 (0.171)	0.001
Majority-Male	0.384 (0.197)	0.608 (0.163)	0.001
p-value	0.001	0.0090	
All-Female	0.605 (0.221)	0.507 (0.182)	0.001
All-Male	0.346 (0.238)	0.648 (0.179)	0.001

continued

Table A3.15 *continued*

Political Institution	Feminine	Masculine	p-value
p-value	0.001	0.001	
Majority-Female	0.644 (0.195)	0.545 (0.171)	0.001
All-Female	0.605 (0.221)	0.507 (0.182)	0.001
p-value	0.1781	0.0090	
Majority-Male	0.384 (0.197)	0.608 (0.163)	0.001
All-Male	0.346 (0.238)	0.648 (0.179)	0.001
p-value	0.2361	0.1094	

All t-tests are two-tailed.

Chapter 4 Appendix

Table A4.1 Sample Characteristics

	Women of Color City Council	Diversified City Council Experiment	Women of Color Executive Office
Sample	MTurk	Prolific	Prolific
% Female	61.33%	46.10%	50.25%
Age (Mean)	38.17 years (SD = 14.45 years)	34.55 years (11.35 years)	Modal Category: 33.99% 25–34 years old
% Ethnorace Minority	27.73%	93.53% 37.97% Black 29.15% AAPI 15.59% Latino 9.83% Other minority	37.88%
College Degree	60.16%	59.66%	77.5%
% Democrat	58.20%	60.34%	46.31%

Table A4.2 Diversified City Council Experiment, Balance Checks

	Assignment to Condition
Woman Participant	0.151 (0.278)
Participant Age	0.002 (0.010)
Participant Income	0.002 (0.067)
Participant Education	−0.070 (0.119)
Racial/Ethnicity Minority Group	0.290 (0.299)
Marital Status	−0.094 (0.333)
Employment Status	−0.221 (0.293)
Democrat	0.384 (0.317)

continued

Table A4.2 *continued*

	Assignment to Condition
Republican	0.463
	(0.407)
Constant	0.056
	(0.655)
Observations	254
Pseudo R^2	0.012

Standard errors in parentheses
* $p < 0.10$, ** $p < 0.05$, *** $p < 0.01$

Table A4.3 WOC City Council, Study Conditions, and N = 256

Conditions	Non-White Participants	White-Participants	N
Majority-Women	30	89	119
Majority-Women of Color	41	96	137

WOC City Council Experimental Design and Results

Majority-Women of Color Condition

New City Council Elected

When the new city council takes over next year, the majority of its members will be women of color. Indeed, women of color will hold over 50 percent of seats in the city council. Residents are looking forward to seeing what new policies the majority-women of color city council puts into place next year.

Majority-Women Conditions

New City Council Elected

A new city council takes over next year. Residents are looking forward to seeing the new policies the city council puts into place next year.

Trait Measures

Sometimes we think about people as having certain traits, and sometimes we also think about objects and institutions as having traits too. Think about the city council you read about earlier, how well do you think the traits below describe the city council as an institution?

> **Masculine Traits:** Assertive, Coarse, Tough, Aggressive, Stern, Masculine, Rational, Self-Confident
> **Feminine Traits:** Warm, Gentle, Feminine, Sensitive, Talkative, Cautious, Empathetic, Caring
> **Response Options:** Very well, Somewhat well, A little bit, Not Well at All

Table A4.4 WOC City Council Experiment, Stereotypic Trait Comparisons

Conditions	Feminine Traits	Masculine Traits	p-value
Majority-Women of Color	0.6392 (0.1532)	0.4051 (0.1130)	0.0001
Majority-Women	0.4598 (0.1841)	0.4013 (0.1347)	0.0001
p-value	0.0001	0.8039	

WOC City Council Experiment, Stereotypic Trait Comparisons

Majority-Women of Color Condition			
	Feminine Traits	Masculine Traits	p-value
Non-White Participants	0.6806 (0.1211)	0.3933 (0.1314)	0.0001
White Participants	0.6215 (0.1624)	0.4102 (0.1044)	0.0001
p-value	0.0383	0.4526	

Majority-Women Condition			
	Feminine Traits	Masculine Traits	p-value
Non-White Participants	0.4889 (0.1635)	0.4458 (0.1332)	0.2039
White Participants	0.4500 (0.1903)	0.3862 (0.1326)	0.0001
p-value	0.3186	0.0356	

Diversified City Council Experimental Design and Results

City Council Election Results

When the new city council takes over next year, the majority of its members will be women of color. Indeed, women of color will hold over 50 percent of seats in the city council. Residents are looking forward to seeing what new policies the majority-women of color city council puts into place next year.

City Council Election Results

When the new city council takes over next year, the majority of its members will be women. Indeed, women will hold over 50 percent of seats in the city council. Residents are looking forward to seeing what new policies the majority-women city council puts into place next year.

City Council Election Results

When the new city council takes over next year, the majority of its members will be people of color. Indeed, people of color will hold over 50 percent of seats in the city council. Residents are looking forward to seeing what new policies the majority-people of color city council puts into place next year.

Trait Measures

Sometimes we think about people as having certain traits, and sometimes we also think about objects and institutions as having traits too. Think about the city council you read about earlier, how well do you think the traits below describe the city council as an institution?

Masculine Traits: Assertive, Coarse, Tough, Aggressive, Stern, Masculine, Rational, Self-Confident

Feminine Traits: Warm, Gentle, Feminine, Sensitive, Talkative, Cautious, Empathetic, Caring

Response Options: Very well, Somewhat well, A little bit, Not Well at All

Issue Priorities

Which types of issues do you think the newly elected city council you read about earlier will prioritize in the upcoming year?

Education, Minimum wage, Childcare, Infrastructure, Criminal justice reform, Healthcare, Sanitation, Housing, Immigration

Very high priority, medium priority, low priority

Group Representation

Please rate how well you think the city council will represent the interests of various groups below.

Black Americans, Latinos, Black women, Latinas, People of color, Asian American or Pacific Islander women, Working class voters, the Wealthy

Very well, Somewhat well, Somewhat unwell, Very unwell

Table A4.5 Diversified City Council, Study Conditions, and N = 295

Conditions	N
Majority-Women	100
Majority-Women of Color	101
People of Color	94

Table A4.6 Diversified City Council Experiment, Balance Checks

	Assignment to Conditions
Majority Women Condition	
Woman Participant	−0.010
	(0.291)
Participant Age	−0.007
	(0.012)
Participant Education	0.312
	(0.280)
Racial/Ethnic Minority Group	−0.076
	(0.099)
Democrat	0.197
	(0.392)
Republican	0.055
	(0.399)
Constant	−0.041
	(0.753)
People of Color Condition	
Woman Participant	0.287
	(0.301)
Participant Age	−0.013
	(0.013)
Participant Education	0.756***
	(0.273)
Racial/Ethnic Minority Group	−0.119
	(0.103)
Democrat	0.431
	(0.427)
Republican	0.345
	(0.430)
Constant	−0.775
	(0.795)
Women of Color Condition (base category)	
Observations	295
Pseudo R^2	0.020

Standard errors in parentheses
*p < 0.10, **p < 0.05, ***p < 0.01

Table A4.7 Diversified CC Experiment, Stereotypic Trait Comparisons

Conditions	Feminine Traits	Masculine Traits	p-value
Majority-Women	0.5871 (0.2056)	0.4980 (0.1787)	0.0001
Majority-Women of Color	0.6002 (0.1891)	0.5041 (0.1820)	0.0001
People of Color	0.5270 (0.2048)	0.5328 (0.2048)	0.7762

Majority-WOC vs. Majority-Women Comparisons

Conditions	Feminine Traits	Masculine Traits
Majority-Women	0.5871 (0.2056)	0.4980 (0.1787)
Majority-Women of Color	0.6002 (0.1891)	0.5041 (0.1820)
p-value	0.6372	0.8074

Majority-WOC vs. People of Color Comparisons

	Feminine Traits	Masculine Traits
Majority-Women of Color	0.6002 (0.1891)	0.5041 (0.1820)
People of Color	0.5270 (0.2048)	0.5328 (0.2048)
p-value	0.0102	0.2602

Table A4.8 Differences in Feminine Stereotyping across Participant Gender, Diversified CC Experiment

Gender Composition	Women	Men	p-value
Majority-Women	0.6061 (0.2093)	0.5721 (0.2034)	0.4162
Majority-Women of Color	0.6114 (0.1966)	0.5909 (0.1839)	0.5899
People of Color	0.5525 (0.1901)	0.5026 (0.2172)	0.2395

Differences in Masculine Stereotyping across Participant Gender

Gender Composition	Women	Men	p-value
Majority-Women	0.4981 (0.1942)	0.4978 (0.1673)	0.9926
Majority-Women of Color	0.5226 (0.1705)	0.4886 (0.1912)	0.3521
People of Color	0.5389 (0.1860)	0.5269 (0.1591)	0.7363

Table A4.9 Differences in Feminine Stereotyping across Participant Party, Diversified CC Experiment

Gender Composition	Democrat	Republican	p-value
Majority-Women	0.5948 (0.1982)	0.5746 (0.2194)	0.6360
Majority-Women of Color	0.6405 (0.1585)	0.5363 (0.2168)	0.0064
People of Color	0.5309 (0.2142)	0.5219 (0.1941)	0.8347

Differences in Masculine Stereotyping across Participant Gender

Gender Composition	Democrat	Republican	p-value
Majority-Women	0.5215 (0.1480)	0.4594 (0.2165)	0.0919
Majority-Women of Color	0.5403 (0.1581)	0.4466 (0.2037)	0.0110
People of Color	0.5208 (0.1734)	0.5490 (0.1709)	0.4360

Table A4.10 Diversified City Council Experiment, Issue Priorities

Issues	Majority-Women	Majority-WOC	p-value[*]	Majority-POC	p-value[**]
Feminine	0.8133 (0.2510)	0.8119 (0.2546)	0.9676	0.6826 (0.2689)	0.0007
Race-Focused	0.6275 (0.2599)	0.6733 (0.2318)	0.1891	0.6290 (0.2563)	0.2068
p-value	0.0001	0.0275		0.0001	

Note:
[*] compares the majority-women to the majority-WOC conditions.
[**] compares the majority-WOC to the majority-POC conditions.

Table A4.11 Diversified City Council Experiment, Issue Priorities, By Participant Party

Majority-Women Institutions			
Issues	Democrat	Republican	p-value
Feminine	0.8495 (0.2390)	0.7544 (0.2621)	0.0657
Race-Focused	0.6109 (0.2418)	0.6546 (0.2883)	0.4170
p-value	0.001	0.0187	

Majority-Women of Color Institutions			
Issues	Democrat	Republican	p-value
Feminine	0.7469 (0.2329)	0.5958 (0.2921)	0.0064
Race-Focused	0.6736 (0.2296)	0.5688 (0.2803)	0.0493
p-value	0.0191	0.4878	

Majority-People of Color Institutions			
Issues	Democrat	Republican	p-value
Feminine	0.8602 (0.2380)	0.7350 (0.2641)	0.0154
Race-Focused	0.7056 (0.2207)	0.6218 (0.2425)	0.0766
p-value	0.0001	0.0189	

Table A4.12 Diversified City Council Experiment, Issue Priorities, By Participant Gender

Majority-Women Institutions			
Issues	Women	Men	p-value
Feminine	0.8598 (0.2094)	0.7769 (0.2757)	0.1007
Race-Focused	0.7102 (0.2362)	0.5625 (0.26111)	0.0042
p-value	0.0001	0.0001	

Majority-Women of Color Institutions			
Issues	**Women**	**Men**	**p-value**
Feminine	0.7319 (0.2732)	0.6354 (0.2588)	0.0821
Race-Focused	0.6549 (0.2624)	0.6042 (0.25044)	0.3401
p-value	0.0283	0.3597	

Majority-People of Color Institutions			
Issues	**Women**	**Men**	**p-value**
Feminine	0.7862 (0.2759)	0.8333 (0.2357)	0.3571
Race-Focused	0.6739 (0.2289)	0.6727 (0.2363)	0.9797
p-value	0.0032	0.0001	

Table A4.13 Diversified City Council Experiment, Group Representation

Issues	Majority-Women	Majority-WOC	p-value[*]	Majority-POC	p-value[**]
Blacks	0.6100 (0.2682)	0.7756 (0.2314)	0.0001	0.7589 (0.2365)	0.6187
Latinos	0.6067 (0.2611)	0.6865 (0.2349)	0.0238	0.7132 (0.2061)	0.4011
Black Women	0.67 (0.2862)	0.8185 (0.2286)	0.0001	0.7319	0.0092
Latinas	0.6633 (0.2686)	0.7162 (0.2280)	0.1319	0.7025	0.6735
People of Color	0.6333 (0.2701)	0.8020 (0.2220)	0.0001	0.7837 (0.2277)	0.5708
AAPI Women	0.6433 (0.2813)	0.6502 (0.3000)	0.8678	0.6600 (0.2292)	0.8067
Working Class	0.62 (0.2722)	0.7063 (0.2720)	0.0257	0.7092 (0.2504)	0.9374
The Wealthy	0.6633 (0.2862)	0.4851 (0.2810)	0.0001	0.4858 (0.3117)	0.9875

Note:
[*]compares the majority-women to the majority-WOC conditions.
[**]compares the majority-WOC to the majority-POC conditions.

Table A4.14 Diversified City Council Experiment, Group Representation, by Participant Party

Majority-Women			
Group Representation	**Democrats**	**Republicans**	**p-value**
Blacks	0.6022 (0.2821)	0.6228 (0.2472)	0.7106
Latinos	0.6129 (0.2712)	0.5965 (0.2470)	0.7620
Black Women	0.6559 (0.3134)	0.6930 (0.2373)	0.5323
Latinas	0.6667 (0.2957)	0.6579 (0.2121)	0.8737
People of Color	0.6183 (0.2821)	0.6579 (0.2510)	0.4793
AAPI Women	0.6559 (0.2893)	0.6228 (0.2704)	0.5705
Working Class	0.6140 (0.2631)	0.6140 (0.2631)	0.8648
the Wealthy	0.6559 (0.2830)	0.6754 (0.2950)	0.7424

Majority-Women of Color			
Group Representation	**Democrats**	**Republicans**	**p-value**
Blacks	0.7654 (0.2301)	0.75 (0.2475)	0.7563
Latinos	0.7233 (0.1932)	0.7 (0.2240)	0.5926
Black Women	0.7407 (0.2212)	0.7193 (0.2392)	0.6591
Latinas	0.7037 (0.2115)	0.7009 (0.2393)	0.9518
People of Color	0.8272 (0.19140	0.725 (0.2603)	0.0308
AAPI Women	0.6976 (0.2075)	0.6083 (0.2491)	0.0617
Working Class	0.7407 (0.2394)	0.6667 (0.2615)	0.1572
the Wealthy	0.5062 (0.3088)	0.4583 (0.3175)	0.4649

Group Representation	Majority-People of Color		
	Democrats	Republicans	p-value
Blacks	0.8172 (0.2063)	0.7094 (0.2557)	0.0219
Latinos	0.7258 (0.2136)	0.6239 (0.2557)	0.0331
Black Women	0.8495 (0.1972)	0.7692 (0.2666)	0.0860
Latinas	0.7473 (0.1973)	0.6667 (0.2649)	0.0835
People of Color	0.8441 (0.1976)	0.7350 (0.2440)	0.0155
AAPI Women	0.6935 (0.2510)	0.5812 (0.3564)	0.0662
Working Class	0.7742 (0.2071)	0.5983 (0.3261)	0.0013
the Wealthy	0.4409 (0.2615)	0.5556 (0.2994)	0.0452

Table A4.15 Diversified City Council Experiment, Group Representation across Institutions within Partisanship, Mean(SD)

Groups	Democratic Participants				
	Majority-Women of Color	Majority-Women	p-value[*]	Majority-People of Color	p-value[**]
Blacks	0.8172 (0.2062)	0.6022 (0.2821)	0.0001	0.7654 (0.2301)	0.2039
Latinos	0.7258 (0.2136)	0.6129 (0.2712)	0.0112	0.7233 (0.1932)	0.9473
Black Women	0.8495 (0.1972)	0.6559 (0.3134)	0.0001	0.7193 (0.2666)	0.3902
Latinas	0.7473 (0.1973)	0.6667 (0.2957)	0.0765	0.7037 (0.2115)	0.2532
People of Color	0.8441 (0.1976)	0.6183 (0.2821)	0.0001	0.8272 (0.1976)	0.6415
AAPI Women	0.6935 (0.2510)	0.6559 (0.2893)	0.4406	0.6975 (0.2075)	0.9266
Working Class	0.7742 (0.2071)	0.6237 (0.2796)	0.0009	0.7407 (0.2394)	0.4213
the Wealthy	0.4409 (0.2615)	0.6559 (0.2829)	0.0001	0.5062 (0.3088)	0.2199

continued

Table A4.15 *continued*

Issues	Majority-Women of Color	Majority-Women	p-value*	Majority-People of Color	p-value**
		Republican Participants			
Blacks	0.7094 (0.2557)	0.6228 (0.2472)	0.1351	0.75 (0.2480)	0.4755
Latinos	0.6239 (0.2557)	0.5965 (0.2470)	0.6335	0.7 (0.2239)	0.1632
Black Women	0.7652 (0.2666)	0.6930 (0.2734)	0.1894	0.7193 (0.2392)	0.3902
Latinas	0.6667 (0.2650)	0.6579 (0.2121)	0.8732	0.7009 (0.2393)	0.5516
People of Color	0.7350 (0.2440)	0.6579 (0.2510)	0.1755	0.725 (0.2603)	0.8601
AAPI Women	0.5812 (0.3564)	0.6228 (0.2704)	0.5663	0.6083 (0.2491)	0.6953
Working Class	0.5983 (0.3261)	0.6140 (0.2631)	0.8165	0.6667 (0.2615)	0.3064
the Wealthy	0.5556 (0.2994)	0.6754 (0.2950)	0.0809	0.4583 (0.3175)	0.1657

Note:
*compares the majority-women to the majority-WOC conditions.
**compares the majority-WOC to the majority-POC conditions.

Table A4.16 Diversified City Council Experiment, Group Representation, by Gender

Group Representation	Women	Men	p-value
	Majority-Women		
Blacks	0.6742 (0.2094)	0.5595 (0.2987)	0.0331
Latinos	0.6591 (0.2214)	0.5655 (0.2837)	0.0750
Black Women	0.6970 (0.2364)	0.6488 (0.3205)	0.4063
Latinas	0.6894 (0.2204)	0.6429 (0.2972)	0.3877
People of Color	0.7121 (0.2107)	0.5714 (0.2962)	0.0090
AAPI Women	0.6970 (0.2252)	0.6011 (0.3141)	0.0911

Working Class	0.6894 (0.2083)	0.5655 (0.3043)	0.0231
The Wealthy	0.5985 (0.2745)	0.7143 (0.2873)	0.0440

Majority-Women of Color

Group Representation	Women	Men	p-value
Blacks	0.7754 (0.22280	0.7431 (0.2502)	0.5108
Latinos	0.7536 (0.2041)	0.6738 (0.2025)	0.0614
Black Women	0.7630 (0.2204)	0.7021 (0.2330)	0.2020
Latinas	0.7609 (0.2068)	0.6454 (0.2242)	0.0115
People of Color	0.7899 (0.2262)	0.7778 (0.2315)	0.7987
AAPI Women	0.6956 (0.2203)	0.625 (0.2344)	0.1359
Working Class	0.7609 (0.2400)	0.6597 (0.2525)	0.0497
The Wealthy	0.5217 (0.3035)	0.4514 (0.3188)	0.2764

Majority-People of Color

Group Representation	Women	Men	p-value
Blacks	0.7899 (0.2032)	0.7636 (0.2540)	0.5734
Latinos	0.6957 (0.2417)	0.6788 (0.2310)	0.7212
Black Women	0.8333 (0.2079)	0.8061 (0.2079)	0.5532
Latinas	0.7319 (0.2290)	0.7030 (0.2284)	0.5291
People of Color	0.8406 (0.2077)	0.7697 (0.2302)	0.1104
AAPI Women	0.6957 (0.2706)	0.6121 (0.3192)	0.1639
Working Class	0.7174 (0.2431)	0.6970 (0.2959)	0.7091
The Wealthy	0.4855 (0.2505)	0.4848 (0.3064)	0.9907

Table A4.17 Diversified City Council Experiment, Group Representation across Institutions within Gender, M(SD)

		Women Participants			
Groups	Majority-Women of Color	Majority-Women	p-value*	Majority-People of Color	p-value**
Blacks	0.7899 (0.2032)	0.6742 (0.2094)	0.0093	0.7754 (0.2229)	0.7452
Latinos	0.6591 (0.2214)	0.6591 (0.2417)	0.4569	0.7536 (0.2041)	0.2171
Black Women	0.8333 (0.2079)	0.6970 (0.2364)	0.0046	0.7630 (0.2204)	0.1207
Latinas	0.7319 (0.2290)	0.6893 (0.2204)	0.3726	0.7609 (0.2068)	0.5257
People of Color	0.8406 (0.2077)	0.7121 (0.2107)	0.0045	0.7899 (0.2262)	0.2656
AAPI Women	0.6957 (0.2706)	0.6970 (0.2253)	0.9801	0.6957 (0.2203)	1.000
Working Class	0.7174 (0.2431)	0.6893 (0.2083)	0.5597	0.7609 (0.2400)	0.3903
The Wealthy	0.4855 (0.2005)	0.5985 (0.2745)	0.0442	0.5217 (0.3035)	0.5339

		Men Participants			
Issues	Majority-Women of Color	Majority-Women	p-value*	Majority-People of Color	p-value**
Blacks	0.7636 (0.2540)	0.5595 (0.2989)	0.0002	0.7431 (0.2540)	0.6804
Latinos	0.6788 (0.2310)	0.5655 (0.2837)	0.0230	0.6738 (0.2025)	0.9079
Black Women	0.8061 (0.2458)	0.6488 (0.3205)	0.0046	0.7021 (0.2330)	0.0316
Latinas	0.7030 (0.2284)	0.6429 (0.2972)	0.2348	0.6454 (0.2242)	0.2030
People of Color	0.7697 (0.2302)	0.5714 (0.2962)	0.0001	0.7778 (0.2315)	0.8596
AAPI Women	0.625 (0.2344)	0.6012 (0.3141)	0.8561	0.6121 (0.3192)	0.8182
Working Class	0.6970 (0.2959)	0.5655 (0.3043)	0.0229	0.6597 (0.2525)	0.4969
The Wealthy	0.4848 (0.3064)	0.7143 (0.2873)	0.0001	0.4514 (0.3188)	0.5886

Note:
*compares the majority-women to the majority-WOC conditions.
**compares the majority-WOC to the majority-POC conditions.

Woman of Color Mayor Experimental Design and Results

New Mayor Elected

When the new mayor takes over in a few days, there will be a woman of color in the executive office. The mayor's inauguration will take place later this week, and she will start working on her policy agenda for the next year. The city is looking forward to having a woman of color in the city's top job.

New Mayor Elected

When the new mayor takes over in a few days, there will be a man of color in the executive office. The mayor's inauguration will take place later this week, and he will start working on his policy agenda for the next year. The city is looking forward to having a man of color in the city's top job.

Trait Measures

Sometimes we think about people as having certain traits, and sometimes we also think about objects and institutions as having traits too. Think about the city council you read about earlier, how well do you think the traits below describe the city council as an institution?

> **Masculine Traits:** Assertive, Coarse, Tough, Aggressive, Stern, Masculine, Rational, Self-Confident
> **Feminine Traits:** Warm, Gentle, Feminine, Sensitive, Talkative, Cautious, Empathetic, Caring
> **Response Options:** Very well, Somewhat well, A little bit, Not Well at All

Issue Priorities

Which types of issues do you think the newly elected city council you read about earlier will prioritize in the upcoming year?

> Education, Minimum wage, Childcare, Infrastructure, Criminal justice reform, Healthcare, Sanitation, Housing, Immigration
> Very high priority, medium priority, low priority

Group Representation

Please rate how well you think the city council will represent the interests of various groups below.

> Black Americans, Latinos, Black women, Latinas, People of color, Asian American or Pacific Islander women, Working class voters, The Wealthy
> Very well, Somewhat well, Somewhat unwell, Very unwell

Table A4.18 WOC Mayor, N = 203

Conditions	N
Woman of Color Mayor	107
Man of Color Mayor	96

Table A4.19 Balance Checks, WOC Mayoral Experiment

	Woman of Color Mayor
Partisanship	−0.125
	(0.299)
Political Interest	0.202*
	(0.105)
Age	−0.157
	(0.120)
Woman Participant	0.475
	(0.296)
Ethnorace	0.240
	(0.316)
Education	−0.579
	(0.379)
Region	−0.095
	(0.143)
Constant	0.042
	(0.854)
Observations	199
Pseudo R^2	0.035

Standard errors in parentheses
$^*p < 0.10$, $^{**}p < 0.05$, $^{***}p < 0.01$,

Table A4.20 Full Means and Standard Deviations, Feminine and Masculine Stereotypes, Mean (SD) Woman of Color Mayor

	Woman of Color	Man of Color	p-value
Feminine Stereotypes	0.6881	0.5512	0.0001
	(0.2020)	(0.2161)	
Masculine Stereotypes	0.5748	0.5748	0.1845
	(0.1727)	(0.1727)	
p-value	0.0001	0.0033	

Table A4.21 Differences in Gender Stereotyping across Participant Party, Woman of Color Mayor Experiment

Differences in Feminine Stereotyping across Participant Party			
Gender Composition	**Democrats**	**Non-Democrats**	**p-value**
Woman of Color	0.6947 (0.1911)	0.6827 (0.2120)	0.7661
Man of Color	0.5506 (0.1887)	0.5517 (0.1386)	0.9813

Differences in Masculine Stereotyping across Participant Party			
Gender Composition	**Democrats**	**Non-Democrats**	**p-value**
Woman of Color	0.5625 (0.1778)	0.5847 (0.1694)	0.5175
Man of Color	0.6141 (0.1868)	0.6092 (0.2304)	0.9118

Table A4.22 Differences in Gender Stereotyping across Participant Party, Woman of Color Mayor Experiment

Differences in Feminine Stereotyping across Participant Party			
Gender Composition	**Women Participants**	**Men Participants**	**p-value**
Woman of Color	0.7016 (0.2024)	0.6720 (0.2026)	0.4608
Man of Color	0.5598 (0.2002)	0.5448 (0.2288)	0.7439

Differences in Masculine Stereotyping across Participant Party			
Gender Composition	**Women Participants**	**Men Participants**	**p-value**
Woman of Color	0.5636 (0.1931)	0.5877 (0.1469)	0.4838
Man of Color	0.6075 (0.1855)	0.6142 (0.2281)	0.8807

Table A4.23 Full Means and Standard Deviations, Issues, Mean (SD) Woman of Color Mayor

	Woman of Color	Man of Color	p-value
Feminine Issues	0.5452 (0.3674)	0.5521 (0.3128)	0.8861
Race-Focused Issues	0.4673 (0.2936)	0.4714 (0.2936)	0.9212

Table A4.24 Differences in issues across Participant Party, Woman of Color Mayor Experiment

Differences in Feminine Issues across Participant Party			
Gender Composition	**Democrats**	**Non-Democrats**	**p-value**
Woman of Color	0.56 (0.3952)	0.5322 (0.3772)	0.6977
Man of Color	0.6316 (0.3123)	0.5 (0.3061)	0.0760

Differences in Race-Focused Issues across Participant Party			
Gender Composition	**Democrats**	**Non-Democrats**	**p-value**
Woman of Color	0.49 (0.2855)	0.4474 (0.3015)	0.4562
Man of Color	0.5057 (0.3120)	0.4423 (0.2694)	0.2882

Table A4.25 Differences in Issues across Participant Gender Woman of Color Mayor Experiment

Differences in Feminine Issues across Participant Gender			
Gender Composition	**Women Participants**	**Men Participants**	**p-value**
Woman of Color	0.5833 (0.3318)	0.5033 (0.4021)	0.2622
Man of Color	0.5641 (0.3167)	0.5439 (0.3126)	0.7573

Differences in Race-Focused Issues across Participant Gender			
Gender Composition	**Women Participants**	**Men Participants**	**p-value**
Woman of Color	0.4911 (0.2989)	0.4412 (0.2983)	0.3824
Man of Color	0.4743 (0.2856)	0.4693 (0.2953)	0.9336

Chapter 5 Appendix

Questions and Response Options

Political Engagement Outcomes

With this newly elected [state legislature/city councilor/governor/mayor], how likely are you to do the following activities?

Contact elected representative
Talk about politics with a friend
Run for political office
Very likely, Somewhat unlikely, Somewhat likely, Very unlikely

Institutional Evaluation Outcomes

Please rate how productive you think the newly elected [state legislature/city councilor/governor/mayor] will be.

Very Productive, Somewhat productive, Somewhat unproductive, Very Unproductive
How much trust do you have in the newly elected [state legislature/city councilor/governor/mayor]?
A great deal, A lot, A moderate amount, A little, None at all

Table A5.1 Full Means and Standard Deviations

	City Councils		
	Majority-Women	Majority-Men	p-value
Contact Rep	0.6306 (0.2504)	0.5159 (0.2564)	0.0003
Talk about Politics	0.6772 (0.2562)	0.6131 (0.2522)	0.0431
Run for Office	0.4776 (0.2681)	0.4663 (0.2799)	0.7389
Trust	0.6090 (0.2020)	0.4968 (0.1972)	0.0001
Productivity	0.3228 (0.3586)	0.3572 (0.3600)	0.4412

State Legislature		
	Majority-Women	**Majority-Men**	**p-value**

	Majority-Women	Majority-Men	p-value
Contact Rep	0.5492 (0.2564)	0.538 (02440)	0. 7258
Talk about Politics	0.6189 (0.2712)	0.576 (0.2680)	0. 2128
Run for Office	0.3689 (0.2208)	0.37 (0.2213)	0.9675
Trust	0.6090 (0.2020)	0.4968 (0.1957)	0. 0001
Productivity	0.3648 (0.3723)	0.382 (0.3628)	0.7127

Mayors		

	Woman	Man	p-value
Contact Rep	0.5789 (0.2704)	0.5325 (0.2478)	0.1589
Talk about Politics	0.6280 (0.2707)	0.6220 (0.2608)	0.8585
Run for Office	0.4489 (0.2630)	0.4277 (0.2591)	0.5296
Trust	0.5953 (0.2054)	0.4878 (0.2083)	0. 0001
Productivity	0.3425 (0.3737)	0.2967 (0.3555)	0.3224

Governors		

	Woman	Man	p-value
Contact Rep	0.5512 (0.2590)	0.5393 (0.2305)	0.7039
Talk about Politics	0.6270 (0.2536)	0.6054 (0.2536)	0. 5370
Run for Office	0.4685 (0.2672)	0.4533 (0.2704)	0.6542
Trust	0.5623 (0.2278)	0.4942 (0.2339)	0.0223
Productivity	0.3115 (0.3540)	0.2975 (0.3540)	0.7589

Table A5.2 Full Means and Standard Deviations, by Participant Party

	City Councils, Contact		
	Majority-Women	Majority-Men	p-value
Democratic Participant	0.6716 (0.2573)	0.5691 (0.2254)	0.0394
Republican Participant	0.6054 (0.2442)	0.4842 (0.2696)	0.0031
p-value	0.1382	0.0719	

	State Legislature, Contact		
	Majority-Women	Majority-Men	p-value
Democratic Participant	0.5581 (0.2719)	0.5318 (0.2408)	0.6131
Republican Participant	0.5443 (0.2492)	0.5429 (0.2481)	0.9718
p-value	0.7772	0.8029	

	Mayors, Contact		
	Woman	Man	p-value
Democratic Participant	0.6202 (0.2399)	0.5640 (0.2321)	0.2514
Republican Participant	0.55 (0.2877)	0.5156 (0.2527)	0.4298
p-value	0.1510	0.3003	

	Governors, Contact		
	Woman	Man	p-value
Democratic Participant	0.59 (0.2563)	0.5667 (0.2223)	0.6384
Republican Participant	0.5243 (0.2592)	0.5230 (0.2352)	0.9749
p-value	0.1692	0.3162	

	City Councils, Talk		
	Majority-Women	Majority-Men	p-value
Democratic Participant	0.75 (0.2398)	0.6596 (0.2298)	0.0601
Republican Participant	0.6325 (0.2622)	0.5854 (0.2622)	0.2501
p-value	0.0094	0.1109	

State Legislature, Talk			
	Majority-Women	**Majority-Men**	**p-value**
Democratic Participant	0.6570 (0.2674)	0.5727 (0.2708)	0.1276
Republican Participant	0.5981 (0.2727)	0.5786 (0.2676)	0.6605
p-value	0.2537	0.9042	

Mayors, Talk			
	Woman	**Man**	**p-value**
Democratic Participant	0.6971 (0.2681)	0.5872 (0.2371)	0.0389
Republican Participant	0.58 (0.2637)	0.6406 (0.2722)	0.1615
p-value	0.0159	0.2805	

Governors, Talk			
	Woman	**Man**	**p-value**
Democratic Participant	0.64 (0.2952)	0.6333 (0.2477)	0.9059
Republican Participant	0.6181 (0.2906)	0.5888 (0.2572)	0.5174
p-value	0.6843	0.3529	

City Councils, Run			
	Majority-Women	**Majority-Men**	**p-value**
Democratic Participant	0.4363 (0.2542)	0.4840 (0.2874)	0.3849
Republican Participant	0.5030 (0.2767)	0.4557 (0.2767)	0.2764
p-value	0.1626	0.5846	

State Legislature, Run			
	Majority-Women	**Majority-Men**	**p-value**
Democratic Participant	0.3721 (0.2522)	0.3909 (0.2296)	0.7007
Republican Participant	0.3671 (0.2035)	0.3536 (0.2149)	0.6940
p-value	0.9054	0.3513	

continued

Table A5.2 *continued*

	Mayor, Run		
	Majority-Women	**Majority-Men**	**p-value**
Democratic Participant	0.4856 (0.2685)	0.4361 (0.2678)	0.3725
Republican Participant	0.4567 (0.2675)	0.4625 (0.2730)	0.8934
p-value	0.5510	0.4720	

	Governor, Run		
	Majority-Women	**Majority-Men**	**p-value**
Democratic Participant	0.44 (0.2345)	0.4056 (0.2400)	0.4815
Republican Participant	0.4549 (0.2825)	0.4408 (0.2704)	0.7573
p-value	0.7603	0.4720	

Table A5.3 Institutional Evaluation Measures, by Participant Party

	City Councils, Productivity		
	Majority-Women	**Majority-Men**	**p-value**
Democratic Participant	0.3530 (0.3974)	0.4415 (0.3730)	0.2593
Republican Participant	0.3042 (0.3337)	0.3070 (0.3443)	0.9590
p-value	0.4471	0.0419	

	State Legislature, Productivity		
	Majority-Women	**Majority-Men**	**p-value**
Democratic Participant	0.3663 (0.3871)	0.3682 (0.3660)	0.9802
Republican Participant	0.3639 (0.3665)	0.3929 (0.3626)	0.6295
p-value	0.9735	0.7075	

	Mayor, Productivity		
	Majority-Women	**Majority-Men**	**p-value**
Democratic Participant	0.3798 (0.3819)	0.3953 (0.3905)	0.8455
Republican Participant	0.3167 (0.3684)	0.2438 (0.3255)	0.1929

p-value	0.3512	0.0235	

Governor, Productivity			
	Majority-Women	**Majority-Men**	**p-value**
Democratic Participant	0.28 (0.3594)	0.2889 (0.3534)	0.9037
Republican Participant	0.3333 (0.3511)	0.3026 (0.3566)	0.5987
p-value	0.4154	0.8375	

City Councils, Trust			
	Majority-Women	**Majority-Men**	**p-value**
Democratic Participant	0.7098 (0.1803)	0.4979 (0.1713)	0.0001
Republican Participant	0.5470 (0.1902)	0.4962 (0.2121)	0.1102
p-value	0.0001	0.9635	

State Legislature, Trust			
	Majority-Women	**Majority-Men**	**p-value**
Democratic Participant	0.7070 (0.1710)	0.4764 (0.1563)	0.0001
Republican Participant	0.4937 (0.2238)	0.4514 (0.2034)	0.2321
p-value	0.0001	0.4540	

Mayor, Trust			
	Majority-Women	**Majority-Men**	**p-value**
Democratic Participant	0.7115 (0.1745)	0.5860 (0.1971)	0.0014
Republican Participant	0.5147 (0.1865)	0.435 (0.1956)	0.0105
p-value	0.0001	0.0001	

Governor, Trust			
	Majority-Women	**Majority-Men**	**p-value**
Democratic Participant	0.652 (0.2013)	0.5067 (0.2071)	0.0008
Republican Participant	0.5 (0.2252)	0.4868 (0.2494)	0.7372
p-value	0.0002	0.6542	

Table A5.4 Full Means and Standard Deviations, by Participant Gender

	City Councils, Contact		
	Majority-Women	Majority-Men	p-value
Woman	0.5955 (0.2332)	0.5372 (0.2444)	0.2218
Man	0.6551 (0.2701)	0.5404 (0.2578)	0.6996
p-value	0.1762	0.9033	

	State Legislature, Contact		
	Majority-Women	Majority-Men	p-value
Woman	0.5904 (0.2298)	0.5351 (0.2287)	0.2232
Man	0.5233 (0.2701)	0.5404 (0.2578)	0.6996
p-value	0.1605	0.9033	

	Mayors, Contact		
	Woman	Man	p-value
Woman	0.6161 (0.2521)	0.5565 (0.2577)	0.2074
Man	0.5493 (0.2823)	0.5082 (0.2326)	0.3679
p-value	0.1680	0.2781	

	Governors, Contact		
	Woman	Man	p-value
Woman	0.5585 (0.2719)	0.5288 (0.2356)	0.5623
Man	0.5467 (0.2523)	0.5471 (0.2280)	0.9914
p-value	0.8070	0.6681	

	City Councils, Talk		
	Majority-Women	Majority-Men	p-value
Woman	0.7045 (0.2361)	0.6117 (0.2200)	0.0438
Man	0.6582 (0.2691)	0.6139 (0.2709)	0.3040
p-value	0.3050	0.9621	

	State Legislature, Talk		
	Majority-Women	**Majority-Men**	**p-value**
Woman	0.6223 (0.2600)	0.6009 (0.2538)	0.6721
Man	0.6167 (0.2798)	0.5551 (0.2794)	0.1910
p-value	0.9110	0.3440	

	Mayors, Talk		
	Woman	**Man**	**p-value**
Woman	0.6429 (0.2502)	0.6452 (0.2648)	0.9613
Man	0.6162 (0.2766)	0.5984 (0.2711)	0.7099
p-value	0.5836	0.3216	

	Governors, Talk		
	Woman	**Man**	**p-value**
Woman	0.6277 (0.3034)	0.5866 (0.2368)	0.4518
Man	0.6267 (0.2859)	0.6196 (0.2664)	0.8779
p-value	0.9855	0.4806	

	City Councils, Run		
	Majority-Women	**Majority-Men**	**p-value**
Woman	0.4955 (0.2613)	0.4894 (0.2707)	0.9083
Man	0.4652 (0.2737)	0.4525 (0.2861)	0.7767
p-value	0.5223	0.4773	

	State Legislature, Run		
	Majority-Women	**Majority-Men**	**p-value**
Woman	0.4043 (0.2245)	0.3904 (0.2410)	0.7633
Man	0.3467 (0.2171)	0.3529 (0.2037)	0.8592
p-value	0.1619	0.3487	

continued

Table A5.4 *continued*

	Mayor, Run		
	Majority-Women	**Majority-Men**	**p-value**
Woman	0.4866 (0.2797)	0.4960 (0.2916)	0.8594
Man	0.4542 (0.2582)	0.4098 (0.2417)	0.3123
p-value	0.5000	0.0772	

	Governor, Run		
	Majority-Women	**Majority-Men**	**p-value**
Woman	0.4574 (0.2870)	0.4423 (0.2648)	0.7855
Man	0.4433 (0.2486)	0.4167 (0.2561)	0.5271
p-value	0.7743	0.5920	

Table A5.5 Institutional Evaluation Measures, by Participant Gender

	City Councils, Productivity		
	Majority-Women	**Majority-Men**	**p-value**
Woman	0.3 (0.3613)	0.4255 (0.3230)	0.0788
Man	0.3386 (0.3581)	0.3165 (0.3619)	0.6995
p-value	0.5418	0.1000	

	State Legislature, Productivity		
	Majority-Women	**Majority-Men**	**p-value**
Woman	0.2926 (0.3310)	0.3860 (0.3572)	0.1859
Man	0.41 (0.3913)	0.3787 (0.3549)	0.6181
p-value	0.0900	0.9115	

	Mayor, Productivity		
	Majority-Women	**Majority-Men**	**p-value**
Woman	0.375 (0.3599)	0.2661 (0.3503)	0.0988
Man	0.3169 (0.3849)	0.3279 (0.3610)	0.8669

p-value	0.3865	0.3376	

Governor Productivity			
	Majority-Women	**Majority-Men**	**p-value**
Woman	0.2766 (0.3467)	0.3221 (0.3512)	0.5186
Man	0.3333 (0.3591)	0.2790 (0.3575)	0.3648
p-value	0.3912	0.5093	

City Councils, Trust			
	Majority-Women	**Majority-Men**	**p-value**
Woman	0.5527 (0.1999)	0.5447 (0.1987)	0.8394
Man	0.6481 (0.1954)	0.4684 (0.1918)	0.0001
p-value	0.0067	0.0351	

State Legislature, Trust			
	Majority-Women	**Majority-Men**	**p-value**
Woman	0.5490 (0.2376)	0.4667 (0.2082)	0.0628
Man	0.5813 (0.2258)	0.4588 (0.1623)	0.0003
p-value	0.4513	0.8134	

Mayor, Trust			
	Majority-Women	**Majority-Men**	**p-value**
Woman	0.5786 (0.2278)	0.5129 (0.2161)	0.1109
Man	0.6085 (0.1865)	0.4623 (0.1985)	0.0001
p-value	0.4179	0.1789	

Governor, Trust			
	Majority-Women	**Majority-Men**	**p-value**
Woman	0.5277 (0.2482)	0.5077 (0.2359)	0.6825
Man	0.584 (0.2125)	0.4841 (0.2337)	0.0080
p-value	0.1844	0.5843	

Table A5.6 PAQ Traits, City Councils

	Contact	Talk	Run	Trust	Productivity
PAQ	−0.054	0.024	0.109*	−0.044	−0.043
	(0.059)	(0.063)	(0.059)	(0.045)	(0.087)
Majority-Women Institutions	0.006	−0.002	−0.018	0.046***	0.031
	(0.020)	(0.022)	(0.020)	(0.016)	(0.030)
Majority-Women Institutions × PAQ	0.153*	−0.014	−0.022	−0.013	0.216*
	(0.082)	(0.087)	(0.083)	(0.063)	(0.121)
City Councils	0.010	0.023	0.041	0.032	0.061
	(0.031)	(0.033)	(0.031)	(0.024)	(0.046)
City Councils × PAQ	0.140	0.057	0.168	0.093	−0.029
	(0.118)	(0.126)	(0.119)	(0.091)	(0.174)
Majority-Women Institutions × City Councils	0.047	0.015	−0.021	−0.019	−0.063
	(0.039)	(0.041)	(0.039)	(0.030)	(0.057)
Majority-Women Institutions × City Councils × PAQ	−0.212	−0.072	−0.111	−0.119	−0.221
	(0.162)	(0.173)	(0.164)	(0.125)	(0.240)
State Legislature Condition	−0.011	−0.030	−0.083***	−0.020	0.065**
	(0.022)	(0.024)	(0.023)	(0.017)	(0.033)
Mayoral Condition	0.011	0.004	0.004	0.008	0.019
	(0.022)	(0.024)	(0.022)	(0.017)	(0.033)
Women Participants	0.021	0.017	0.027	0.009	−0.005
	(0.017)	(0.018)	(0.017)	(0.013)	(0.025)
Nonbinary Gender Identity	−0.041	−0.072	−0.047	0.028	−0.064
	(0.067)	(0.072)	(0.068)	(0.052)	(0.099)
Democratic	0.012	0.017	−0.057***	0.081***	0.023
	(0.022)	(0.023)	(0.022)	(0.017)	(0.032)
Independent	−0.024	−0.011	−0.054**	−0.017	−0.008
	(0.021)	(0.023)	(0.022)	(0.017)	(0.032)
Household Income	0.031***	0.027**	0.048***	0.039***	−0.025
	(0.010)	(0.011)	(0.011)	(0.008)	(0.015)
Marital Status	−0.004	0.005	0.003	−0.006*	0.004
	(0.004)	(0.005)	(0.004)	(0.003)	(0.006)
Racial/Ethnic Minority	0.037**	0.025	0.037**	0.009	0.061**
	(0.017)	(0.018)	(0.017)	(0.013)	(0.026)
Education Level	0.033***	0.027**	0.011	0.065***	0.023
	(0.011)	(0.012)	(0.011)	(0.008)	(0.016)
Employment Status	0.021	0.025	0.065***	0.012	−0.006
	(0.016)	(0.017)	(0.016)	(0.012)	(0.023)
Registered Voter	0.056**	0.093***	−0.015	0.031	0.055
	(0.026)	(0.028)	(0.027)	(0.020)	(0.039)
Constant	0.309***	0.348***	0.302***	0.172***	0.212***
	(0.046)	(0.049)	(0.046)	(0.035)	(0.067)

	Contact	Talk	Run	Trust	Productivity
Observations	985	985	985	985	985
R^2	0.082	0.064	0.111	0.266	0.024
Adjusted R^2	0.064	0.046	0.094	0.251	0.005

Standard errors in parentheses
* p<0.10, **p<0.05, ***p<0.01

Table A5.7 PAQ Traits, State Legislatures

	Contact	Talk	Run	Trust	Productivity
PAQ	0.044	0.045	0.159***	−0.004	−0.132
	(0.060)	(0.064)	(0.060)	(0.046)	(0.088)
Majority-Women Institutions	0.021	−0.004	−0.014	0.042***	0.030
	(0.020)	(0.021)	(0.020)	(0.015)	(0.030)
Majority-Women Institutions × PAQ	−0.015	−0.069	−0.052	−0.052	0.227**
	(0.082)	(0.088)	(0.083)	(0.063)	(0.122)
State Legislature Condition	−0.007	−0.039	−0.066**	−0.022	0.105**
	(0.030)	(0.032)	(0.031)	(0.023)	(0.045)
State Legislatures × PAQ	−0.258**	−0.024	−0.048	−0.065	0.306*
	(0.112)	(0.120)	(0.114)	(0.087)	(0.166)
Majority-Women Institutions × State Legislatures	−0.023	0.023	−0.043	−0.007	−0.048
	(0.038)	(0.041)	(0.039)	(0.030)	(0.057)
Majority-Women Institutions × State Legislatures × PAQ	0.443***	0.145	0.031	0.034	−0.254
	(0.159)	(0.170)	(0.161)	(0.123)	(0.236)
City Council Condition	0.026	0.027	0.019	0.018	0.042
	(0.022)	(0.024)	(0.022)	(0.017)	(0.033)
Mayoral Condition	0.006	0.003	0.003	0.007	0.021
	(0.022)	(0.024)	(0.023)	(0.017)	(0.033)
Women Participants	0.022	0.017	0.027	0.009	−0.010
	(0.016)	(0.018)	(0.017)	(0.013)	(0.024)
Nonbinary Gender Identity	−0.048	−0.079	−0.050	0.029	−0.058
	(0.067)	(0.071)	(0.068)	(0.052)	(0.099)
Democrat	0.008	0.017	−0.058***	0.082***	0.026
	(0.022)	(0.023)	(0.022)	(0.017)	(0.032)
Independent	−0.028	−0.011	−0.056***	−0.017	−0.006
	(0.021)	(0.023)	(0.022)	(0.017)	(0.032)
Household Income	0.034***	0.027**	0.050***	0.039***	−0.026*
	(0.010)	(0.011)	(0.011)	(0.008)	(0.015)

continued

Table A5.7 *continued*

	Contact	Talk	Run	Trust	Productivity
Marital Status	−0.004	0.005	0.003	−0.006*	0.005
	(0.004)	(0.005)	(0.004)	(0.003)	(0.006)
Racial/Ethnic Minority	0.035**	0.025	0.037**	0.009	0.063**
	(0.017)	(0.018)	(0.017)	(0.013)	(0.026)
Education Level	0.033***	0.027**	0.011	0.065***	0.024
	(0.011)	(0.012)	(0.011)	(0.008)	(0.016)
Employment Status	0.022	0.025	0.064***	0.011	−0.008
	(0.016)	(0.017)	(0.016)	(0.012)	(0.023)
Registered Voter	0.054**	0.091***	−0.016	0.030	0.054
	(0.026)	(0.028)	(0.027)	(0.020)	(0.039)
Constant	0.304***	0.350***	0.303***	0.176***	0.206***
	(0.045)	(0.049)	(0.046)	(0.035)	(0.067)
Observations	985	985	985	985	985
R^2	0.087	0.065	0.111	0.265	0.024
Adjusted R^2	0.069	0.046	0.093	0.251	0.005

Standard errors in parentheses
*$p<0.10$, **$p<0.05$, ***$p<0.01$

Table A5.8 PAQ Traits, Mayor

	Contact	Talk	Run	Trust	Productivity
PAQ	−0.018	0.006	0.188***	−0.010	0.027
	(0.058)	(0.061)	(0.058)	(0.044)	(0.085)
Majority-Women Institutions	0.015	0.019	−0.034*	0.030*	−0.008
	(0.020)	(0.022)	(0.021)	(0.016)	(0.030)
Majority-Women Institutions × PAQ	0.112	0.068	−0.080	−0.065	0.067
	(0.081)	(0.086)	(0.082)	(0.062)	(0.120)
Mayor	0.002	0.037	−0.027	−0.015	−0.042
	(0.031)	(0.033)	(0.031)	(0.024)	(0.046)
Mayor × PAQ	−0.018	0.150	−0.177	−0.054	−0.335*
	(0.123)	(0.130)	(0.124)	(0.094)	(0.181)
Majority-Women Institutions × Mayor	0.008	−0.067	0.041	0.042	0.090
	(0.039)	(0.041)	(0.039)	(0.030)	(0.057)
Majority-Women Institutions × Mayor × PAQ	−0.046	−0.400**	0.153	0.091	0.380
	(0.166)	(0.177)	(0.168)	(0.128)	(0.245)
City Council Condition	0.030	0.030	0.019	0.018	0.039
	(0.022)	(0.023)	(0.022)	(0.017)	(0.033)
State Legislature Condition	−0.012	−0.028	−0.085***	−0.022	0.062*
	(0.022)	(0.024)	(0.023)	(0.017)	(0.033)

	Contact	Talk	Run	Trust	Productivity
Women Participants	0.022	0.014	0.028*	0.009	−0.007
	(0.017)	(0.018)	(0.017)	(0.013)	(0.025)
Nonbinary Gender Identity	−0.049	−0.074	−0.051	0.027	−0.049
	(0.067)	(0.071)	(0.068)	(0.051)	(0.099)
Democrat	0.015	0.021	−0.057***	0.081***	0.024
	(0.022)	(0.023)	(0.022)	(0.017)	(0.032)
Independent	−0.023	−0.010	−0.054**	−0.017	−0.005
	(0.021)	(0.023)	(0.022)	(0.016)	(0.032)
Household Income	0.032***	0.028**	0.049***	0.039***	−0.025
	(0.010)	(0.011)	(0.011)	(0.008)	(0.015)
Marital Status	−0.004	0.005	0.003	−0.006*	0.004
	(0.004)	(0.005)	(0.004)	(0.003)	(0.006)
Racial/Ethnic Minority	0.035**	0.022	0.039**	0.010	0.064**
	(0.017)	(0.018)	(0.017)	(0.013)	(0.026)
Education Level	0.034***	0.027**	0.010	0.065***	0.023
	(0.011)	(0.012)	(0.011)	(0.008)	(0.016)
Employment Status	0.021	0.024	0.065***	0.011	−0.007
	(0.016)	(0.017)	(0.016)	(0.012)	(0.023)
Registered Voter	0.054**	0.089***	−0.016	0.030	0.055
	(0.027)	(0.028)	(0.027)	(0.020)	(0.039)
Constant	0.302***	0.340***	0.315***	0.180***	0.232***
	(0.045)	(0.048)	(0.046)	(0.035)	(0.067)
Observations	985	985	985	985	985
R^2	0.078	0.070	0.112	0.266	0.025
Adjusted R^2	0.060	0.051	0.094	0.252	0.006

Standard errors in parentheses
*p<0.10, **p<0.05, ***p<0.01

Table A5.9 PAQ Traits, Governor

	Contact	Talk	Run	Trust	Productivity
PAQ	−0.061	0.080	0.137**	−0.028	−0.048
	(0.060)	(0.064)	(0.060)	(0.046)	(0.089
Majority-Women Institutions	0.026	−0.005	−0.030	0.045***	0.009
	(0.020)	(0.021)	(0.020)	(0.015)	(0.030)
Majority-Women Institutions × PAQ	0.148*	−0.110	−0.029	−0.040	0.118
	(0.081)	(0.086)	(0.082)	(0.062)	(0.120)
Governor	0.021	−0.025	−0.014	0.005	−0.027
	(0.032)	(0.035)	(0.033)	(0.025)	(0.048)

continued

Table A5.9 *continued*

	Contact	Talk	Run	Trust	Productivity
Governor × PAQ	0.154	−0.162	0.032	0.033	−0.001
	(0.116)	(0.123)	(0.117)	(0.089)	(0.171)
Majority-Women Institutions × Governor	−0.043	0.032	0.024	−0.020	0.025
	(0.040)	(0.043)	(0.041)	(0.031)	(0.059)
Majority-Women Institutions × Governor × PAQ	−0.197	0.333*	−0.062	−0.010	0.175
	(0.166)	(0.177)	(0.168)	(0.128)	(0.246)
City Council Conditions	0.020	0.024	0.016	0.011	0.021
	(0.022)	(0.023)	(0.022)	(0.017)	(0.032)
State Legislature Conditions	−0.021	−0.034	−0.088***	−0.028*	0.046
	(0.022)	(0.024)	(0.022)	(0.017)	(0.033)
Women Participants	0.024	0.016	0.028*	0.009	−0.008
	(0.017)	(0.018)	(0.017)	(0.013)	(0.025)
Nonbinary Gender Identity	−0.050	−0.073	−0.056	0.029	−0.051
	(0.067)	(0.071)	(0.068)	(0.052)	(0.099)
Democrat	0.016	0.017	−0.056***	0.083***	0.026
	(0.022)	(0.023)	(0.022)	(0.017)	(0.032)
Independent	−0.022	−0.011	−0.054**	−0.016	−0.006
	(0.021)	(0.023)	(0.022)	(0.016)	(0.032)
Household Income	0.032***	0.028**	0.049***	0.039***	−0.024
	(0.011)	(0.011)	(0.011)	(0.008)	(0.016)
Marital Status	−0.004	0.005	0.003	−0.006*	0.004
	(0.004)	(0.005)	(0.004)	(0.003)	(0.006)
Racial/Ethnic Minority	0.036**	0.023	0.037**	0.010	0.060**
	(0.017)	(0.018)	(0.018)	(0.013)	(0.026)
Education Level	0.034***	0.027**	0.011	0.065***	0.022
	(0.011)	(0.012)	(0.011)	(0.008)	(0.016)
Employment Status	0.020	0.025	0.065***	0.010	−0.008
	(0.016)	(0.017)	(0.016)	(0.012)	(0.023)
Registered Voter	0.054**	0.092***	−0.015	0.029	0.054
	(0.027)	(0.028)	(0.027)	(0.020)	(0.039)
Constant	0.303***	0.355***	0.311***	0.181***	0.239***
	(0.045)	(0.048)	(0.046)	(0.035)	(0.067)
Observations	985	985	985	985	985
R^2	0.079	0.067	0.110	0.265	0.022
Adjusted R^2	0.061	0.048	0.092	0.251	0.002

Standard errors in parentheses
*p<0.10, **p<0.05, ***p<0.01

Diversified City Council Engagement Results

Engagement Measures

With this new city council, how likely are you to attend a city council meeting?
How likely are you to contact a member of the newly elected city council?
Would you consider running for the city council yourself?
Response Options: Very likely, Somewhat likely, Somewhat unlikely, Very unlikely

Institutional Evaluations

How much trust do you have in the decisions the newly elected city council will make?
A lot of trust, Some trust, Very little Trust, No Trust at all
How productive do you think the newly elected city council will be?
Very productive, Somewhat productive, Somewhat unproductive, Very unproductive

Table A5.10 Diversified City Council Experiment, Political Engagement and Institutional Evaluations

	Majority-Women	Majority-WOC	p-value[*]	Majority-POC	p-value[**]
Contact Rep	0.46 (0.3754)	0.4851 (0.3110)	0.6054	0.4787 (0.3371)	0.8900
Vote	0.7733 (0.3066)	0.6997 (0.3667)	0.1241	0.7163 (0.3128)	0.7344
Run for Office	0.6933 (0.0909)	0.6667 (0.1000)	0.6390	0.7305 (0.1319)	0.0663
Trust	0.66 (0.2881)	0.6865 (0.2531)	0.4896	0.6631 (0.2102)	0.4860
Productivity	0.77 (0.2306)	0.8086 (0.2126)	0.2190	0.7447 (0.1920)	0.0292

Table A5.11 Women of Color Mayor Experiment Political Engagement and Institutional Evaluations

	Majority-WOC	Majority-POC	p-value[*]
Contact Rep	0.5762 (0.2503)	0.5921 (0.2308)	0.6418å
Talk about Politics	0.7452 (0.2246)	0.7553 (0.2187)	0.7500

continued

Table A5.11 *continued*

	Majority-WOC	Majority-POC	p-value[*]
Run for Office	0.4835	0.4947	0.7572
	(0.2588)	(0.2552)	
Trust	0.5206	0.4702	0.2921
	(0.3457)	(0.3280)	
Productivity	0.7651	0.7439	0.5027
	(0.2354)	(0.2089)	

Chapter 6 Appendix

Gendered Processes Content Analysis Coding Procedures

To ascertain the way that journalists use gendered process frames to discuss congressional procedures, outcomes, and relationships with other government actors, a team of researchers read and coded 1400 news articles from the *New York Times* between 2007 through 2020 which encompasses the 110th through 116th congressional terms. I restrict the analyses to the *New York Times* following current scholarship analyzing news coverage of key political events, polarization, and candidate news coverage (Boydstun 2013; Krupnikov and Ryan 2022). Analyses are restricted to the *New York Times* given that this is widely accepted as the "newspaper of record." Next, I developed a set of search terms to identify articles about congressional processes and procedures. Simply searching for Congress in archived *New York Times* coverage will lead to an unwieldy and larger number of articles. The key search terms used to identify the most relevant articles were "congress" plus Budget OR Appropriations OR Defense OR Legislation OR Bill; the search encompassed time periods when Congress, the House or the Senate, was in session and actively considering legislation. This initial search for articles yielded approximately 1000–2000 articles for each of the fourteen congressional sessions in the designated time frame. This is still a very large set of articles to code. As a next step, I followed approaches from past scholarship (Levendusky and Malhotra 2016) and pulled a random sample of 100 articles from each congressional term. This gave a set of 1400 articles to code.

Two independent research assistants read each article. The first step was for the researcher to determine if the article was, in fact, about congressional processes. While the seat of search terms used was meant to restrict the search to process articles, the search terms are not perfect. For example, several obituaries about congressional leaders made their way into our dataset and these obituaries quite reasonably used a combination of our search terms. We also excluded editorials, op-eds, book reviews, and other news coverage that does not fit into the rubric of "hard" news about congressional process (Cook 1997). Next, the articles were coded for the extent to which they embodied elements as feminine or masculine stereotypes in describing the *process* of conducting congressional business.

Feminine process frames are those that talk about compromise, collaboration, consensus-building, or bipartisanship and discuss the communal or caregiving motives of congressional actors. Masculine process frames talk use win/loss frames, war and/or sports metaphors, discuss strategy and tactics, and focus on the agentic or power-seeking motives of congressional actors. I chose these particular metrics based on behaviors and qualities that fit into feminine and masculine stereotypes, including the feminine stereotypic of women in leadership roles (Prentice and Carranza 2002; Eagly and Carli 2003a). Each coder separately identified whether these elements appeared in the news articles about congressional processes. The inter-coder reliability values indicate a moderate level of agreement for feminine process frames and a substantial level of agreement for masculine frames.

Table A6.1 Intercoder Reliability for Gendered Process Content Analysis

Gendered Process Variables	% Agreement	Cohen's Kappa
Feminine	88.12%	0.4843
Masculine	84.12%	0.6098

Table A6.2 Gendered Sources in Political Process News

	Men Referenced	Men Quoted
Woman Speaker of the House	0.023	0.016
	(0.043)	(0.043)
Proportion of Women Senators	1.644	0.628
	(1.763)	(1.728)
Proportion of Women House Members	−1.438	0.196
	(2.838)	(2.952)
Proportion of Women Authors	−0.014	−0.021
	(0.033)	(0.032)
Divided Government	0.016	0.007
	(0.046)	(0.046)
Logged Length (in words)	0.018	0.013
	(0.023)	(0.023)
Proportion of Women Editors at NYT	−0.031	−0.042
	(0.087)	(0.086)
Constant	0.166	0.096
	(0.313)	(0.326)
Observations	1151	1151
Pseudo R^2	0.0115	0.0065

Note: Standard errors clustered by congressional term.
$^*p < 0.10, ^{**}p < 0.05, ^{***}p < 0.01$

Table A6.3 Gendered Process Frames, Women of Color

	Feminine Process Frames, WOC	Masculine Process Frames, WOC
Woman Speaker of the House	0.269	0.426***
	(0.325)	(0.106)
Proportion of Women of Color in Congress	−8.354	−1.322
	(5.808)	(2.228)
Proportion of Women Authors	0.338	0.014
	(0.270)	(0.174)

	Feminine Process Frames, WOC	Masculine Process Frames, WOC
Divided Government	−0.145	−0.120
	(0.298)	(0.108)
Logged Length (in words)	−0.195	−0.018
	(0.159)	(0.113)
Proportion of Women Editors at NYT	−0.289	0.615***
	(0.618)	(0.167)
Constant	0.214	−0.874
	(1.241)	(0.811)
Observations	1151	1151
Pseudo R^2	0.012	0.007

Standard errors in parentheses
*p < 0.10, **p < 0.05, ***p < 0.01

Table A6.4 Gendered Sourcing, WOC

	WOC, Women Referenced	WOC, Women Quoted	WOC, Men Referenced	WOC, Men Quoted
Woman Speaker of the House	0.032*	0.019	0.013	0.011
	(0.017)	(0.017)	(0.043)	(0.042)
Proportion of Women of Color in Congress	1.515***	1.477***	0.882	0.929
	(0.298)	(0.288)	(0.827)	(0.829)
Proportion of Women Authors	0.035***	0.037**	−0.011	−0.018
	(0.013)	(0.016)	(0.033)	(0.032)
Divided Government	0.015	0.021	0.022	0.005
	(0.016)	(0.016)	(0.038)	(0.037)
Logged Length (in words)	−0.001	0.002	0.021	0.016
	(0.008)	(0.007)	(0.023)	(0.023)
Proportion of Women Editors at NYT	0.026	−0.025	−0.008	−0.034
	(0.034)	(0.031)	(0.078)	(0.072)
Constant	−0.044	−0.052	0.147	0.186
	(0.071)	(0.068)	(0.165)	(0.168)
Observations	1151	1151	1151	1151

Standard errors in parentheses
*p < 0.10, **p < 0.05, ***p < 0.01

References

Aaldering, Loes, and Daphne Joanna van der Pas. 2020. "Political Leadership in the Media: Gender Bias in Leader Stereotypes during Campaign and Routine Times." *British Journal of Political Science* 50 (3):911–931. doi: https://doi.org/10.1017/S0007123417000795.

ABA. 2017. A Current Glance at Women in the Law. In *ABA, Commission on Women in the Professsion*. Chicago, IL: American Bar Association.

Acharya, Avidit, Matthew Blackwell, and Maya Sen. 2018. *Deep Roots: How Slavery Still Shapes Southern Politics*. Princeton, NJ: Princeton University Press.

Acker, Joan. 1990. "Hierarchies, Jobs, Bodies: A Theory of Gendered Organizations." *Gender & Society* 4 (2):139–158.

Acker, Joan. 1992. "From Sex Roles to Gendered Institutions." *Contemporary Sociology* 21 (5):565–569.

Aday, Sean, and James Devitt. 2001. "Style over Substance: Newspaper Coverage of Elizabeth Dole's Presidential Bid." *The International Journal of Press/Politics* 6 (2):52–73. doi: 10.1177/108118001129172134.

Alexander, Deborah, and Kristi Anderson. 1993. "Gender as a Factor in the Attribution of Leadership Traits." *Political Research Quarterly* 46 (3):527–545.

Althaus, Scott L., and David Tewksbury. 2002. "Agenda Setting and the "New" News: Patterns of Issue Importance among Readers of the Paper and Online Versions of the New York Times." *Communication Research* 29 (2):180–207. doi: 10.1177/0093650202029002.

Ansolabehere, Stephen, and Phillip Jones. 2010. "Constituents' Responses to Congressional Roll-Call Voting." *American Journal of Political Science* 54:583–597.

Ansolabehere, Stephen, and Shiro Kuriwaki. 2022. "Congressional Representation: Accountability from the Constituent's Perspective." *American Journal of Political Science* 66 (1): 123–139.

Anzia, Sarah F., and Rachel Bernhard. 2022. "Gender Stereotyping and the Electoral Success of Women Candidates: New Evidence from Local Elections in the United States." *British Journal of Political Science* 52 (4):1544–1563. doi: 10.1017/S0007123421000570

Anzia, Sarah F., and Christopher R. Berry. 2011. "The Jackie (and Jill) Robinson Effect: Why Do Congresswomen Outperform Congressmen?" *American Journal of Political Science* 55 (3):478–493. doi: 10.1111/j.1540-5907.2011.00512.x.

Archetti, Cristina. 2008. "News Coverage of 9/11 and the Demise of the Media Flows, Globalization and Localization Hypotheses." *International Communication Gazette* 70 (6): 463–485. doi: 10.1177/1748048508096143.

Armstrong, Cory L., and Michael P. Boyle. 2011. "Views from the Margins: News Coverage of Women in Abortion Protests, 1960–2006." *Mass Communication and Society* 14:153–177. https://doi.org/10.1080/15205431003615901.

Armstrong, Cory. L. 2004. "The Influence of Reporter Gender on Source Selection in Newspaper Stories." *Journalism and Mass Communication Quarterly* 81:139–154). doi: 10.1177/107769900408100110.

Arnesen, Sveinung, and Yvette Peters. 2018. "The Legitimacy of Representation: How Descriptive, Formal, and Responsiveness Representation Affect the Acceptability of Political Decisions." *Comparative Political Studies* 51 (7):868–899.

Atkeson, Lonna Rae. 2003. "Not All Cues Are Created Equal: The Conditional Impact of Female Candidates on Political Engagement." *The Journal of Politics* 65 (4):1040–1061.

Atkinson, Mary Layton, and Jason H. Windett. 2019. "Gender Stereotypes and the Policy Priorities of Women in Congress." *Political Behavior* 41 (3):769–789. doi: https://doi.org/10.1007/s11109-018-9471-7.

Baitinger, Gail. 2015. "Meet the Press or Meet the Men? Examining Women's Presence in American News Media." *Political Research Quarterly* 68 (3):579–592. doi: https://doi.org/10.1177/1065912915586632.

Bankert, Alexa. 2020. "Let's Talk about Sexism: The Differential Effects of Gender Discrimination on Liberal and Conservative Women's Political Engagement." *American Politics Resaerch* 48 (6):779–791. doi: 10.1177/1532673X20939503.

Barnes, Tiffany D. 2016. *Gendering Legislative Behavior: Institutional Constraints and Collaboration.* New York: Cambridge University Press.

Barnes, Tiffany D., and Emily Beaulieu. 2014. "Gender Stereotypes and Corruption: How Candidates Affect Perceptions of Election Fraud." *Politics & Gender* 10:365–391.

Barnes, Tiffany D., Victoria D. Beall, and Mirya R. Holman. 2021. "Pink-Collar Representation and Budgetary Outcomes in US States." *Legislative Studies Quarterly* 46 (1): 119–154. doi: 10.1111/lsq.12286.

Barnes, Tiffany D., and Emily Beaulieu. 2019. "Women Politicians, Institutions, and Perceptions of Corruption." *Comparative Political Studies* 52 (1):134–167. doi: https://doi.org/10.1177/0010414018774355.

Barnes, Tiffany D., Emily Beaulieu, and Gregory W. Saxton. 2020. "Sex and Corruption: How Sexism Shapes Voters' Responses to Scandal." *Politics, Groups, and Identities* 8 (1): 103–121.

Barnes, Tiffany D., Regina P. Branton, and Erin C. Cassese. 2017. "A Re-Examination of Women's Electoral Success in Open Seat Elections: the Conditioning Effect of Electoral Competition." *Journal of Women, Politics & Policy* 38 (3):298–317.

Barnes, Tiffany D., and Mirya R. Holman. 2020. "Gender Quotas, Women's Representation, and Legislative Diversity." *Journal of Politics* 82 (4):1271–1286.

Barnes, Tiffany D., Yann Kerevel, and Gregory W. Saxton. 2024. *Working Class Inclusion: Evaluations of Democratic Institutions in Latin America.* New York: Cambridge University Press.

Barnes, Tiffany D., and Gregory W. Saxton. 2019. "Working-Class Legislators and Perceptions of Representation in Latin America." *Political Research Quarterly* 72 (4):910–928.

Barnes, Tiffany D., and Michelle M. Taylor-Robinson. 2018. "Women Cabinet Ministers in Highly Visible Posts and Empowerment of Women: Are the Two Related?" In *Measuring Women's Political Empowerment across the Globe*, edited by Amy Alexander, Catherine Bolzendahl, and Farida Jalazai, 229–255. New York: Springer.

Barnett, Bernice McNair. 1993. "Invisible Southern Black Women Leaders in the Civil Rights Movement: The Triple Constraints of Gender, Race, and Class." *Gender & Society* 7 (2): 162–182.

Batto, Nathan F., and Emily Beaulieu. 2020. "Partisan Conflict and Citizens' Democratic Attitudes: How Partisanship Shapes Reactions to Legislative Brawls." *Journal of Politics* 82 (1):315–328.

Bauer, Nichole M. 2015a. "Emotional, Sensitive, and Unfit for Office: Gender Stereotype Activation and Support for Female Candidates." *Political Psychology* 36 (6):691–708. doi: 10.1111/pops.12186.

Bauer, Nichole M. 2015b. "Who Stereotypes Female Candidates? Identifying Individual Differences in Feminine Stereotype Reliance." *Politics, Groups, and Identities* 3 (1):94–110. doi: https://doi.org/10.1080/21565503.2014.992794.

Bauer, Nichole M. 2017. "The Effects of Counter-Stereotypic Gender Strategies on Candidate Evaluations." *Political Psychology* 38 (2):279–295. doi: 10.1111/pops.12351.

Bauer, Nichole M. 2018. "Untangling the Relationship between Partisanship, Gender Stereotypes, and Support for Female Candidates." *Journal of Women, Politics & Policy* 39 (1):1–25.

Bauer, Nichole M. 2019. "The Effects of Partisan Trespassing Strategies across Candidate Sex." *Political Behavior* 41 (4):897–915. doi: https://doi.org/10.1007/s11109-018-9475-3.

Bauer, Nichole M. 2020a. *The Qualification Gap: Why Women Must Be More Qualified than Men to Win Political Office*. New York, NY: Cambridge University Press.

Bauer, Nichole M. 2020b. "Running Local: Gender Stereotyping and Female Candidates in Local Elections." *Urban Affairs Review* 56 (1):96–123.

Bauer, Nichole M. 2020c. "Shifting Standards: How Voters Evaluate the Qualifications of Female and Male Candidates." *Journal of Politics* 82 (1):1–12. doi: 10.1086/705817.

Bauer, Nichole M. 2024a. "Gendered Self-Promotion: Differences in How Voters Evaluate Women and Men Who Highlight Their Legislative Accomplishments." *Political Research Quarterly* 77 (1):344–358. doi: https://doi.org/10.1177/106591292312091.

Bauer, Nichole M. 2024b. "Who Covers the Qualifications of Female Candidates? Examining Gender Bias in News Coverage across National and Local Newspapers." *Journalism & Mass Communication Quarterly* 101 (3):657–678. doi: https://doi.org/10.1177/10776990221100514.

Bauer, Nichole M., and Ivy A. M. Cargile. 2023. "Women Get the Job Done: The Constituency Service of Non-White and White Women Legislators." *Politics & Gender* 19 (4):1110–1133. doi: 10.1017/S1743923X23000259.

Bauer, Nichole M., and Colleen Carpinella. 2018. "Visual Communication and Candidate Evaluation: The Influence of Feminine and Masculine Images on Support for Female Candidates." *Political Research Quarterly* 71 (2):395–407. doi: 10.1177/1065912917738579.

Bauer, Nichole M., Anna Gunderson, Jeong Hyun Kim, Elizabeth Lane, Belinda Davis, and Kathleen Searles. 2025. "Gendered Expectations: Do Voters Reward Women for Supporting Women's Interests?" *British Journal of Political Science* 55 (80).

Bauer, Nichole M., Cana Kim, Kenlea Barnes, Khaleel Ouedraogo, and Elise Strain. 2024. "Still a Boy's Club: Women Journalists & Political News Coverage." *Journalism Studies* 25 (13):1654–1675. doi: https://doi.org/10.1080/1461670X.2024.2373910.

Bauer, Nichole M., Eugene B. Lee-Johnson, and Dan Qi. 2025. "Tough and Aggressive: How Women of Color Strategically Emphasize Masculine Stereotypes in Campaign Messages." In *Masculinity in American Politics*, edited by Monika L. McDermott and Dan Cassino, 76–98. New York: NYU Press.

Bauer, Nichole M., and Martina Santia. 2021. "Going Feminine: Identifying How and When Female Candidates Emphasize Feminine & Masculine Traits on the Campaign Trail." *Political Research Quarterly* 75 (3):691–705. doi: 10.1177/10659129211020257.

Bauer, Nichole M., and Martina Santia. 2023. "Gendered Times: How Gendered Contexts Shape Campaign Messages of Female Candidates." *Journal of Communication* 73 (4):329–341. doi: https://doi.org/10.1093/joc/jqac052.

Bauer, Nichole M., and Tatum Taylor. 2023. "Selling Them Short? Differences in News Coverage of Female and Male Candidate Qualifications." *Political Research Quarterly* 76 (1):308–322. doi: https://doi.org/10.1177/10659129221086024.

Bauer, Nichole M., Laurel Yong Harbridge, and Yanna Krupnikov. 2017. "Who is Punished? Conditions Affecting Voter Evaluations of Legislators Who Do Not Compromise." *Political Behavior* 39 (2):379–400. doi: DOI 10.1007/s11109-016-9356-6.

Bejarano, Christina. 2013. *The Latina Advantage: Gender, Race, and Political Success*. Austin: University of Texas Press.

Bejarano, Christina, Nadia E. Brown, Sarah Allen Gershon, and Celeste Montoya. 2021. "Shared Identities: Intersectionality, Linked Fate, and Perceptions of Political Candidates." *Political Research Quarterly* 74 (4):970–985.

Bejarano, Christina, and Wendy Smooth. 2022. "Women of Color Mobilizing: Sistahs Are Doing It for Themselves from GOTV to Running Candidates for Political Office." *Journal of Women, Politics & Policy* 43 (1):8–24.

Bem, Sandra Lipsitz. 1981. "Gender Schema Theory: A Cognitive Account of Sex Typing." *Psychological Review* 88 (4):354–364.

Bergersen, Meghan, Samara Klar, and Elizabeth Schmitt. 2018. "Intersectionality and Engagement among the LGBTQ+ Community." *Journal of Women, Politics & Policy* 39 (2):169–219. doi: 10.1080/1554477X.2018.1449527.

Berinsky, Adam J., Gregory A. Huber, and Gabriel S. Lenz. 2012. "Evaluating Online Labor Markets for Experimental Research: Amazon.com's Mechanical Turk." *Political Analysis* 20 (3):351–368.

Berinsky, Adam J., Vincent L. Hutchings, Tali Mendelberg, Lee Shaker, and Nicholas A. Valentino. 2011. "Sex and Race: Are Black Canddiates More Likely to Be Disadvantaged by Sex Scandals?" *Political Behavior* 33:179–202.

Bernhard, Rachel, Shauna Shames, and Dawn Langan Teele. 2021. "To Emerge? Breadwinning, Motherhood, and Women's Decisions to Run for Office." *American Political Science Review* 115 (2):379–394. doi: https://doi.org/10.1017/S0003055420000970.

Bigler, Rebecca S., Andrea E. Arthur, Julie Milligan Hughes, and Meagan M. Patterson. 2008. "The Politics of Race and Gender: Children's Perceptions of Discrimination and the U.S. Presidency." *Analyses of Social Issues and Public Policy* 8 (1):83–112.

Bishin, Benjamin G., Daniel Stevens, and Christian Wilson. 2006. "Character Counts: Honesty and Fairness in Election 2000." *Public Opinion Quarterly* 70 (2):235–248.

Bittner, Amanda, and Elizabeth Goodyear-Grant. 2017. "Sex Isn't Gender: Reforming Concepts and Measurements in the Study of Public Opinion." *Political Behavior* 39 (4):1019–1041. doi: 10.1007/s11109-017-9391-y.

Bligh, Michelle C., Michele M. Shlehofer, Bettina J. Casad, and Amber M. Gaffney. 2012. "Competent Enough, but Would You Vote for Her? Gender Stereotypes and Media Influences on Perceptions of Women Politicians." *Journal of Applied Social Psychology* 42 (3):560–597. doi: https://doi.org/10.1111/j.1559-1816.2011.00781.x

BLS, Bureau of Labor Statistics. 2000. Changes in Women's Labor Force Participation in the 20th Century. https://www.bls.gov/opub/ted/2000/feb/wk3/art03.htm#:~:text=In%201950%20about%20one%20in,with%2059.8%20percent%20in%201998.: Bureau of Labor Statistics.

Bobo, Lawrence D., and David Mickey-Pabello. 2020. "Ethnoracial Exclusion and Social Inequality." *Du Bois Review* 16 (2):285–289.

Bonneau, Chris W., and Kristin Kanthak. 2020. "Stronger Together: Political Ambition and the Presentation of Women Running for Office." *Politics, Groups, and Identities* 8 (3):576–594.

Bos, Angela L., Bas W. Doorn, and Kjersten Nelson. 2018. "Who Is in the Picture? The Gender Composition of Images of Congress in Party Caucus Twitter Feeds and Online Media." *Politics, Groups, and Identities* 6 (4):788–801.

Bos, Angela L., Jill S. Greenlee, Mirya R. Holman, Zoe M. Oxley, and Celeste J. Lay. 2022. "This One's for the Boys: How Gendered Political Socialization Limits Girls' Political Ambition and Interest." *American Political Science Review* 116 (2):484–501. doi: https://doi.org/10.1017/S0003055421001027.

Bos, Angela L., Monica C. Schneider, and Brittany L. Utz. 2017. "Gender Stereotypes and Prejudice in U.S. Elections." In *APA Handbook of the Psychology of Women* edited by Cheryl Travis and Jackie White, 367–384. Washington, DC: American Psychological Assocaition.

Boussalis, Constantine, Travis G. Coan, Mirya Holman, and Stefan Muller. 2021. "Gender, Candidate Emotional Expression, and Voter Reactions during Televised Debates."

American Political Science Review 115 (4):1242–1257. doi: https://doi.org/10.1017/ S0003055421000666.

Boydstun, Amber E. 2013. *Making the News: Politics, the Media, and Agenda Setting.* Chicago: University of Chicago Press.

Bracic, Ana, Mackenzie Israel-Trummel, and Allyson Shortle. 2019. "Is Sexism for White People? Gender Stereotypes, Race, and the 2016 Presidential Election." *Political Behavior* 41 (2):281–307. doi: doi.org/10.1007/s1110.

Branton, Regina, Ashley English, Samantha Pettey, and Tiffany D. Barnes. 2018. "The Impact of Gender and Quality Opposition on the Relative Assessment of Candidate Competency." *Electoral Studies* 54:35–43. doi: doi: 10.1016/j.electstud.2018.04.002.

Bratton, Kathleen A. 2006. "The Behavior and Success of Latino Legislators: Evidence from the States." *Social Science Quarterly* 87 (5):1136–1157.

Bratton, Kathleen A., Karry L. Haynie, and Beth Reingold. 2007. "Agenda Setting and African-American Women in State Legislatures." *Women, Politics, and Policy* 71 (Summer/Fall): 71–96.

Bratton, Kathleen A., and Kerry L. Haynie. 1999. "Agenda Setting and Legislative Success in State Legislatures: The Effects of Gender and Race." *Journal of Politics* 61 (3):658. doi: 10.2307/2647822.

Broockman, David E. 2014. "Do Female Politicians Empower Women to Vote or Run for Office? A Regression Discontinuity Approach." *Electoral Studies* 34:190–204.

Brown, Nadia. 2014a. *Sisters in the Statehouse: Black Women and Legislative Decision Making.* New York: Oxford University Press.

Brown, Nadia, and Kira Hudson Banks. 2014. "Black Women's Agenda Asetting in the Maryland State Legislature." *Journal of African American Studies* 18 (2):264–180.

Brown, Nadia E. 2014b. "Political Participation of Women of Color: An Intersectional Analysis." *Journal of Women, Politics & Policy* 35 (4):315–348. doi: 10.1080/ 1554477X.2014.955406.

Brown, Nadia E., and Sarah Allen Gershon. 2017. "Examining Intersectionality and Symbolic Representation." *Politics, Groups, and Identities* 5 (3):500–505. doi: https://doi.org/10.1080/ 21565503.2017.1321995.

Brown, Nadia, and Danielle Casarez Lemi. 2021. *Sister Style: The Politics of Appearance for Black Women Political Elites.* New York: Oxford University Press.

Bryant, Lisa A., and Julia Marin Hellwege. 2018. "Working Mothers Represent: How Children Affect the Legislative Agenda of Women in Congress." *American Politics Research* 47 (3):447–470.

Burden, Barry C., Yoshikuni Ono, and Masahiro Yamada. 2017. "Reassessing Public Support for a Female President." *Journal of Politics* 79 (3):1–7.

Burrell, Barbara C. 1994. *A Woman's Place Is in the House.* Michigan: University of Michigan Press.

Burris, Kimberly, Roya Ayman, Yi Che, and Hanyi Min. 2013. "Asian Americans' and Caucasians' Implicit Leadership Theories: Asian Stereotypes, Transformational, and Authentic Leadership." *Asian American Journal of Psychology* 4 (4):258–266.

Bush, Sarah Sunn. 2011. "International Politics and the Spread of Quotas for Women in Legislatures." *International Organization* 65 (1):103–137.

Bush, Sarah Sunn, and Pär Zetterberg. 2021. "Gender Quotas and International Reputation." *American Journal of Political Science* 65 (2):326–341. doi: 10.1111/ajps.12557.

Butler, Daniel M., Elin Naurin, and Patrik Öhberg. 2022. "Constituents Ask Female Legislators to Do More." *Journal of Politics* 84 (4):2278–2282.

Bystrom, Dianne G., M. C. Banwart, Lynda Lee Kaid, and Terry A. Robertson. 2005. *Gender and Candidate Communication: Videostyle, Webstyle, Newsstyle.* New York: Routledge.

Campbell, David, and Christina Wolbrecht. 2020. "The Resistance as Role Model: Disillusionment and Protest among American Adolescents After 2016." *Political Behavior* 42 (4):1143–1168.

Campbell, David E., and Christina Wolbrecht. 2006. "See Jane Run: Women Politicians as Role Models for Adolescents." *Journal of Politics* 68 (2):233–247.

Campi, Ashleigh, and Jane Junn. 2019. "Racial Linked Fate and Gender in U.S. Politics." *Politics, Groups, and Identities* 7 (3):654–662. doi: 10.1080/21565503.2019.1638805.

Cappella, Joseph N., and Kathleen Hall Jamieson. 1996. "News Frames, Political Cynicism, and Media Cynicism." *Annals of the American Academy of Political and Social Science* 546:71–84.

Cargile, Ivy A. M. 2023. "Stereotyping Latinas: Candidate Gender and Ethnicity on the Political Stage." *Politics, Groups, and Identities* 11 (2):207–225. doi: https://doi.org/10.1080/21565503.2021.1946097.

Cargile, Ivy A. M. 2016. "Latina Issues: An Analysis of the Policy Issue Competencies of Latina Candidates." In *Distinct Identities: Minority Women in U.S. Politics*, edited by Nadia E. Brown and Sarah A. Gershon, 134–150. New York: Routledge.

Cargile, Ivy A. M., Jennifer Merolla, and Jean Reith Schroedel. 2016. "Intersectionality and Latino/a Candidate Evaluation." In *Latinas in American Politics*, edited by Sharon Navarro, Sharon Hernandez, and Leslie A. Navarro, 39–60. London: Lexington in American Politics.

Carnes, Nicholas, and Noam Lupu. 2016. "Do Voters Dislike Working-Class Candidates? Voter Biases and the Descriptive Underrepresentation of the Working Class." *American Political Science Review* 110 (4):832–845.

Carpinella, Colleen, and Nichole M. Bauer. 2021. "A Visual Analysis of Gender Stereotypes in Campaign Advertising." *Politics, Groups, and Identities* 9 (2):369–386. doi: doi.org/10.1080/21565503.2019.1637353.

Carroll, Susan J., and Kira Sanbonmatsu. 2013. *More Women Can Run: Gender and Pathways to the State Legislatures*. New York: Oxford University Press.

Cassese, Erin C. 2019. "Intersectional Stereotyping in Political Decision Making "In *Oxford Research Encyclopedia of Political Decision Making*, edited by David Redlawsk. Oxford: Oxford University Press. Available at https://oxfordre.com/politics/view/10.1093/acrefore/9780190228637.001.0001/acrefore-9780190228637-e-773

Cassese, Erin C., and Mirya R. Holman. 2019. "Playing the Woman Card: Ambivalent Sexism in the 2016 U.S. Presidential Race." *Political Psychology* 40 (1):55–74.

Cassese, Erin C., and Tiffany D. Barnes. 2019. "Reconciling Sexism and Women's Support for Republican Candidates: A Look at Gender, Class, and Whiteness in the 2012 and 2016 Presidential Races." *Political Behavior* 41 (2):677–700.

Cassese, Erin C., and Mirya R. Holman. 2018. "Party and Gender Stereotypes in Campaign Attacks." *Political Behavior* 40 (3):785–807. doi: DOI 10.1007/s11109-017-9423-7.

Castle, Jeremiah, Shannon Jenkins, Candice D. Ortbals, Lori Poloni-Staudinger, and J. Cherie Strachan. 2020. "The Effect of the #MeToo Movement on Political Engagement and Ambition in 2018." *Political Research Quarterly* 73 (4):926–941. doi: 10.1177/1065912920924824.

Castorena, Oscar. 2023. "Female Officeholders and Women's Political Engagement: The Role of Parties." *Political Behavior* 45(4): 1609–1631.

Chanley, Virginia A., Thomas J. Rudolph, and Wendy M. Rahn. 2000. "The Origins and Consequences of Public Trust in Government." *Public Opinion Quarterly* 64:239–256.

Childs, Sarah, and Mona Lena Krook. 2006. "Should Feminists Give Up on Critical Mass? A Contingent Yes." *Politics & Gender* 4 (2):522–530.

Childs, Sarah, and Mona Lena Krook. 2008. "Critical Mass Theory and Women's Political Representation." *Political Studies* 56:725–736.

Childs, Sarah, and Mona Lena Krook. 2009. "Analysing Women's Substantive Representation: From Critical Mass to Critical Actors." *Government and Opposition* 44 (2):125–145. doi: 10.1111/j.1477-7053.2009.01279.x.

Clark, Christopher. 2019. *Gaining Voice: The Causes and Consequences of Black Representation in the American States.* New York: Oxford University Press.

Clayton, Amanda. 2018. "Do Gender Quotas Really Reduce Bias? Evidence from a Policy Experiment in Southern Africa." *Journal of Experimental Political Science* 5 (3): 182–194.

Clayton, Amanda, Diana Z. O'Brien, and Jennifer Piscopo, M. 2019. "All Male Panels? Representation and Democratic Legitimacy." *American Journal of Political Science* 63 (1):113–129. doi: 10.1111/ajps.12391.

Clayton, Amanda, Diana Z. O'Brien, and Jennifer Piscopo, M. 2023a. "Electoral Gender Quotas and Democratic Legitimacy." Mini-Conference on Gender, Race, and Diversity in Representation, University of Houston.

Clayton, Amanda, Diana Z. O'Brien, and Jennifer Piscopo, M. 2023b. "Women Grab Back: Exclusion, Policy Threat, and Women's Political Ambition." *American Political Science Review* 117 (4):1465–1485.

Clayton, Amanda, Diana Z. O'Brien, and Jennifer Piscopo, M. 2024. "Founding Narratives and Men's Political Ambition: Experimental Evidence from US Civics Lessons." *British Journal of Political Science* 54 (1):129–151. doi: 10.1017/S0007123423000340.

Connor, Rachael A., and Susan T. Fiske. 2019. "Not Minding the Gap: How Hostile Sexism Encourages Choice Explanations for the Gender Income Gap." *Psychology of Women Quarterly* 43 (1):22–36.

Conroy, Meredith 2015. *Masculinity, Media, and the American Presidency.* New York: Palgrave McMillan.

Conroy, Meredith, and Jon Green. 2020. "It Takes a Motive: Communal and Agentic Articulated Interest and Candidate Emergence." *Political Research Quarterly* 73 (4):942–956.

Conroy, Meredith, and Sarah Oliver. 2020. *Who Runs? The Masculine Advantage in Candidate Emergence.* Ann Arbor: University of Michigan Press.

Cook, Elizabeth Adell, and Clyde Wilcox. 1994. *The Year of the Woman: Myths and Realities.* Boulder: Westview Press.

Cook, Timothy E. 1997. *Governing with the News: The News Media as a Political Institution.* Chicago, IL: University of Chicago Press. Reprint, 2nd edition.

Cooperman, Rosalyn. 2020. "On the Money: Assessing the Campaign-Finance Networks of Women Congressional Candidates." In *Politicking While Female: The Political Lives of Women*, edited by Nichole M. Bauer, 71–90. Baton Rouge: Louisiana State University Press.

Cox, Gary, and Matthew McCubbins. 1993. *Legislative Leviathan: Party Government in the House.* Berkeley: University of California Press.

Craft, Stephanie, and Wayne Wanta. 2004. "Women in the Newsroom: Influence of Female Editors and Reporters on the News Agenda." *Journalism and Mass Communication Quarterly* 81:124–138.

Crenshaw, Kimberlé. 1991. "Mapping the Margins: Intersectionality, Identity Politics, and Violence against Women of Color." *Stanford Law Review* 43 (6):1241–1299. doi: 10.2307/1229039.

Crowder-Meyer, Melody. 2013. "Gendered Recruitment without Trying: How Local Party Recruiters Affect Women's Representation." *Politics & Gender* 9:390–413.

Crowder-Meyer, Melody. 2020. "Baker, Bus Driver, Babysitter, Candidate? Revealing the Gendered Development of Political Ambition among Ordinary Americans." *Political Behavior* 42:359–384.

Crowder-Meyer, Melody, and Rosalyn Cooperman. 2018. "Can't Buy Them Love: How Party Culture among Donors Contributes to the Party Gap in Women's Representation." *Journal of Politics* 80 (4):1211–1224. doi: 10.1086/698848.

Crowder-Meyer, Melody, Shana Kushner Gadarian, and Jessica Trounstine. 2015. "Electoral Institutions, Gender Stereotypes, and Women's Local Representation." *Politics, Groups, and Identities* 3 (2):318–334.

Crowder-Meyer, Melody, and Benjamin Lauderdale. 2014. "A Partisan Gap in the Supply of Female Potential Candidates in the United States." *Research and Politics* 1:1–7.

Crowder-Meyer, Melody, and Adrienne R. Smith. 2015. "How the Strategic Context Affects Women's Emergence and Success in Local Legislative Elections." *Politics, Groups, and Identities* 3 (2):295–317.

Dahlerup, Drude. 2006. "The Story of the Theory of Critical Mass." *Politics & Gender* 4 (2):511–522.

Darr, Joshua P., Matthew P. Hitt, and Johanna L. Dunaway. 2021. *Home Style Opinion: How Local Newspapers Can Slow Polarization.* New York: Cambridge University Press: Elements in Political Communication.

Davis, Belinda Creel, Michelle Livermore, and Younghee Lim. 2011. "The Extended Reach of Minority Political Power: The Interaction of Descriptive Representation, Managerial Networking, and Race." *Journal of Politics* 73 (2):494–507.

Dawson, Michael C. 2001. *Behind the Mule: Race and Class in African-American Politics.* Princeton: Princeton University Press.

De Benedictis-Kessner, Justin, Diana Da In Lee, Yamil R. Velez, and Christopher Warshaw. 2023. "American Local Government Elections Database." *Scientific Data* 10 (1):912.

de Bruin, Marjan. 2000. "Gender, Organizational and Professional Identities in Journalism." *Journalism* 1 (2):217–238.

Dearing, James W., and Everett M. Rogers. 1996. *Agenda-Setting.* Thousand Oaks, CA: Sage.

Deaux, Kay, and Laurie L. Lewis. 1984. "Structure of Gender Stereotypes: Interrelationships among Components and Gender Labels." *Journal of Personality and Social Psychology* 46 (5):991–1004.

Delli Carpini, Michael X., and Scott Keeter. 1996. *What Americans Know about Politics and Why It Matter.* New Haven: Yale University Press.

Diekman, Amanda B., and Alice H. Eagly. 2000. "Stereotypes as Dynamic Constructs: Women and Men of the Past, Present, and Future." *Personality and Social Psychology Bulletin* 26 (10):1171–1188.

Dietrich, Bryce J., Matthew Hayes, and Diana Z. O'Brien. 2019. "Pitch Perfect: Vocal Pitch and the Emotional Intensity of Congressional Speech on Women." *American Political Science Review* 113 (4):941–962. doi: 10.1017/S0003055419000467.

Ditonto, Tessa. 2019. "Direct and Indirect Effects of Prejudice: Sexism, Information, and Voting Behavior in Political Campaigns." *Politics, Groups, and Identities* 7 (3):590–609. doi: 10.1080/21565503.2019.1632065.

Ditonto, Tessa M. 2017. "A High Bar or a Double Standard? Gender, Competence, and Information in Political Campaigns." *Political Behavior* 39 (2):301–325. doi: 10.1007/s11109-016-9357-5.

Ditonto, Tessa M., Allison J. Hamilton, and David P. Redlawsk. 2014. "Gender Stereotypes, Information Search, and Voting Behavior in Political Campaigns." *Political Behavior* 36 (2):335–358. doi: 10.1007/s11109-013-9232-6.

Dittmar, Kelly. 2015. *Navigating Gendered Terrain: Stereotypes and Strategy in Political Campaigns.* Philadelphia: Temple University Press.

Dittmar, Kelly, Kira Sanbonmatsu, and Susan J. Carroll. 2018. *A Seat at the Table.* New York: Oxford University Press.

Dolan, Julie, and Paru Shah. 2020. "She Persisted: Gender, Electoral Loss, and the Decision to Run Again." *Political Research Quarterly* 73 (4):957–966. doi: 10.1177/1065912920934869.

Dolan, Kathleen. 2006. "Symbolic Mobilization? The Impact of Candidate Sex in American Election." *American Politics Research* 34 (6):687–704.

Dolan, Kathleen. 2010. "The Impact of Gender Stereotyped Evaluations on Support for Women Candidates." *Political Behavior* 32 (1):69–88. doi: 10.1007/s11109-009-9090-4.

Dolan, Kathleen. 2014. *When Does Gender Matter? Women Candidates & Gender Stereotypes in American Elections.* New York: Oxford University Press.

Dolan, Kathleen, and Timothy Lynch. 2016. "The Impact of Gender Stereotypes on Voting for Women Candidates by Level and Type of Office." *Politics & Gender* 12 (3):573–595.

Dolan, Kathleen, and Kira Sanbonmatsu. 2009. "Gender Stereotypes and Attitudes toward Gender Balance in Government." *American Politics Research* 37 (3):409–428.

Dovi, Suzanne. 2002. "Preferable Descriptive Representatives: Will Just Any Woman, Black, or Latino Do?" *American Political Science Review* 96 (4):729–743.

Druckman, James N. 2001. "On the Limits of Framing Effects." *Journal of Politics* 63 (4): 1041–1066.

Druckman, James N., and Elizabeth A. Sharrow. 2023. *Equality Unfulfilled: How Title IX's Policy Design Undermines Change to College Sports.* New York: Cambridge University Press.

Duerst-Lahti, Georgia. 2007. "Masculinity on the Campaign Trail." In *Rethinking Madam President: Are We Ready for a Woman in the White House?*, edited by Lori Cox Han and Caroline Heldman, 87–112. Boulder, CO: Lynne Rienner Publishers.

Dunaway, Johanna L. 2008. "Markets, Ownership, and the Quality of Campaign News Coverage." *Journal of Politics* 70 (4):1193–1202. doi: 10.1017/S0022381608081140.

Dunaway, Johanna, and Regina G. Lawrence. 2015. "What Predicts the Game Frame? Media Ownership, Electoral Context, and Campagin News." *Political Communication* 32 (1): 43–60. doi: 10.1080/10584609.2014.880975.

Dunaway, Johanna, Regina G. Lawrence, Melody Rose, and Christopher R. Weber. 2013. "Traits versus Issues: How Female Candidates Shape Coverage of Senate and Gubernatorial Races." *Political Research Quarterly* 66 (3):715–726. doi: https://doi.org/10.1177/1065912913491464.

Dynes, Adam M., Hans J.G. Hassell, Matthew R. Miles, and Jessica Robinson Preece. 2021. "Personality and Gendered Selection Processes in the Political Pipeline." *Politics & Gender* 17 (1):53–73.

Eagly, A. H. 1987. *Sex Differences in Social Behavior: A Social Role Interpretation.* Hillsdale, NJ: L. Erlbaum Associates.

Eagly, Alice H., and Linda L. Carli. 2003a. "The Female Leadership Advantage: An Evaluation of the Evidence." *The Leadership Quarterly* 14:807–834.

Eagly, Alice H., and Linda L. Carli. 2003b. "Finding Gender Advantage and Disadvantage: Systematic Research Integration Is the Solution." *The Leadership Quarterly* 14:851–859. doi: 10.1016/j.leaqua.2003.09.003.

Eagly, Alice H., and Steve J. Karau. 2002. "Role Congruity Theory of Prejudice toward Female Leaders." *Psychological Review* 109 (3):573–594. doi: 10.1037//0033-295X.109.3.573.

Eagly, Alice H., Christa Nater, David I. Miller, Michele Kaufmann, and Sabine Sczesny. 2020. "Gender Stereotypes Have Changed: A Cross-Temporal Meta-Analysis of U.S. Public Opinion Polls, 1946–2018." *American Psychologist* 75 (3):301–315.

Eatough, Mandi, and Jessica R. Preece. 2025. "Crediting Invisible Work: Congress and the Lawmaking Productivity Metric (LawProM)." *American Political Science Review* 119 (2): 566–584. doi: https://doi.org/10.1017/S0003055424000224

Enders, Adam M., and Jamil S. Scott. 2019. "The Increasing Racialization of American Electoral Politics, 1988-2016." *American Politics Resaerch* 47 (2):275–303. doi: https://doi.org/10.1177/1532673X18755654.

Fenno, Richard F. 1962. "The House Appropriations Committee as a Political System." *American Political Science Review* 56:310–324.

Filler, Nicole, and Pei-te Lien. 2016. "Asian Pacific Americans in U.S. Politics: Gender and Pathways to Elected Office." In *Distinct Identities: Minority Women in U.S. Politics*, edited by Nadia E. Brown and Sarah Allen Gershon, 218–233. New York, NY: Routledge, Taylor & Francis Group.

Filler, Nicole, and Pei-te Lien. 2023. "Asian Americans Making Waves in City Halls and Beyond." In *Distict Identities*, edited by Nadia Brown and Sarah Gershon, 115–130.

Fine, Marlene G. 2009. "Women Leaders' Discursive Constructions of Leadership." *Women's Studies in Communication* 32 (2):180–202.

Fiske, Susan T. 2018. "Stereotype Content: Warmth and Competence Endure." *Current Directions in Psychological Science* 27 (2):67–73. doi: https://doi.org/10.1177/0963721417738825.

Fletcher, Holly Berkley. 2008. *Gender and the American Temperance Movement of the Nineteenth Century*. New York: Routledge.

Flores, Andrew, Dakota Strode, and Donald P. Haider-Markel. 2025. "Political Psychology and the Study of LGBTQI+ Groups, Politics, and Policy: Existing Research and Future Directions." *Advances in Political Psychology*. 46 213–249 S1 doi:https://doi.org/10.1111/pops.12989

Ford Dowe, Pearl K. 2020. "Resisting Marginalization: Black Women's Political Ambition and Agency." *PS: Political Science & Politics*:697–701. doi: 10.1017/S1049096520000554.

Fox, Richard L., and Jennifer L. Lawless. 2011. "Gendered Perceptions and Political Candidacies: A Central Barrier to Women's Equality in Electoral Politics." *American Journal of Political Science* 55 (1):59–73.

Fox, Richard L., and Zoe M. Oxley. 2003. "Gender Stereotyping in State Executive Elections: Candidate Selection and Success." *Journal of Politics* 65 (3):833–850.

Fraga, Luis, Linda Lopez, Valerie Martinez-Ebers, and Ricardo Ramirez. 2006. "Gender and Ethnicity: Patterns of Electoral Success and Legislative Advocacy among Latina and Latino State Officials in Four States." *Journal of Women, Politics & Policy* 28 (3-4):131–145.

Frederick, Angela. 2013. "Bringing Narrative In: Race-Gender Storytelling, Political Ambition, and Women's Paths to Public Office." *Journal of Women, Politics & Policy* 34 (2):113–137.

Fridkin, Kim L., and Patrick J. Kenney. 2014. "How the Gender of U.S. Senators Influences People's Understanding of Politics." *The Journal of Politics* 76 (4):1017–1031.

Fulton, Sarah A. 2012. "Running Backwards and in High Heels: The Gendered Quality Gap and Incumbent Electoral Success." *Political Research Quarterly* 65 (2):303–314. doi: 10.1177/1065912911401419.

Fulton, Sarah A., and Kostanca Dhima. 2021. "The Gendered Politics of Congressional Elections." *Political Behavior* 43 (4):1611–1637.

Funk, Carolyn L. 1999. "Bringing the Candidate into Models of Candidate Evaluation." *Journal of Politics* 61 (3):700–720.

Galtung, Johan, and Mari Holmboe Ruge. 1965. "The Structure of Foreign News: The Presentation of the Congo, Cuba, and Cyprus Crises in Four Norweigan Newspapers." *Journal of Peace Research* 2 (1):64–91.

Gans, Herbert J. 1980. *Deciding What's News*. New York: Vintage.

Gay, Claudine, and Katherine Tate. 1998. "Doubly Bound: The Impact of Gender and Race on the Politics of Black Women." *Political Psychology* 19 (1):169–184.

Gershon, Sarah Allen, and Jessica Lavariega Monforti. 2021. "Intersecting Campaigns: Candidate Race, Ethnicity, Gender and Voter Evaluations." *Politics, Groups, and Identities* 9 (3):439–463. doi: 10.1080/21565503.2019.1584752.

Gershon, Sarah Allen, Celeste Montoya, Christina Bejarano, and Nadia Brown. 2019. "Intersectional Linked Fate and Political Representation." *Politics, Groups, and Identities* 7 (3):642–653. doi: 10.1080/21565503.2019.1639520.

Ghosh, Shreenita, Min-Hsin Su, Jiyoun Suk, Chau Tong, Kruthika Kamath, Ornella Hills, Teresa Correa, Christine Garlough, Porismita Borah, and Dhavan Shah. 2022. "Covering #MeToo across the News Spectrum: Political Accusation and Public Events as Drivers of Press Attention." *International Journal of Press/Politics* 27 (1):158–185. doi: https://doi.org/10.1177/1940161220968081.

Gill, Rebecca, Jennie Sweet-Cushman, and Christopher Zorn. 2024. "Public Beliefs about Gender Representation in Legislative Bodies." American Political Science Association's Annual Meeting, Philadelphia, PA.

Givens, Sonja M. Brown, and Jennifer L. Monahan. 2005. "Priming Mammies, Jezebels, and Other Controlling Images: An Examination of the Influence of Mediated Stereotypes on Perceptions of an African American Woman." *Media Psychology* 7 (1):87–106.

Glick, Peter. 1991. "Trait-Based and Sex-Based Discrimination in Occupational Prestige, Occupational Salary, and Hiring." *Sex Roles* 25 (5/6):351–378.

Glick, Peter, and Susan T. Fiske. 1996. "The Ambivalent Sexism Inventory: Differentiating Hostile and Benevolent Sexism." *Journal of Personality and Social Psychology* 86:713–728.

Glick, Peter, Korin Wilk, and Michele Perreault. 1995. "Images of Occupations: Components of Gender and Status in Occupational Stereotypes." *Sex Roles* 32 (9/10):565–582.

Golebiowska, Ewa A. 2003. "When to Tell?: Disclosure of Concealable Group Membership, Stereotypes, and Political Evaluation." *Political Behavior* 25 (4):313–337.

Gonzalez, Sylvia I., and Nichole M. Bauer. 2022. "Strong and Caring? The Stereotypic Traits of Women of Color in Politics." *Politics, Groups, and Identities* 12 (1):124–141. doi: https://doi.org/10.1080/21565503.2022.2144389.

Gottfredson, Linda S. 1981. "Circumscription and Compromise: A Developmental Theory of Occupational Aspirations." *Journal of Counseling Psychology Monograph* 28 (6):545–580.

Goyal, Tanushree, and Cameron Sells. 2024. "Descriptive Representation and Party Building: Evidence from Municipal Governments in Brazil." *American Political Science Review* 118 (4):1840–1855. doi: 10.1017/S0003055423001168.

Grabe, Maria Elizabeth, Lelia Sampson, Asta Zelenkauskaite, and Narine S. Yegiyan. 2011. "Covering Presidential Election Campaigns: Does Reporter Gender Affect the Work Lives of Correspondents and Their Reportage?" *Journal of Broadcasting and Electronic Media* 55 (3):285–306.

Graber, Doris. 1988. *Processing the News*. New York: Longman.

Grant, Jan. 1988. "Women as Managers: What Can They Offer to Organizations?" *Organizational Dynamics* 16 (3):56–63.

Greene, Stacey, Yalidy Matos, and Kira Sanbonmatsu. 2021. "The Politics of "Women of Color": A Group Identity Worth Investigating." *Politics, Groups, and Identities* 11 (3):549–570.

Grey, Sandra. 2006. "Numbers and Beyond: The Relevance of Critical Mass in Gender Research." *Politics & Gender* 2 (4):492–502.

Groenendyk, Eric, and Yanna Krupnikov. 2021. "What Motivates Reasoning? A Theory of Goal-Dependent Political Evaluation." *American Journal of Political Science* 65 (1):180–196.

Grose, Christian R. 2010. *Congress in Black and White: Race and Representation in Washington and at Home*. New York: Cambridge University Press.

Grumbach, Jacob M., Alexander Sahn, and Sarah Staszak. 2022. "Gender, Race, and Intersectionality in Campaign Finance." *Political Behavior* 44:319–340.

Gunderson, Anna, and Laura Huber. 2024. "Blue First and Foremost: Female Descriptive Representation, Rape, and the Justice Gap." *Perspectives on Politics* 22 (1):28–43. doi: 10.1017/S1537592722000974.

Gunderson, Anna, Emily Rains, Nichole Bauer, and Annie Sheehan-Dean. 2025. "Gender Stereotypes across Electoral Contexts." Midwest Political Science Association, Chicago, IL.

Guo, Lei. 2019. "Media Agenda Diversity and Intermedia Agenda Setting in a Controlled Media Environment: A Computational Analysis of China's Online News." *Journalism Studies* 20 (16):2460–2477. doi: https://doi.org/10.1080/1461670X.2019.1601029.

Guttmann, A., and D. Thompson. 2012. *The Spirit of Compromise: Why Governing Demands It and Campaigning Undermines It.* Princeton: Princeton University Press.

Haines, Elizabeth L., Kay Deaux, and Nicole Lofaro. 2016. "The Times They Are a-Changing or Are They Not? A Comparison of Gender Stereotypes, 1983-2014." *Psychology of Women Quarterly.* doi: 10.1177/0361684316634081.

Hamel, Brian T., and Nichole M. Bauer. 2024. "Gender, Issue Stereotypes, and the Electoral Returns to Distributive Politics in the United States." *Politics & Gender* 20 (4):858–878. doi: https://doi.org/10.1017/S1743923X24000321.

Hancock, Ange-Marie. 2007. "Intersectionality as a Normative and Empirical Paradigm." *Politics & Gender* 3 (2):248–254.

Hanitzch, Thomas, and Folker Hanuch. 2012. "Does Gender Determine Journalists' Professional Views? A Reassessment Based on Cross-National Evidence." *European Journal of Communication* 27 (3):257–277. doi: 10.1177/0267323112454804.

Hannagan, Rebecca J., Monica C. Schneider, and Jill S. Greenlee. 2012. "Symposium: Data, Methods, and Theoretical Implications." *PS: Political Science and Politics* 45 (2): 232–237.

Harbridge, Laurel, and Neil Malhotra. 2011. "Electoral Incentives and Partisan Conflict in Congress: Evidence from Survey Experiments." *American Journal of Political Science* 55 (3):494–510.

Harcup, Tony, and Deirdre O'Neill. 2017. "What is News? News Values Revisited (Again)." *Jouranlism Studies* 18 (12): 1470–1488. doi: https://doi.org/10.1080/1461670X.2016. 1150193.

Harris-Perry, Melissa. 2013. *Sister Citizen: Shame, Stereotypes, and Black Women in America.* New Haven: Yale University Press.

Hawkesworth, Mary. 2003. "Congressional Enactments of Race–Gender: Toward a Theory of Raced–Gendered Institutions." *American Political Science Review* 97 (4):529–550. doi: https://doi.org/10.1017/S0003055403000868.

Hayes, Danny. 2005. "Candidate Qualities through a Partisan Lens: A Theory of Trait Ownership." *American Journal of Political Science* 49 (4):908–923. doi: https://doi.org/10.1111/j.1540-5907.2005.00163.x

Hayes, Danny 2011. "When Gender and Party Collide: Stereotyping in Candidate Trait Attribution." *Politics & Gender* 7 (2):133–165. doi: 10.1017/S1743923X11000055.

Hayes, Danny, and Jennifer L. Lawless. 2016. *Women on the Run: Gender, Media, and Political Campaigns in a Polarized Era.* New York: Cambridge University Press.

Haynie, Kerry L. 2001. *African American Legislators in the American States.* New York, NY: Columbia University Press.

Hegelsen, S. 1990. *The Female Advantage.* New York: Double-Day.

Heilman, Madeline. 2012. "Gender Stereotypes and Workplace Bias." *Research in Organizational Behavior* 32:113–135.

Heilman, Madeline E. 2001. "Description and Prescription: How Gender Stereotypes Prevent Women's Ascent up the Organizational Ladder." *Journal of Social Issues* 57 (4): 181–203.

Heilman, Madeline E., Aaron S. Wallen, Daniella Fuchs, and Melinda M. Tamkins. 2004. "Penalties for Success: Reactions to Women Who Succeed at Male Gender-Typed Tasks." *Journal of Applied Psychology* 89 (3):416–427. doi: 10.1037/0021-9010.89.3.416.

Heilman, Madeline E., and Tyler G. Okimoto. 2007. "Why Are Women Penalized for Success at Male Tasks?: The Implied Communality Deficit." *Journal of Applied Psychology* 91 (1): 81–92.

Heldman, Caroline J., Susan J. Carroll, and Stephanie Olson. 2005. "'She Brought Only a Skirt': Print Media Coverage of Elizabeth Dole's Bid for the Republican Presidential Nomination." *Political Communication* 22:315–335. doi: https://doi.org/10.1080/10584600591006564.

Herring, Mary, Jennie Sweet-Cushman, Elizabeth Prough, and Fred Vultee. 2022. "Who Dominates the Conversation? The Effect of Gender, Discussion Medium, and Controversy on Political Discussion." *Feminist Media Studies* 22 (3):522–570. doi: 10.1080/14680777.2020.1808036.

Hetherington, Marc J. 1998. "The Political Relevance of Political Trust." *American Political Science Review* 92 (4):791–808.

Hetherington, Marc J., and Jason A. Husser. 2012. "How Trust Matters: The Changing Political Relevance of Political Trust." *American Journal of Political Science* 56 (2):312–325. doi: I0.1111/j.1540-5907.2011.00548.x.

Hibbing, John R., and Elizabeth Theiss-Morse. 2002. *Stealth Democracy*. New York: Cambridge University Press.

Hilliard, Lacey J., and Lynn S. Liben. 2010. "Differing Levels of Gender Salience in Preschool Classrooms: Effects on Children's Gender Attitudes and Intergroup Bias." *Child Development* 81 (6):1787–1798.

Hilliard, Lacey J., and Lynn S. Liben. 2019. "Addressing Sexism with Children: Young Adults' Beliefs about Bias Socialization." *Child Development* 91 (2):488–507.

Hinojosa, Magda, and Miki Caul Kittilson. 2020. *Seeing Women, Strengthening Democracy: How Women in Politics Foster Connected Citizens*. New York: Oxford University Press.

Hitt, Matthew P., and Kathleen Searles. 2018. "Media Coverage and Public Approval of the U.S. Supreme Court." *Political Communication* 35 (4):566–586. doi: 10.1080/10584609.2018.1467517.

Hochschild, Arlie, and Anne Machung. 1990. *The Second Shift*. New York: Penguin Books.

Holman, Mirya R. 2017. "Women in Local Government: What We Know and Where We Go From Here." *State and Local Government Review* 49 (4):285–296. doi: DOI: 10.1177/0160323X17732608.

Holman, Mirya R., Anna Mahoney, and Emma Hurler. 2022. "Let's Work Together: Bill Success via Women's Cosponsorship in U.S. State Legislatures." *Political Research Quarterly* 75 (3):676–690. doi: https://doi.org/10.1177/10659129211020123.

Holman, Mirya R., Jennifer L. Merolla, Elizabeth J. Zechmeister, and Ding Wang. 2019. "Terrorism, Gender, and the 2016 U.S. Presidential Election." *Electoral Studies* 61:1–8. doi: https://doi.org/10.1016/j.electstud.2019.03.009.

Holman, Mirya R., and Anna Mitchell Mahoney. 2019. "Stop, Collaborate, and Listen: Women's Collaboration in US State Legislatures." *Legislative Studies Quarterly* 43 (2): 179–206. doi: 10.1111/lsq.12199.

Holman, Mirya R., Jennifer L. Merolla, and Elizabeth J. Zechmeister. 2016. "Terrorist Threat, Male Stereotypes, and Candidate Evaluations." *Political Research Quarterly* 69 (1):134–147. doi: https://doi.org/10.1177/1065912915624018.

Holman, Mirya R., Jennifer L. Merolla, and Elizabeth J. Zechmeister. 2021. "The Curious Case of Theresa May and the Public That Did not Rally: Gendered Reactions to Terrorist Attacks Can Cause Slumps not Bumps." *American Political Science Review* 116 (1):249–264. doi: 10.1017/S0003055421000861.

Holman, Mirya R., and Monica C. Schneider. 2018. "Gender, Race, and Political Ambition: How Intersectionality and Frames Influence Interest in Political Office." *Politics, Groups, and Identities* 6 (2):264–280.

Homola, Jonathan. 2022. "The Effects of Women's Descriptive Representation on Government Behavior." *Legislative Studies Quarterly* 47 (2):295–308. doi: 10.1111/lsq.12330.

Huber, Laura, and Anna Gunderson. 2023. "Putting a Fresh Face Forward: Does the Gender of a Police Chief Affect Public Perceptions?" *Political Research Quarterly* 76 (3):1418–1432. doi: https://doi-org.libezp.lib.lsu.edu/10.1177/10659129221142598.

Huber, Laura, Lindsey Pruett, and Sabrina Karim. 2022. "The Commando Effect: How Priming Masculinity Shapes Tolerance for Security Force Misconduct." American Political Science Association's Annual Meeting, Montreal, Canada.

Huddy, Leonie, and Nayda Terkildsen. 1993a. "The Consequences of Gender Stereotypes for Women Candidates at Different Levels and Types of Office." *Political Research Quarterly* 46 (3):503–525.

Huddy, Leonie, and Nayda Terkildsen. 1993b. "Gender Stereotypes and the Perception of Male and Female Candidates." *American Journal of Political Science* 37 (1):119–147.

Iyengar, Shanto, and Donald R. Kinder. 1987. *News That Matters: Television and American Opinion, Updated Edition, Chicago Studies in American Politics.* Chicago, IL: University of Chicago Press.

Jaramillo, Patricia. 2010. "Building a Theory, Measuring a Concept: Exploring Intersectionality and Latina Activism at the Individual Level." *Journal of Women, Politics & Policy* 31 (3):193–216.

Jardina, Ashley 2019. *White Identity Politics.* New York Cambridge University Press.

Johnson Carew, Jessica D. 2016. "How Do You See Me? Stereotyping of Black Women and How It Affects Them in an Electoral Context." In *Distinct Identities: Minority Women in U.S. Politics*, edited by Nadia Brown and Sarah Gershon. New York: Routledge, 95–115.

Jones, Jennifer J. 2016. "Talk "Like a Man": The Linguistic Styles of Hillary Clinton, 1992–2013." *Perspectives on Politics* 14 (3):625–643.

Jones, Phillip Edward. 2022. "Respectability Politics and Straight Support for LGB Rights." *Political Research Quarterly* 75 (4):935–949. doi: https://doi.org/10.1177/10659129211035834.

Junn, Jane. 2017. "The Trump Majority: White Womanhood and the Making of Female Voters in the U.S." *Politics, Groups, and Identities* 5 (2):343–352.

Kahn, Kim F. 1996. *The Political Consequences of Being a Woman: How Stereotypes Influence the Conduct and Consequences of Political Campaigns.* New York: Columbia University Press.

Kanter, Rosabeth Moss. 1977a. *Men and Women of the Corporation.* New York, NY: Basic Books.

Kanter, Rosabeth Moss. 1977b. "Some Effects of Proportions on Group Life: Skewed Sex Ratios and Responses to Token Women." *American Journal of Sociology* 82 (5):965–990.

Kanthak, Kristin, and Jonathon Woon. 2015. "Women Don't Run: Election Aversion and Candidate Entry." *American Journal of Political Science* 59 (3):595–612.

Kao, Kristen, Ellen Lust, Marwa Shalaby, and Chagai M. Weiss. 2024. "Female Representation and Legitimacy: Evidence from a Harmonized Experiment in Jordan, Morocco, and Tunisia." *American Political Science Review* 118 (1):495–503. doi: 10.1017/S0003055423000357.

Karp, Jeffrey A., and Susan A. Banducci. 2008. "When Politics Is Not Just a Man's Game: Women's Representation and Political Engagement." *Electoral Studies* 27 (1):105–115.

Karpowitz, Christopher F., and Tali Mendelberg. 2014. *The Silent Sex: Gender, Deliberation, and Institutions.* Princeton, NJ: Princeton University Press.

Karpowitz, Christopher F., J. Quin Monson, Jessica R. Preece, and Alejandra Aldridge. 2024. "Selecting for Masculinity: Women's Under-Representation in the Republican Party." *American Political Science Review* 118 (4):1873–1894. doi: 10.1017/S0003055423000783.

Kaslovsky, Jaclyn, and Jon C. Rogoswki. 2022. "Under the Microscope: Gender and Accountability in the US Congress." *American Political Science Review* 116 (2):516–532. doi: 10.1017/S0003055421001118.

Katsuo, Nishikawa, Terri L. Towner, Rosalee A. Clawson, and Eric N. Walternberg. 2009. "Interviewing the Interviewers: Journalistic Norms and Racial Diversity in the Newsroom." *Howard Journal of Communication* 20 (3):242–259. doi: 10.1080/10646170903070175.

Katz, D., and K. Braly. 1933. "Racial Stereotypes of One Hundred College Students." *Jouranl of Abnormal and Social Psychology* 28 (3):280–290.

Kawahara, Debra M. 2007a. "Asian American Women Leaders: The Intersection of Race, Gender, and Leadership." In *Women and Leadership: Transforming Vision and Diverse Voices*, edited by Jean Lau Chine, Bernice Lott, Joy K. Rice, and Janis Sanchez-Hucles, 297–313. Hoboken, NJ: Blackwell Publishing.

Kawahara, Debra M. 2007b. "Making a Difference: Asian American Women Leaders." *Women & Therapy* 30 (3–4):17–33. doi: 10.1300/J015v30n03_03.

Keiser, Lael R. 2010. "Understanding Street-Level Bureaucrats' Decision Making: Determining Eligibility in the Social Security Disability Program." *Public Administration Review* 70 (2):247–257.

Keiser, Lael R., Vicky M. Wilkins, Kenneth J. Meier, and Catherine A. Holland. 2002. "Lipstick and Logarithms: Gender, Institutional Context, and Representative Bureaucracy." *American Political Science Review* 96 (3):553–564. doi: https://doi.org/10.1017/S0003055402000321.

Keiser, Lael R., and Vicky M. Wilkins. 2004. "Linking Passive and Active Representation by Gender: The Case of Child Support Agencies." *Journal of Public Administration Research and Theory* 16:87–102.

Keum, Brian TaeHyuk, Jennifer L. Brady, Rajni Sharma, Yun Lu, Young Hwa Kim, and Christina J. Thai. 2018. "Gendered Racial Microaggressions Scale for Asian American Women: Development and Initial Validation." *Journal of Counseling Psychology* 65 (5): 571–585. doi: 10.1037/cou0000305.

Kim, Jeong. 2019. "Direct Democracy and Women's Political Engagement." *American Journal of Political Science* 63 (3):594–610.

Kim, Jeong Hyun. 2022. "Voting in Referendums Increases Internal Political Efficacy of Men but not Women: Evidence from Ireland's 2018 Abortion Referendum." *Journal of Elections, Public Opinion, and Parties* 32 (3):707–726. doi: 10.1080/17457289.2021.1929258.

Kim, Jeong Hyun, Anna Gunderson, Elizabeth Lane, and Nichole M. Bauer. 2023. "State Courts, State Legislatures, and Setting Abortion Policy." *Journal of Health Politics, Policy, and Law* 48 (4):569–592.

Kiousis, Spiro. 2011. "Agenda-Setting and Attitudes." *Journalism Studies* 12 (3):359–374. doi: 10.1080/1461670x.2010.501149.

Klar, Samara, and Yanna Krupnikov. 2016. *Independent Politics: How American Disdain for Parties Leads to Political Inaction.* New York: Cambridge University Press.

Koenig, Anne M., Alice H. Eagly, Abigail A. Mitchell, and Tiina Ristikari. 2011. "Are Leader Stereotypes Masculine? A Meta-Analysis of Three Research Paradigms." *Psychological Bulletin* 137 (4):616–642.

Krefting, Linda A., Philip K. Berger, and Marc J. Wallace Jr. 1978. "The Contribution of Sex Distribution, Job Content, and Occupational Classification to Job Sextyping: Two Studies." *Journal of Vocational Behavior* 13: 181–191.

Krehbiel, Keith. 1990. "Seniority, Commitment, and Self-Governing Groups." *Journal of Law, Economics, & Organization* 6 (ArticleType: research-article/Issue Title: Special Issue:

[Papers from the Organization of Political Institutions Conference, April 1990]/Full publication date: 1990/Copyright ¬© 1990 Oxford University Press):73–77.

Kreitzer, Rebecca, and Tracy Osborn. 2019. "The Emergence and Activities of Women's Recruiting Groups in the U.S." *Politics, Groups, and Identities* 7 (4): 842–852.

Krosnick, Jon A., and Laura A. Brannon. 1993. "The Impact of the Gulf War on the Ingredients of Presidential Evaluations: Multidimensional Effects of Political Involvement." *The American Political Science Review* 87 (4):963–975. doi: 10.2307/2938828.

Krupnikov, Yanna, and Nichole M. Bauer. 2014. "The Relationship between Campaign Negativity, Gender and Campaign Context." *Political Behavior* 36 (1):167–188. doi: 10.1007/s11109-013-9221-9.

Krupnikov, Yanna, Spencer Piston, and Nichole M. Bauer. 2016. "Saving Face: Identifying Voter Responses to Black and Female Candidates." *Political Psychology* 37 (2):253–273. doi: 10.1111/pops.12261.

Krupnikov, Yanna, and John Barry Ryan. 2022. *The Other Divide: Polarization and Disengagement in American Politics.* New York Cambridge University Press.

Ladam, Christina, Jeffrey Harden, J., and Jason H. Windett. 2018. "Prominent Role Models: High-Profile Female Politicians and the Emergence of Women as Candidates for Public Office." *American Journal of Political Science* 62 (2):369–381.

Lavariega Monforti, Jessica. 2017. "The Latina/o Gender Gap in the 2016 Election." *Aztlan* 42 (2):229–248.

Lawless, Jennifer L. 2004. "Politics of Presence? Congresswomen and Symbolic Representation." *Political Research Quarterly* 57 (1):81–99.

Lawless, Jennifer L. 2012. *Becoming a Candidate: Political Ambition and the Decision to Run for Office.* New York: Cambridge University Press.

Lawless, Jennifer L., and Richard L. Fox. 2005. *It Takes a Candidate: Why Women Don't Run for Office.* New York: Cambridge University Press.

Lawrence, Regina, and Melody Rose. 2010. *Hillary Clinton's Race for the White House: Gender Politics and the Media on the Campaign Trail.* Boulder, Colorado: Lynne Rienner Publishers.

Lay, Celeste J., Mirya R. Holman, Angela L. Bos, Jill S. Greenlee, Zoe M. Oxley, and Allison Buffett. 2021. "TIME for Kids to Learn Gender Stereotypes: Analysis of Gender and Political Leadership in a Common Social Studies Resource for Children." *Politics & Gender* 17 (1): 1–22.

Layman, Geoffrey C., and Thomas M. Carsey. 2002. "Party Polarization and Conflict Extension in the American Electorate." *American Journal of Political Science* 46:786–802.

Lazarus, Jeffrey, and Amy Steigerwalt. 2018. *Gendered Vulnerability: How Women Work Harder to Stay in Office.* Ann Arbor: University of Michigan Press.

Lazarus, Jeffrey, Amy Steigerwalt, and Micalya Clark. 2023. "Time Spent in the House: Gender and the Political Careers of U.S. House Members." *Politics & Gender* 19 (1):97–132. doi: 10.1017/S1743923X21000428.

Lee, Tiane L., and Susan T. Fiske. 2006. "Not an Outgroup, not yet an Ingroup: Immigrants in the Stereotype Content Model." *International Journal of Intercultural Relations* 30 (6): 751–768. doi: https://doi.org/10.1016/j.ijintrel.2006.06.005.

Lemi, Danielle Casarez. 2019. "Melanin and Curls: Evaluation of Black Women Candidates." *Journal of Race, Ethnicity, and Politics* 4:259–296. doi: 10.1017/rep.2019.18.

Lemi, Danielle Casarez. 2020. "Voting for Multiracial Women." In *Politicking while Female: The Political Lives of Women,* edited by Nichole M. Bauer. Baton Rouge: LSU Press, 55–70.

Levanon, Asaf, Paula England, and Paul Allison. 2009. "Occupational Feminization and Pay: Assessing Causal Dynamics Using 1950–2000 U.S. Census Data." *Social Forces* 88 (2): 865–891.

Levendusky, Matthew, and Neil Malhotra. 2016. "Does Media Coverage of Partisan Polarization Affect Political Attitudes?" *Political Communication* 33 (2):283–301. doi: 10.1080/10584609.2015.1038455.

Li, Peggy. 2014. "Hitting the Ceiling: An Examination of Barriers to Success for Asian American Women." *Berkeley Journal of Gender, Law & Justice* 29 (1):140–167.

Liben, Lynn S., Rebecca S. Bigler, and Holleen R. Krogh. 2001. "Pink and Blue Collar Jobs: Children's Judgments of Job Status and Job Aspirations in Relation to Sex of Worker." *Journal of Experimental Child Psychology* 79:346–363.

Lien, Pei-te, and Nicole Filler. 2022. *Contesting the Last Frontier: Race, Gender, Ethnicity, and Political Representation of Asian Americans.* New York, NY: Oxford University Press.

Lippman, Walter. 1922. *Public Opinion.* New York: Free Press Paperbacks.

Long, J. Scott. 1997. *Regression Models for Categorical and Limited Dependent Variables Advanced Quantitative Techniques in the Social Sciences.* Thousand Oaks, CA: Sage Publications.

Lowande, Kenneth, Melinda Ritchie, and Erinn Lauterbach. 2019. "Descriptive and Substantive Representation in Congress: Evidence from 80,000 Congressional Inquiries." *American Journal of Political Science* 63 (3):644–659. doi: 10.1111/ajps.12443.

Lupia, Arthur, and Mathew D. McCubbins. 1998. *The Democratic Dilemma: Can Citizens Learn What They Need to Know.* New York: Cambridge University Press.

MacDonald, Jason A., and Erin E. O'Brien. 2011. "Quasi-Experimental Design, Constituency, and Advancing Women's Interests: Reexamining the Influence of Gender on Substantive Representation." *Political Research Quarterly* 64 (2):472–486. doi: 10.1177/1065912909354703.

Maestas, Cherie D., Sarah A. Fulton, L. Sandy Maisel, and Walter J. Stone. 2006. "When to Risk It? Institutions, Ambition, and the Decision to Run for the U.S. House." *American Political Science Review* 199 (2):195–208.

Mahoney, Anna Mitchell. 2018. *Women Take Their Place in State Legislatures: The Creation of Women's Caucuses.* New Jersey: Temple University Press.

Mahoney, Anna Mitchell, Meghan Kearney, and Carly Megan Shaffer. 2020. "#MeToo in the State House." In *Politicking while Female: The Political Lives of Women*, edited by Nichole M. Bauer. Baton Rouge: LSU Press, 158–180.

Mansbridge, Jane. 1985. "Myth and Reality: The ERA and the Gender Gap in the 1980 Election." *Public Opinion Quarterly* 49 (2):164–178.

Mansbridge, Jane. 1986. *Why We Lost the ERA.* Chicago: University of Chicago Press.

Mansbridge, Jane. 1999. "Should Blacks Represent Blacks and Women Represent Women? A Contingent "Yes."" *The Journal of Politics* 61 (3):628–657.

Mansbridge, Jane. 2003. "Rethinking Representation." *American Political Science Review* 97 (4):515–528.

Matos, Yalidy, Stacey Greene, and Kira Sanbonmatsu. 2020. "Do Women Seek "Women of Color" for Public Office? Exploring Women's Support for Electing Women of Color." *Political Research Quarterly* 74 (2):259–273. doi: 10.1177/1065912920971793.

Matos, Yalidy, and Kira Sanbonmatsu. 2024. "Men of Color, Linked Fate, and Support for Women of Color Candidates." *Journal of Race, Ethnicity, and Politics* 9 (3):600–619. doi: https://doi.org/10.1017/rep.2024.10.

Mayhew, David R. 1974. *Congress: The Electoral Connection.* New Haven: Yale University Press.

McCombs, Maxwell E., and Donald L. Shaw. 1972. "The Agenda-Setting Function of the Press." *Public Opinion Quarterly* 36:176–187.

McConnaughy, Corrine 2013. *The Woman Suffrage Movement in America: A Reassessment.* New York: Cambridge University Press.

McDermott, Monika L. 2016. *Masculinity, Feminity, and American Political Behavior*. New York: Oxford University Press.

McLaughlin, Peter. 2023. "More Money, Less Credit? Legislator Gender and the Effects of Congressional Credit Claiming." *Politics & Gender* 20 (2):346–362.

Mechkova, Valeriya, and Steven L. Wilson. 2021. "Norms and Rage: Gender and Social Media in the 2018 U.S. Mid-Term Elections." *Electoral Studies* 69 (102268):1–13. doi: 10.1016/j.electstud.2020.102268.

Meeks, Lindsey. 2012. "Is She "Man Enough"? Women Candidates, Executive Political Offices, and News Coverage." *Journal of Communication* 62:175–193. doi: https://doi.org/10.1111/j.1460-2466.2011.01621.x

Meeks, Lindsey. 2013. "He Wrote, She Wrote: Journalist Gender, Political Office, and Campaign News." *Journalism and Mass Communication Quarterly* 90 (1):58–74. doi: 10.1177/1077699012468695.

Mendelberg, Tali, and Christopher Karpowitz. 2016. "Power, Gender, and Group Discussion." *Advances in Political Psychology* 37 (1):23–60.

Mendelberg, Tali, Christopher Karpowitz, and Nicholas Goedert. 2014. "Does Descriptive Representation Facilitate Women's Distinctive Voice? How Gender Composition and Decision Rules Affect Deliberation." *American Journal of Political Science* 58 (2):291–306.

Mills, Kay. 1997. "What Difference Do Women Journalists Make?" In *Women, Media, and Politics*, edited by Pippa Norris. New York: Oxford University Press, 41–55.

Milyo, Jeffrey, and Samantha Schlosberg. 2000. "Gender Bias and Selection Bias in House Elections." *Public Choice* 105 (1/2):41–59.

Montoya, Celeste M., Christina Bejarano, Nadia Brown, and Sarah Allen Gershon. 2022. "The Intersectional Dynamics of Descriptive Representation." *Politics & Gender* 18 (2):483–512. doi: 10.1017/S1743923X20000744.

Morehouse Mendez, Jeanette, and Tracy Osborn. 2010. "Gender and the Perception of Knowledge in Political Discussion." *Political Research Quarterly* 63 (2):269–279.

Morton, Rebecca B., and Kenneth C. Williams. 2010. *Experimental Political Science and the Study of Causality: From Nature to the Lab*. New York: Cambridge University Press.

Moureau, Julie, Stephen Nuño-Pérez, and Lisa M. Sanchez. 2019. "Intersectionality, Linked Fate, and LGBTQ Latinx Political Participation." *Political Research Quarterly* 72 (4): 976–990.

Moyer, Laura P. 2025. "Does Descriptive Representation of Women on the Bench Improve Institutional Trust?" *Journal of Law and Courts* forthcoming. doi: 10.1017/jlc.2025.8.

Mukkamala, Shruti, and Karen L. Suyemoto. 2018. "Racialized Sexism/Sexualized Racism: A Multimethod Study of Intersectional Experiences of Discrimination for Asian American Women." *Asian American Journal of Psychology* 9 (1):32–46.

Mullinix, Kevin J., Thomas J. Leeper, James N. Druckman, and Jeremy Freese. 2015. "The Generalizability of Survey Experiments." *Journal of Experimental Political Science* 2: 109–138.

Mutz, Diana C. 2011. *Population Based Survey Experiments*. Princeton, NJ: Princeton University Press.

Mutz, Diana C. 2015. *In Your Face Politics: The Consequences of Incivility*. Princeton: Princeton University Press.

Mutz, Diana C., and Byron Reeves. 2005. "The New Videomalaise: Effects of Televised Incivility on Political Trust." *American Political Science Review* 99 (1):1–15.

Naunov, Martin. 2025. "The Effect of Protesters' Gender on Public Reactions to Protests and Protest Repression." *American Political Science Review* 119 (1):135–151.

North, Louise. 2016a. "The Gender of 'Soft' and 'Hard' News: Female Journalists' Views on Gendered Story Allocations." *Journalism Studies* 17 (3):356–373.

North, Louise. 2016b. "Still a "Blokes Club": The Motherhood Dilemma in Journalism." *Journalism* 17 (3):315–330.

Nugent, Mary K. 2019. "When Does He Speak for She? Men Representing Women in Parliaments." PhD, Political Science, Rutgers University.

Oden, Ayla, Nichole M. Bauer, Ke Jiang, and Lance Porter. 2024. "Women's Engagement in Political Discussion on Twitter: The Role of Gender Salience, Resources, and Race/Ethnicity." *Sex Roles* 90:250–266. doi: https://doi.org/10.1007/s11199-023-01439-w.

Oliver, Sarah, and Meredith Conroy. 2017. "Tough Enough for the Job? How Masculinity Predicts Recruitment of City Council Members." *American Politics Research* 46 (6):1094–1122.

Omi, Michael, and Howard Winant. 2014. *Racial Formation in the United States.* New York: Routledge

Ondercin, Heather L. 2017. "Who Is Responsible for the Gender Gap? The Dynamics of Men's and Women's Democratic Macropartisanship, 1950–2012." *Political Research Quarterly* 70 (4):749–761.

Orey, Byron D'Andra, and Yu Zhang. 2019. "Melanated Millennials and the Politics of Black Hair." *Social Science Quarterly* 100 (6):2458–2476.

Osborn, Tracy. 2012. *How Women Represent Women: Political Parties, Gender, and Representation in the State Legislatures.* New York, NY: Oxford University Press.

Owens, Chris. 2005. "Black Substantive Representation in State Legislatures from 1971–1994." *Social Science Quarterly* 86 (4):779–791.

Oxley, Zoe M., Mirya R. Holman, Jill S. Greenlee, Angela L. Bos, and Celeste J. Lay. 2020. "Children's Views of the American Presidency." *Public Opinion Quarterly* 84 (1):141–157.

Padgett, Jeremy, Johanna L. Dunaway, and Joshua P. Darr. 2019. "As Seen on TV? How Gatekeeping Makes the U.S. House Seem More Extreme." *Journal of Communication* 69 (6):696–719.

Paivio, Allan. 1979. *Imagery and Verbal Processes.* Edited by Inc. Publishers Lawrence Erlbaum Associates. Hillsdale, New Jersey.

Paola, Maria De, Vincenzo Scoppa, and Rosetta Lombardo. 2010. "Can Gender Quotas Break Down Negative Stereotypes? Evidence from Canges in Electoral Rules." *Journal of Public Economies* 94 (5–6):344–353.

Patterson, Thomas E. 1997. "The News Media: An Effective Political Actor?" *Political Communication* 14 (4):445–455. doi: 10.1080/105846097199245.

Pearson, Kathryn, and Logan Dancey. 2011. "Speaking for the Underrepresented in the House of Representatives: Voicing Women's Interests in a Partisan Era." *Politics & Gender* 7: 493–519.

Pearson, Kathryn, and Eric McGhee. 2013. "What It Takes to Win: Questioning "Gender Neutral" Outcomes in U.S. House Elections." *Politics & Gender* 9:439–462.

Peffley, Mark, Hurwitz Jon, and Paul M. Sniderman. 1997. "Racial Stereotypes and Whites' Political Views of Blacks in the Context of Welfare and Crime." *American Journal of Political Science* 41 (1):30–60.

Peterson, Paul E. 1981. *City Limits.* Chicago: University of Chicago Press.

Petrocik, John R. 1996. "Issue Ownership in Presidential Elections, with a 1980 Case Study." *American Journal of Political Science* 40 (3):825–850. doi: 10.2307/2111797.

Petrocik, John R., William L. Benoit, and G. J. Hansen. 2003. "Issue Ownership and Presidential Campaigning, 1952–2000." *Political Science Quarterly* 118 (4):599–626.

Phillips, Christian D. 2023. "Nevertheless, He Persisted: White Men and the Links Between Incumbency and Group Descriptive Representation." *Political Research Quarterly* 76 (4):1691–1706. doi: 10.1177/10659129231173340.

Philpot, Tasha S., and Hanes Walton, Jr. 2007. "One of Our Own: Black Female Candidates and the Voters Who Support Them." *American Journal of Political Science* 51 (1):49–62.

Piscopo, Jennifer, M. 2019. "The Limits of Leaning in: Ambition, Recruitment, and Candidate Training in Comparative Perspective." *Politics, Groups, and Identities* 7 (4):817–828.

Pitkin, Hannah. 1967. *The Concept of Representation.* Berkeley: University of California Press.

Plutzer, Eric, and John F. Zipp. 1996. "Identity Politics and Voting for Women Candidates." *The Public Opinion Quarterly* 60 (1):30–57.

Prentice, Deborah A., and Erica Carranza. 2002. "What Women and Men Should Be, Shouldn't Be, Are Allowed to Be, and Don't Have to Be: The Contents of Prescriptive Gender Stereotypes." *Psychology of Women Quarterly* 26 (4):269–291. doi: 10.1111/1471-6402.t01-1-00066.

Qi, Dan, Cana Kim, and Nichole M. Bauer. 2023. "Asian American and Pacific Islander Women Leaders & Political Communication." In *Distinct Identities: Minority Women in American Politics*, edited by Nadia Brown and Sarah Gershon. New York: Routledge, 172–187.

Reingold, Beth, Kerry L. Haynie, and Kirsten Widner. 2021. *Race, Gender, and Political Representation: Toward a More Intersectional Approach.* New York: Oxford University Press.

Reingold, Beth, Rebecca J. Kreitzer, Tracy Osborn, and Michele Swers. 2021. "Anti-abortion Policymaking and Women's Representation." *Political Research Quarterly* 74 (2):403–420.

Reynolds-Dobbs, Wendy, Kecia M. Thomas, and Matthew S. Harrison. 2008. "From Mammy to Superwoman: Images That Hinder Black Women's Career Representation." *Journal of Career Development* 35 (2):129–150.

Rodgers, Shelly, and Esther Thorson. 2003. "A Socialization Perspective on Male and Female Reporting." *Journal of Communication* 53 (4):658–675.

Rohde, David. 1991. *Parties and Leaders in the Postreform House.* Chicago: University of Chicago Press.

Rohrbach, Tobias, Loes Aaldering, and Daphne Joanna Van Der Pas. 2023. "Gender Differences and Similarities in News Media Effects on Political Candidate Evaluations: A Meta-Analysis." *Journal of Communication* 73 (2):101–112. https://doi.org/10.1093/joc/jqac042.

Rosenthal, Cindy Simon. 1995. "The Role of Gender in Descriptive Representation." *Political Research Quarterly* 48 (3):599–611.

Rosenwasser, Shirley Miller, and Norma G. Dean. 1989. "Gender Role and Political Office: Effects of Perceived Masculinity/Feminity of Candidate and Political Office." *Psychology of Women Quarterly* 13 (1):77–85.

Ryan, Michelle K., and S. Alexander Haslam. 2007. "The Glass Cliff: Exploring the Dynamics Surrounding the Appointment of Women to Precarious Leadership Positions." *Academy of Management Review* 32 (2):549–572.

Ryan, Michelle K., S. Alexander Haslam, and Clara Kulich. 2010. "Politics and the Glass Cliff: Evidence That Women Are Preferentially Selected to Contest Hard-To-Win Seats." *Psychology of Women Quarterly* 34:56–64.

Ryan, Michelle K., S. Alexander Haslam, Thekla Morgenroth, Floor Rink, Jana Stoker, and Kim Peters. 2016. "Getting on Top of the Glass Cliff: Reviewing a Decade of Evidence, Explanations, and Impact." *The Leadership Quarterly* 27:446–455.

Sanbonmatsu, Kira. 2002a. "Gender Stereotypes and Vote Choice." *American Journal of Political Science* 46 (1):20–34.

Sanbonmatsu, Kira. 2002b. "Political Parties and the Recruitment of Women to State Legislatures." *The Journal of Politics* 64 (3):791–809.

Sanbonmatsu, Kira. 2006. *Where Women Run: Gender and Party in the American States.* Ann Arbor: University of Michigan Press.

Sanbonmatsu, Kira. 2015. "Electing Women of Color: The Role of Campaign Trainings." *Journal of Women, Politics & Policy* 36 (2):137–160.

Santia, Martina, and Nichole M. Bauer. 2023. "The Intersection of Candidate Gender and Ethnicity: How Voters Respond to Campaign Messages from Latinas." *The International Journal of Press/Politics* 28 (4):975–994. doi: https://doi.org/10.1177/19401612211072697

Schneider, Monica C. 2014. "The Effects of Gender-Bending on Candidate Evaluations." *Journal of Women, Politics & Policy* 35:55–77. doi: https://doi.org/10.1080/1554477X.2014.863697.

Schneider, Monica C., and Angela L. Bos. 2011. "An Exploration of the Content of Stereotypes about Black Politicians." *Political Psychology* 32 (2):205–233.

Schneider, Monica C., and Angela L. Bos. 2019. "The Application of Social Role Theory to the Study of Gender in Politics." *Political Pscyhology* 40 (S1). doi: 10.1111/pops.12573.

Schneider, Monica C., Mirya R. Holman, Amanda B. Diekman, and Thomas McAndrew. 2016. "Power, Conflict, and Community: How Gendered Views of Political Power Influence Women's Political Ambition." *Political Psychology* 37 (4):515–531. doi: 10.1111/pops.12268.

Schneider, Monica C., Jennie Sweet-Cushman, and Taylor Gordon. 2023. "Role Model Do No HARM: Modeling Achievable Success Inspires Social Belonging and Women's Candidate Emergence." *Journal of Women, Politics & Policy* 44 (1):105–120. doi: 10.1080/1554477X.2023.2155775.

Schudson, Michael. 1998. *The Good Citizen: A History of American Public Life.* Cambridge: Harvard University Press.

Schwindt-Bayer, Leslie. 2010. *Political Power and Women's Representation in Latin America.* New York: Oxford University Press.

Schwindt-Bayer, Leslie A., and William Mishler. 2005. "An Integrated Model of Women's Representation." *The Journal of Politics* 67 (2):407–428.

Schwindt-Bayer, Leslie, and Catherine Reyes-Householder. 2017. "Citizen Responses to Female Executives: Is It Sex, Novelty or Both?" *Politics, Groups, and Identities* 5 (3):373–398. doi: 10.1080/21565503.2017.1283238.

Scott, James C. 1969. "Corruption, Machine Politics, and Political Change." *American Political Science Review* 63 (4):1142–1158. doi: https://doi.org/10.2307/1955076.

Scott, Jamil, Nadia Brown, Lorrie Frasure, and Diane Pinderhughes. 2021. "Destined to Run? The Role of Political Participation on Black Women's Decision to Run for Elected Office." *National Review of Black Politics* 2 (1):22–52.

Searles, Kathleen, Yanna Krupnikov, John Barry Ryan, and Hillary Style. 2023. *Constructing Political Expertise in the News.* New York: Cambridge University Press.

Sears, David O., and Nicholas A. Valentino. 2005. "Old Times There Are Not Forgotten: Race and Partisan Realignment in the Contemporary South." *American Journal of Political Science* 49 (3):672–688.

Segev, Elad, and Menahem Blondheim. 2013. "America's Global Standing According to Popular News Sites from around the World." *Political Communication* 30 (1):139–161. doi: 10.1080/10584609.2012.737418.

Senk, Kaitlin. 2023. "When Do Women Represent Women's Rights: Exploring Seniority and Political Security." *Politics, Groups, and Identities* 11 (5):1077–1097. doi: https://doi.org/10.1080/21565503.2022.2080081.

Shah, Paru, Jamil Scott, and Eric Gonzalez Juenke. 2019. "Women of Color Candidates: Examining Emergence and Success in State Legislative Elections." *Politics, Groups, and Identities* 7 (2):429–443.

Shames, Shauna. 2019. *Out of the Running: Why Millennials Reject Political Careers and Why It Matters.* New York: New York University Press.

Shapiro, Matthew A., and Libby Hemphill. 2016. "Politicians and the Policy Agenda: Does Use of Twitter by the U.S. Congress Direct New York Times Content?" *Policy and Internet.* 9(1):109–132. doi: 10.1002/poi3.120.

Shinar, Eva H. 1975. "Sexual Stereotypes of Occupations." *Journal of Occupational Behavior* 7:99–111.

Shor, Eran, Arnout van de Rijt, Alex Miltsov, Vivek Kulkarni, and Steven Skiena. 2015. "A Paper Ceiling: Explaining the Persistent Underrepresentation of Women in Printed News." *American Sociological Review* 80 (5):960–984.

Shortell, Christopher, and Melody E. Valdini. 2022. "The Politics of Women's Presence on High Courts: Bias and the Conditional Nature of Cultivating Legitimacy." *Politics & Gender* 18 (3):858–877. doi: 10.1017/S1743923X21000404.

Sigelman, Carol K., Lee Sigelman, Barbara J. Walkosz, and Michael Nitz. 1995. "Black Candidates, White Voters: Understanding Racial Bias in Political Perceptions." *American Journal of Political Science* 39 (1):243–265.

Silva, Bruno Castanho, and Danielle Pullan. 2025. "Blending in or Standing Out? Gendered Political Communication in 24 Democracies." *American Journal of Political Science* 69 (2):653–668.

Simien, Evelyn M. 2005. "Race, Gender, and Linked Fate." *Journal of Black Studies* 35 (5): 529–550.

Smith, Amy Erica, Katherine Warming, and Valerie M. Hennings. 2016. "Refusing to Know a Woman's Palce: The Causes and Consequences of Rejecting Stereotypes of Women Politicians in the Americas." *Politics, Groups, and Identities* 5(1), 132–151.

Smith, Terry. 2000. "Parties and Transformative Politics." *Columbia Law Review* 100 (3): 845–872.

Splichal, Sigman L., and Bruce Garrison. 1995. "Gender as a Factor in Newsroom Managers' Views on Covering the Private Lives of Politicians." *Mass Communication Review* 22 (1–2):101–108.

Splichal, Sigman L., and Bruce Garrison. 2000. "Covering Public Officials: Gender and Privacy Issue Differences." *Journal of Mass Media Ethics* 15 (3):167–179.

Springer, Frederik, Markus Klein, and Yvonne Ludecke. 2024. "The Impact of Party Quotas on Women's Political Ambition." *Journal of Women, Politics & Policy* 45 (2):213–229. doi: 10.1080/1554477X.2023.2206978.

Staples, Robert. 1978. "Masculinity and Race: The Dual Dilemma of Black Men." *Journal of Social Issues* 34 (1):169–183.

Stauffer, Katelyn E. 2021. "Public Perceptions of Women's Inclusion and Feelings of Political Efficacy." *American Political Science Review* 115 (4):1226–1441. doi: 10.1017/S0003055421000678.

Stoddard, Olga, and Jessica Preece. 2015. "Why Women Don't Run: Experimental Evidence on Gender Differences in Competition Aversion." *Journal of Economic Behavior & Organization* 117:296–308.

Su, Yan, and Porismita Borah. 2019. "Who Is the Agenda Setter? Examining the Intermedia Agenda-Setting Effect between Twitter and Newspapers." *Journal of Information Technology & Politics* 16 (3):236–249. doi: https://doi.org/10.1080/19331681. 2019.1641451.

Sui, Mingxiao, Newly Paul, Paru Shah, Brook Spurlock, Brooksie Chastant, and Johanna L. Dunaway. 2018. "The Role of Minority Journalists, Candidates, and Audiences in Shaping Race-Related Campaign News Coverage." *Journalism and Mass Communication Quarterly* 95 (4):1079–1102. doi: 10.1177/1077699018762078.

Summey, Pamela S., and Marsha Hurst. 1986. "Ob/Gyn on the Rise of the Evolution of Professional Ideology in the Twentieth Century." *Women & Health* 11 (2):103–122. doi: https://doi.org/10.1300/J013v11n02_08.

Sweet-Cushman, Jennie. 2019. "See It; Be It? The Use of Role Models in Campaign Trainings for Women." *Politics, Groups, and Identities* 7 (4):853–863.

Sweet-Cushman, Jennie. 2020. "Where Does the Pipeline Get Leaky? The Progressive Ambition of School Board Members and Personal and Political Network Recruitment." *Politics, Groups, and Identities* 8 (4):762–785. doi: 10.1080/21565503.2018.1541417

Sweet-Cushman, Jennie. 2022. "Legislative vs. Executive Political Offices: How Gender Stereotypes Can Disadvantage Women in Either Office." *Political Behavior* 44:411–434. doi: doi.org/10.1007/s11109-021-09721-x.

Sweet-Cushman, Jennie, Rebecca Gill, and Christopher Zorn. 2025. "Legislating in the First Female Majority State Legislature: Gendered Power, Leadership, and Patterns of Sponsorship and Cosponsorship." *Political Research Quarterly* 78: 1045–1059 3. doi:https://doi.org/10.1177/10659129251338179.

Swers, Michele. 1998. "Are Congresswomen More Likely to Vote for Women's Issue Bills Than Their Male Colleagues?" *Legislative Studies Quarterly* 23:435–448.

Swers, Michele. 2002. *The Difference Women Make: The Policy Impact of Women in Congress.* Chicago: University of Chicago Press.

Swers, Michele. 2013. *Women in the Club.* Chicago: University of Chicago Press.

Takash, Paule C. 1993. "Breaking Barriers to Representation: Chicana/Latina Elected Officials in California." *Urban Anthropology* 22 (3–4):325–360.

Tate, Katherine. 2003. "Black Opinion on the Legitimacy of Racial Redistricting and Majority-Minority Districts." *American Political Science Review* 97 (1):45–56.

Tate, Katherine. 2018. *Black Faces in the Mirror: African Americans and Their Representatives in the US Congress.* Princeton: Princeton University Press.

Taylor-Robinson, Michelle, and Nehemia Geva. 2023. *The Image of Gender and Political Leadership: A Multinational View of Women and Leadership.* New York: Oxford University Press.

Teele, Dawn Langan. 2019. *Forging the Franchise: The Political Origins of the Women's Vote.* Princeton: Princeton University Press.

Terkildsen, Nayda. 1993. "When White Voters Evaluate Black Candidates: The Processing Implications of Candidate Skin Color, Prejudice, and Self-Monitoring." *American Journal of Political Science* 37 (4):1032–1053.

Thomsen, Danielle M., and Aaron S. King. 2020. "Women's Representation and the Gendered Pipeline to Power." *American Political Science Review* 114 (4):989–1000. doi: 10.1017/S0003055420000404.

Tremblay, Manon. 2006. "The Substantive Representation of Women and PR: Some Reflections on the Role of Surrogate Representation and Critical Mass." *Politics & Gender* 2 (4):502–511.

Ulbig, Stacy G. 2007. "Gendering Municipal Government: Female Descriptive Representation and Feelings of Political Trust." *Social Science Quarterly* 88 (5):1106–1123.

Usher, Nikki. 2014. *Making News at the New York Times.* Ann Arbor: University of Michigan Press.

Usher, Nikki, Jesse Holcomb, and Justin Littman. 2018. "Twitter Makes It Worse: Political Journalists, Gendered Echo Chambers, and the Amplification of Gender Bias." *The International Journal of Press/Politics* 23 (3):324–344.

Valentino, Nicholas A., Carly Wayne, and Marzia Oceno. 2018. "Mobilizing Sexism: The Interaction of Emotion and Gender Attitudes in the 2016 US Presidential Election." *Public Opinion Quarterly* 82 (Special Issue 2018):213–235.

Valentino, Nicholas, Vincent L. Hutchings, and Ismail White. 2002. "Cues That Matter: How Political Ads Prime Racial Attitudes During Campaigns." *American Political Science Review* 96 (1):75–90. doi: 10.1017/S0003055402004240.

van der Pas, Daphne Joanna, and Loes Aaldering. 2020. "Gender Differences in Political Media Coverage: A Meta-Analysis." *Journal of Communication* 70 (1):114–143. doi: https://doi.org/10.1093/joc/jqz046.

Van Duyn, Emily, Cynthia Peacock, and Natalie Jomini Stroud. 2019. "The Gender Gap in Online News Comment Sections." *Social Science Computer Review* 39 (2):181–196. doi: 10.1177/0894439319864876.

Varney, Helen, and Joyce Beebe Thompson. 2016. *A History of Midwifery in the United States: The Midwife Said Fear Not.* New York: Springer.

Verge, Tania, Nina Wisehomeier, and Ana Espirito-Santo. 2020. "Framing Symbolic Representation: Exploring How Women's Political Presence Shapes Citizens' Political Attitude." *European Journal of Politics & Gender* 3 (2):257–276.

Vinkenburg, Claartje, Marloes L. van Engen, Alice H. Eagly, and Mary C. Johannesen-Schmidt. 2011. "An Exploration of Stereotypical Beliefs about Leadership Styles: Is Transformational Leadership a Route to Women's Promotion?" *The Leadership Quarterly* 22 (1): 10–21.

Volden, Craig, Alan E. Wiseman, and Dana E. Wittmer. 2013. "When Are Women More Effective Lawmakers than Men?" *American Journal of Political Science* 57:326–341. doi: 10.1111/ajps.12010.

Volden, Craig, Alan E. Wiseman, and Dana E. Wittmer. 2018. "Women's Issues and Their Fates in the U.S. Congress." *Political Science Research Methods* 6 (4):679–696. doi: 10.1017/psrm.2016.32.

Vraga, Emily K. 2017. "Which Candidates Can Be Mavericks? The Effects of Issue Disagreement and Gender on Candidate Evaluations." *Politics & Policy* 45 (1):4–30. doi: https://doi.org/10.1111/polp.12192.

Weaver, David. 1997. "Women as Journalists." In *Women, Media, and Politics*, edited by Pippa Norris. New York: Oxford University Press, 21–40.

Weeks, Ana Catalano. 2022. *Making Gender Salient: From Gender Quota Laws to Policy.* New York: Cambridge University Press.

West, Emily A. 2017. "Descriptive Representation and Political Efficacy: Evidence from Obama and Clinton." *Journal of Politics* 79 (1):351–355.

West, Emily Anne, and Dominik Duell. 2025. "How Political Representation Empowers Women." *Political Behavior* 47: 217–240. https://doi.org/10.1007/s11109-024-09948-4.

White, Ismail K., Chryl N. Laird, and Troy D. Allen. 2014. "Selling Out?: The Politics of Navigating Conflicts between Racial Group Interest and Self-Interest." *American Political Science Review* 108 (4):783–800.

Windett, Jason Harold. 2011. "State Effects and the Emergence and Success of Female Gubernatorial Candidates." *State Politics & Policy Quarterly* 11 (4):460–482.

Winter, James P., and Chaim H. Eyal. 1981. "Agenda Setting for the Civil Right Issue." *The Public Opinion Quarterly* 45 (3):376–383.

Winter, Nicholas J. G. 2008. *Dangerous Frames: How Ideas about Race and Gender Shape Public Opinion.* Chicago: The University of Chicago Press.

Winter, Nicholas J. G. 2010. "Masculine Republicans and Feminine Democrats: Gender and Americans' Explicit and Implicit Images of the Political Parties." *Political Behavior* 32 (4):587–618. doi: 10.1007/s11109-010-9131-z.

Wolak, Jennifer. 2015. "Candidate Gender and the Political Engagement of Women and Men." *American Politics Research* 45 (3):872–896.

Wolak, Jennifer. 2017. "Feelings of Political Efficacy in the Fifty States." *Political Behavior* 40:763–784. doi: 10.1007/s11109-017-9421-9.

Wolak, Jennifer. 2020a. *Compromise in an Age of Party Polarization*. New York: Oxford University Press.

Wolak, Jennifer. 2020b. "Confict Avoidance and Gender Gaps in Political Engagement." *Political Behavior* 44:133–156.

Wolak, Jennifer. 2020c. "Descriptive Representation and the Political Engagement of Women." *Politics & Gender* 16 (2):339–362.

Wolbrecht, Christina. 2000. *The Politics of Women's Rights: Parties, Positions, and Change*. Princeton, NJ: Princeton University Press.

Wolbrecht, Christina. 2002. "Explaining Women's Rights Realignment: Convention Delegates, 1972–1992." *Political Behavior* 24 (3):237–282.

Wolbrecht, Christina, and David E. Campbell. 2017. "Role Models Revisited: Youth, Novelty, and the Impact of Female Candidates." *Politics, Groups, and Identities* 5 (3):418–434. doi: http://dx.doi.org/10.1080/21565503.2016.1268179.

Wood, Wendy, and Alice H. Eagly. 2012. "Biosocial Construction of Sex Differences and Similarities in Behavior." In *Advances in Experimental Social Psychology*, edited by James M. Olson and Mark P. Zanna, 55–123. Burlington: Academic Press.

Wright, Jamie M., Jennifer Hayes Clark, and Heather K. Evans. 2021. "'They Were Laughing': Congressional Framing of Dr. Christine Blasey Ford's Sexual Assault Allegations on Twitter." *Political Research Quarterly* 75 (1):147–159. doi: 10.1177/1065912920987631.

Yoder, Janice, and Thomas L. Schleicher. 1996. "Undergraduates Regard Deviation from Occupational Gender Stereotypes as Costly for Women." *Sex Roles* 34 (3/4): 171–188.

Zipp, John F., and Eric Plutzer. 1985. "Gender Differences in Voting for Female Candidates: Evidence from the 1982 Election." *The Public Opinion Quarterly* 49 (2):179–197.

Zoch, Lynn M., and Judy VanSlyke Turk. 1998. "Women Making News: Gender as a Variable in Source Selection and Use." *Journalism and Mass Communication Quarterly* 75 (4):762–775.

Index

For the benefit of digital users, indexed terms that span two pages (e.g., 52–53) may, on occasion, appear on only one of those pages.